BURLEIGH GRIMES

BURLEIGH GRIMES

Baseball's Last Legal Spitballer

Joe Niese

Foreword by Donald Honig

McFarland & Company, Inc., Publishers
Jefferson, North Carolina, and London

ISBN 978-0-7864-7328-1
softcover : acid free paper ∞

LIBRARY OF CONGRESS CATALOGUING DATA ARE AVAILABLE

BRITISH LIBRARY CATALOGUING DATA ARE AVAILABLE

On the cover: Burleigh Grimes in 1938, during his second and final year
of managing the Brooklyn Dodgers (Charles Clark Photo Collection);
background image iStockphoto/Thinkstock

Manufactured in the United States of America

*McFarland & Company, Inc., Publishers
Box 611, Jefferson, North Carolina 28640
www.mcfarlandpub.com*

For Sara

Contents

Acknowledgments

There are a number of people who are deserving of a thank you for their contributions.

I extend my deepest gratitude to Charles and Ardeth Clark, the procurers of all things Burleigh Grimes. This book wouldn't have been complete without their kindness, generosity and hospitality. The Clarks' enthusiasm for Grimes certainly hasn't waned over the years. Today, nearly three decades after his death, Grimes's memory is alive and well. The Clarks continue to run the Clear Lake Historical Museum, welcoming visitors three days a week from Memorial Day to Labor Day. The museum's breadth of artifacts has garnered it the nickname "The Cooperstown of the Midwest."

I am also grateful to:

Ross Evavold, whose continued encouragement is instrumental in my evolution as a writer.

My parents, Marvin and Mary, who encouraged a love of reading that continues to this day.

My brothers, Andy and Marty, with whom I played endless hours of baseball while growing up.

The legendary Donald Honig, who wrote the foreword to this book. His previous writings on Grimes were an inspiration.

Others who wrote lengthy pieces on Grimes, including Charles and Richard Faber, Jerry Poling and Jason Christopherson.

The outstanding interlibrary loan department at the Indianhead Federated Library System — thank you Maureen Welch, Cheri Case, Gayle Spindler and the entire staff at the Chippewa Falls Public Library.

Several other libraries, historical societies and museums played a role including the Clear Lake Historical Museum, National Baseball Hall of Fame Library in Cooperstown, New York, Chalmer Davee Library at the University of Wisconsin-River Falls Library, Withee (Wisconsin) Public Library, Grundy County (Missouri) Library, Grundy County (Missouri) Historical Museum and the Cleveland Public Library.

There were a number of others who helped me via correspondence or conversation. Thank you, Gary Ashwill, Bob Brown, Chris Brzinksi, Tom Dillie, Darryl Eschete, Bill Kemp, Mary Beth Newbill, Louise Olszewski, Manas Sanyal, Phil Schlarb, Sharon Scott and Mitchell Conrad Stinson.

Most of all, I want to thank my wife Sara and our children, Oliver and Evelyn. I will forever be indebted for your love, patience and sacrifice of family time.

Foreword by Donald Honig

To their peers it soon became evident: Ty Cobb's zeal on the diamond was almost "psychotic"; Lefty Grove's will to win was "terrifying," and for the elderly gentleman sitting serenely next to me the descriptive word for his competitive demeanor was "ferocious," so stated by those of his teammates and opponents I had spoken with through the years.

"Ferocious" seemed incongruous in connection with Burleigh Grimes who this chilly October evening was gazing into a crackling autumnal fire in the living room of his rural Wisconsin home. The antic flames had turned pensive as he summoned and unfolded memories between puffs on a companionable cigar.

So I put to the musing, octogenarian Mr. Grimes the question of his old reputation.

"Ferocious?" he responded quizzically.

"They all said it."

"That seems pretty strong," he said, a bit sternly. He smoked and pondered for a few moments. Then, in a conciliatory tone, "Maybe a little bit mean. Tough, sure."

Bill Hallahan, Burleigh's teammate on the St. Louis Cardinals in the early 1930s, described Grimes as "the toughest guy I ever saw out on the mound. He'd fight you on every pitch."

"Well," Burleigh said, somewhat defensively, "you had to be tough. It was that kind of profession. The jobs were few and the boys were hungry. There was no charity out there. Somebody asked, 'Don't you let up a bit when you're ahead by ten runs?' Well, hell no. The guy up there is swinging the bat, isn't he? He's not letting up. Let up? You show me the pitcher who lets up and I'll show you a guy who's going to be pumping gas or tending bar soon."

Burleigh Grimes played the game as he found it, as others had played it before him and as he would pass it along to his successors. But there was one hazardous difference to Burleigh's game: he had to work his heyday years in

1

baseball's most thunderous offensive decade ever. In the 1920s the National League, Grimes's sphere of employment, dented the baseball for a decade-long *average* of .285.

"It was like pitching in a shooting gallery," he said. "I felt like I had a target painted on me."

It was the decade, of course, that saw the introduction of the lively ball, a shiny, rock-hard grenade of a baseball that in those early years was not even rubbed up before a game. It was hard to get the necessary grip, the "feel," with which to snap off your curve. Compounding this disadvantage for the pitchers was the fact that the batters had all learned their game and mode of attack in the recently interred Dead Ball Era; they were still choking up on the bat and swinging for contact rather than distance, scorching those high-caloried baseballs all around the field. The free-swinging, bottom-of-the-bat strikeout-prone hitters were still a decade away. It was the era of towering batting averages and blood-soaked earned run averages.

It was in the face of this unrelenting target practice that the indomitable Mr. Grimes established his Hall of Fame credentials, winning 20 or more games five times and seven times finishing among the league's top five in strikeouts.

Burleigh's adventures on the National League mounds came well before the advent of bullpen specialists — the set-up men and the closers who today pilot a starting pitcher to his "W." Pitching with that murderously lively ball (which was in use until after the 1930 season), Grimes not only prevailed but endured. He seldom missed a start, leading the league in games started three times and in complete games four times, and in five seasons pitched over 300 innings.

I asked him how, in light of latter-day standards, his arm was able to accommodate so demanding a workload. He answered, with quiet logic, "Well, it was your job. They're paying you to pitch, so you pitch. You do the best you can when you're doing it." Then he laughed. "Listen, some of those guys ahead of us, like McGinnity and Walsh and Chesbro, they'd work up to 400 innings in a season. So they probably thought *we* were sissies. You just fit into whatever's your time and place, that's all."

Again, it was hard to associate this placid old gentleman with the "tough," "ferocious" pitchers of legend. I thought I would try him again.

"Where does it go after the game, after the career?"

"Where does what go?" he asked.

"The ferocity," I said, as playfully as I could.

He brought up the cigar, drew on it and released a haze of languorous gray smoke.

"It doesn't go anywhere," he said. "It stays there."

"Stays where?"

"On the mound. Inside the uniform."

"You mean it comes with the uniform?"

"Well," he said, then paused. Then, "It should, shouldn't it?"

He was immensely proud of his career, and it was a career replete with glories and glittering highlights. He had packed his life with playing, coaching, managing, scouting, always alert to what went on between the white lines, and beyond. When talking about managing he had a particularly telling insight. "A manager should always remember that every player thinks he's better than he really is. Learn that," Burleigh said, "keep it to yourself and you can save yourself a lot of grief."

Burleigh Grimes shared the field and now the history of the game with many of its greats: Honus Wagner, Grover Cleveland Alexander, longtime Dodgers teammate Dazzy Vance, Rogers Hornsby, John McGraw, Paul Waner, and, during his brief stint with the Yankees, Babe Ruth and Lou Gehrig. He crisscrossed the highways and byways of an expanding America in its raucous Jazz Age, plying his trade in the great arenas of Baseball America.

As we sat before the warming fireplace, the chill Wisconsin night beyond the windows, I asked the serene Mr. Grimes if he sometimes missed the roars and shouts of the grandstands, the rips and throbs of baseball passions.

He drew on the cigar, let the smoke weave like a shadow around him, then said, "Oh, I can still hear them." And added, "When I want to."

A baseball biography comes with a certain established structure. We have the page in the record book, permanent and in its context revealing. We have the years, the box scores, and we have the memories of teammates and opponents. We have a sizeable segment of a man's life, where he was and what he was doing for months at a time. But within all of that is the man himself, elusive as men are, and here is where the biographer must work his magic and restore dimensions. Joe Niese has done this. Through diligent research, with skilled craftsmanship and thoughtful insights into the man and his time he has illuminated the past and returned Burleigh Grimes from the shadows and back into the light of center stage. Here we have the Hall of Fame pitcher and multi-faceted personality in season and out. Mr. Niese gives us a book about a baseball player, and more.

Donald Honig is a novelist and baseball historian. His works include *Baseball When the Grass Was Real*, *Baseball America* and *The Fifth Season*.

Preface

Burleigh Grimes. The name sounds fictitious, a character out of lumberjack folklore, mingling with Paul Bunyan and Babe the Blue Ox. Grimes's origins aren't far off from a tall tale. He was born and raised at the end of Northern Wisconsin's lumber era, working as a lumberjack as a teen and nearly losing his life in a lumber accident. He brought the rough-and-tumble mentality of a logger to the pitcher's mound, where he carved out a Hall of Fame career over parts of 19 big league seasons.

There aren't enough words in a thesaurus to describe Grimes's boorish behavior on the mound, but one would be hard pressed to find a team that wouldn't have been happy to have Grimes in its uniform. He nearly made a full tour of the National League during his playing days, spending time with the Pittsburgh Pirates (three stints), Brooklyn Dodgers, New York Giants, Boston Braves, St. Louis Cardinals (two stints) and Chicago Cubs. He was also briefly an American Leaguer, throwing 18 innings in 10 games for the New York Yankees. When all was said and done, Grimes had won 270 ballgames, pitched in four World Series (winning one), and played alongside the most Hall of Famers of any player, 36.

Probably one of the most famous photographs of Grimes (Charles Clark Photo Collection).

5

Off the field Grimes was described as congenial, enjoying the camaraderie that baseball brought. Away from the game, he loved any outdoor activity, including farming and raising horses, cattle and pigs.

For most of my life I knew very little about Burleigh Grimes. I was aware that he started his professional baseball journey in my hometown of Eau Claire, Wisconsin, in 1912. He is often overshadowed by Henry Aaron, who started his ascent to the majors in the same western Wisconsin town 40 years later. It wasn't until the fall of 2009 while reading Jerry Poling's *A Summer Up North*, centering on Aaron's 1952 season in Eau Claire, that I was given a more thorough introduction to Grimes.

The fact that Grimes's career started a century ago and spanned 19 seasons over three decades made researching this book an arduous process. In addition, Grimes was prone to telling a fable or two in the hundreds of interviews he did over the years, which made it feel at times as though I was trying to piece together the life and times of a folk hero. It quickly became a labor of love, though, as I utilized a mix of modern and old-fashioned research methods. There are of course some great Internet sources that have made researching baseball much easier (retrosheet.org, baseball-almanac.com, baseball-reference.com and a variety of content available to members of SABR, the Society for American Baseball Research). I also went through dozens of microfilm reels as I researched each year of his career, perused a number of books about his contemporaries and the era he played in, and made contact or traveled to numerous libraries, archives and history centers. Finally, I gained invaluable insight from many visits with Grimes's close friends Charles and Ardeth Clark, who run the Clear Lake Historical Museum in Clear Lake, which houses a terrific collection of Grimes memorabilia.

It has been nearly 80 years since Burleigh Grimes threw his last pitch in the major leagues, and almost 50 since he was inducted into the National Baseball Hall of Fame. Several substantial pieces have been written on the life of Grimes, yet there has never been a full biography. This book fills that void by covering his entire life, from his childhood days in Clear Lake, Wisconsin, to his death in the same small town. In between is the story of one of baseball's great competitors.

Introduction

Burleigh Grimes was most comfortable when he was talking about either horses or baseball. Both activities had been a part of his life for as long as he could remember, and while Grimes probably had a greater affinity for horses (maintaining into old age that he would take a good saddle horse over a motorcar any day), baseball was what brought him fame. Over the years he had given hundreds if not thousands of interviews regarding baseball, but on the morning of July 27, 1964, Grimes seemed to be at a loss for words. Less than a month from his seventy-first birthday, he stepped to the podium in Cooperstown, New York, to accept Major League Baseball's highest individual honor: enshrinement into the National Baseball Hall of Fame.

> Mr. Chairman, I started my career before the Hall of Fame was started. It's been wonderful. I don't know how a fellow can get old so fast. It impresses me here. I don't know whether I'm nervous or whether I'm ice cold, or both. But I'll tell you this — it's great to be here. I want to thank everybody. Opponents that helped beat me, players that were on the club that I played on. Newspapermen, press, television, radio. I want to thank the good friends at Clear Lake, Wisconsin, and Trenton, Missouri. I'm happy to be here and I'm happy that it came soon enough that I could receive this plaque. I thank you.[1]

Grimes during his acceptance speech on the front steps of the National Baseball Hall of Fame and Museum on July 27, 1964 (Charles Clark Photo Collection).

It's easy to understand why if Grimes might have wondered whether he would ever see this day. Just shy of three decades since his career as a professional baseball player ended (1934), and nearly as long since he first appeared on the Hall of Fame ballot (1937), Grimes had been up for election 14 times and never received more than 5.8 percent of the votes (1948). Finally some momentum started in the late 1950s before peaking in 1960 with 34.2 percent of the votes of the Base Ball Writers Association of America. In 1964 he was handed over to the Veterans Committee, made up of his contemporaries, and was promptly voted in.[2]

On the evening of his enshrinement Grimes seemed emotionally spent as he stood in the lobby of Cooperstown's historic Otesaga Hotel with close friend Charles Clark, waiting for their wives to go out for a dinner celebration. The pair was reliving the day's events when the local news ran a story on the induction ceremony. Clark, who was transfixed by the first color television he had ever seen, said to Grimes without looking at him, "What were you thinking about Burleigh?" There was a pause, and then Grimes replied in a hushed tone, "I wish my parents could have been here today." His emotions finally got the best of him. With tears in his eyes he looked over at Clark, who had never before and would never again see his good friend display that type of emotion. "You know, that plaque is for all of us up there," said a moved Grimes.[3] "There" was Clear Lake, Wisconsin, where Grimes's baseball journey had begun.

1

Northwoods Roots

It's unclear what prompted Elias Grimes to move his young family from Clara, Pennsylvania, to Emerald, Wisconsin. Perhaps it was Wisconsin's lumber trade, which had begun to emerge as a major industry a few decades earlier. Maybe it was the farming opportunities in the state, which were accommodating the lumber trade. Whatever the reason, Elias, his wife Jane and their young children, John and Lula, made the nearly 1,000-mile trek westward to start a new life in the fall of 1864.

As one of the first white settlers in the area, Grimes hacked out a family homestead in the heavily wooded Emerald Township in western Wisconsin's St. Croix County. Elias soon got the urge to re-enlist in the Union Army. He had previously served as a private in the 150th Pennsylvania Voluntary Infantry "Bucktails" Regiment from September 2 to October 4, 1862, when he was given a disability discharge. This time he enlisted as a wagoner in the 51st Wisconsin Volunteer Infantry Regiment, shortly after it entered federal service in March 1865. Once again he had an abbreviated stint, mustering out on May 6, almost a month after Confederate General Robert E. Lee surrendered to Union General Ulysses S. Grant at Appomattox Court House in Appomattox, Virginia.

In the post–Civil War years the Grimes family continued to grow. In addition to their son John and daughter Lula they had three more boys — Wila, Cecil and Burdette — as they settled into life on their farm in Emerald. Elias Grimes supplemented his farming income by dabbling in bootleg liquor and selling animal pelts from his regular hunting expeditions. As time went on, he gained a reputation as a backwoods character. Seldom one to cut his hair or beard, he was said to spend his summers barefoot, wearing a gunnysack cloth while roaming the western Wisconsin wilderness.

As Elias and Jane Grimes's sons grew to manhood, all of them worked in some capacity in the ever-expanding northern Wisconsin lumber trade. By the 1880s there were Wisconsin mills turning out 500,000 feet of lumber a day, compared to 5,000 just thirty years earlier. Due to the seasonal nature of lumbering, many farmers worked in the industry for part of the year, leaving for the woods right after the fall harvest and returning in time to plant crops in the spring. The abundance of farmers heading to the woods each fall to supplement their income drove down the pay of the lumberjack, who averaged anywhere from $12 to $25 a month.

The lumber trade wasn't the only activity that expanded in the years after the war. Long an informal pastime, the popularity of "base ball" grew by leaps and bounds in the years immediately following the Civil War. Soon every town had a ball team to root for and adults and children alike devoured the game. One of those boys was Cecil Grimes (better known as "Nick"), who joined his brother Burdette in playing the game whenever and wherever possible. While the U.S. Census may have listed his occupation as a "day laborer" or "farmer," Nick was a baseball man at heart. He played for a number of town teams, starting in Emerald and then branching out to other towns in St. Croix and Polk County.

In between his farming duties and playing baseball Nick Grimes found time to court Ruth Tuttle from nearby Glenwood City. In March 1892 the couple married. Ruth, who had been briefly married in the late 1880s, had moved across the state from Wrightstown (near Green Bay) with her mother Hanna and several of her eighteen siblings after her father William's death in 1883. William S. Tuttle had been an accomplished man, having been a master of a vessel on the Great Lakes as well as serving in the Wisconsin legislature, where he became "The first man to introduce a bill relating to the lien law and was successful in carrying it through."[1] Prior to his death the family had run the Sherman House in Wrightstown.

Nick and Ruth Grimes settled in Emerald, where Nick continued working as a day laborer. On August 18, 1893, they welcomed their first child, Burleigh Arland Grimes. The name "Burleigh" was chosen by Ruth, who had been reading about the aristocracy of the British Isles, including a section on William Cecil, known as Lord Burleigh.[2] For the next decade the Grimes family led a nomadic life, moving from farm to farm around St. Croix and neighboring Polk County. During these years the other two Grimes children were born: a daughter Hazel in 1895 and a son Shurleigh in 1900.

By the time Burleigh was five his father had already taught him how to throw, catch and hit a baseball. He also faithfully served as batboy for the Nick Grimes–managed Clear Lake Yellow Jackets. The players on the Yellow Jackets were Grimes's baseball idols. Years later he said he had "never heard of Honus Wagner or John McGraw or Christy Mathewson or any of those fellows. The news hadn't got through the timber yet."[3]

It was during this time that Burleigh Grimes began his lifelong allegiance to Clear Lake, which he always identified as his hometown. Clear Lake, with a population of nearly 800, was located in southeast Polk County in Wisconsin's "Lake Country," and its name derived from a beautiful spring-fed lake just outside of town. A fire had devastated Clear Lake in the spring of 1898, but a few years into the new century the town's dirt roads and wooden sidewalks were once again a hub of activity, thanks to the lumber trade and the Chicago and Northwestern Railway that ran through town.

Around that time, the Grimes family settled on a farm in the township of Black Brook, almost three miles from Clear Lake. It was a family affair as Nick and his brother Burdette (also known as "Birch" or "Bird") had a large head of cattle that they maintained in addition to their crops. Not even ten years old yet, Burleigh had already been heavily involved in working on the family farm — he plowed fields, pitched hay, milked cows, and dug up stumps and stones. He even wielded a baseball bat as part of the farm's varmint control. His skills with a horse also were growing and he soon would be earning a nickel a day to wrangle cattle.

Baseball was also a priority on the farm. Nick kept a patch of the hay field trimmed low so that he and his sons could play ball. At the end of a long day of work on the farm they headed to the field and Nick put his boys through a number of drills. It was during one of these sessions that a neighbor saw Burleigh in action. Impressed with his talent, he urged Nick to let his son play ball rather than be a batboy for the Yellow Jackets. Nick Grimes took the neighbor's advice and in the summer of 1903 Burleigh began playing for the Clear Lake Red Jackets.

The Red Jackets were made up of 10-, 11- and 12-year-olds and they received as much press coverage as the Yellow Jackets. The boys had uniforms paid for by local donations and a large fan base that followed them as they took on teams from surrounding towns such as Turtle Lake, Amery, New Richmond, and even Osceola. Today the trip to Osceola takes 45 minutes by car, but back then the trip was made on a horse-led 3-seater rig. The boys would "leave home at 5:45 on a Sunday morning and not get back until 2 the following morning."[4]

During the summer of 1903, it became apparent that the Red Jackets' chief rival was to be the New Richmond Brownies. Like the Clear Lake boys, the Brownies received considerable local attention and were adorned with uniforms provided by the New Richmond town folk. The Brownies were coached by the future owner of the Minneapolis Millers, Mike Cantillon, who was living in New Richmond and had a few nephews on the team. The teams split the first two games, with each winning by a run. The Clear Lake victory included a strong pitching performance from nine-year-old Burleigh Grimes, who struck out a dozen Brownies in four innings. Having yet to discover the pitch that would make him famous, Grimes dominated the Brownies with one pitch — an effectively wild fastball.

For the rubber match Grimes again took the mound for the Red Jackets in front of a crowd of several hundred at the New Richmond Fair Grounds. During Grimes's previous appearance against the Brownies, Cantillon had preached to his players that they didn't even need to take their bats off their shoulders against the wild pitches of Grimes. The team hadn't adhered to those warnings, but this time they did so and young Burleigh once again had control issues. According to William McNally, Grimes was "pitching his heart out, with tears streaming down his face," unable to find the plate during the 11–5 defeat.[5]

According to the Brownies' team records kept by their 10-year-old secretary Miles McNally, the tears continued after the game:

> The third game the Red Jackets came down here and we skinned them Berly [sic] got mad and pitched bum there was a lad hollering for us and he got the Red Jackets up in the air and they couldn't play good. After the game Berly began to cry and the kids laughed at him and he got mad and said he wouldn't never play no more.[6]

Young Grimes's life wasn't all baseball and farming. Away from the homestead and ball field he hunted, fished, spent hours riding his horse around and swimming in Clear Lake and the French Lakes. In the winter he walked, skied or snow-shoed to school across the frozen Clear Lake. His ability with horses allowed him to earn some extra money by driving horses for Dr. Lorne Campbell when the doctor made his calls in the country. He also had a keen interest in boxing from an early age, inspired by his uncle John, who at one point had been described as "the coming man in the middleweight class."[7] For a while Burleigh also aspired to be a professional boxer before being discouraged by his family.[8]

As a youth, Grimes had a mischievous side that was often accompanied by a large grin. In his later years he and Gaylord Nelson, a fellow Clear Lake native and a future governor of Wisconsin, recounted an infamous adventure that had become town folklore. According to Nelson's version:

> At Clear Lake the village butcher kept a kennel of bloodhounds, including "one old mean one" who grabbed all the bones from the other dogs in the pen. One day Grimes fixed it up so the other dogs got a chance to get a bone or two. Grabbing a stone, he fired from about 75 feet and hit the big one on the head. While the old bloodhound lay unconscious to the world the other bloodhounds got their fill of bones. Ever after, the moral of the story goes, the old bloodhound shared the feast with the rest of the kennel.[9]

Grimes did not follow through on his petulant vow to quit baseball. By the summer of 1906, the twelve year old was still throwing his unpredictable fastball for the Red Jackets and continuing to put in a full day's work on the family farm in Black Brook. By midsummer, grass supplies had dwindled, which was often a cue for farmers to sell off some of their cattle. Early one morning Nick Grimes, his brother Birch and his son Burleigh herded a substantial head of cattle three miles to the train depot in Clear Lake, where they loaded their freight into cattle cars headed for the St. Paul stockyards. The Grimes brothers usually made the annual trip to Minnesota, but Nick was unable to make this year's venture. In his place he sent Burleigh, giving the lad an opportunity to see a part of the family trade that he would more than likely take over one day.

Birch and Burleigh's business at the St. Paul stockyards didn't last much past noon. As the pair headed back to the train depot for the journey home, Burleigh suggested they watch a baseball game at Lexington Park. His uncle obliged and the pair boarded a streetcar — something that Burleigh had never seen before and headed for Lexington Park. Hopping off at the southwest corner of Lexington Avenue and University Avenue they entered the park, where the St. Paul Saints were taking on the Minneapolis Millers. As a pitcher, the attention of young Grimes was immediately drawn to the Millers' pitcher, Hank Gehring, who kept bringing the ball close to his mouth in between pitches. Burleigh asked his uncle what Gehring was doing. "Throwing a spitball," the uncle replied, going on to explain to his nephew the intricacies of the pitch. For the rest of the game Burleigh was fixated on Gehring and the trick pitch.

When Grimes and his uncle returned to Black Brook, he tried to emulate what he had seen in St. Paul. Starting with a mouthful of grass, the ball moved a little differently than usual. He had just thrown his first spitball. Soon he was making the trek into Clear Lake, where he worked on his pitching with Clear Lake Yellow Jackets veteran catcher E.E. Church during his lunch break at the post office. Church, who in a few years would be catching Grimes for the Yellow Jackets, said of those sessions that he had "never seen a kid with more desire."[10]

The spitball was being touted as the chic new pitch during the first decade of the twentieth century. Much like other non–fastball pitches such as the curveball, slider and knuckleball, it's difficult to pinpoint an exact origin. There were pitchers dating back to the 1860s who were said to have doctored the ball with saliva in order to get more movement on pitches. In the early 1900s, however, the spitball really started to catch on. Two pitchers used the pitch to great effect: Jack Chesbro won 41 games for the New York Highlanders (soon to be Yankees) in 1904 and Ed Walsh tallied 40 in 1908 for the Chicago White Sox.

When thrown properly, the spitball leaves the hand with no spin, rather like a knuckleball with more velocity. As physics professor Robert Adair explained, "The application of a lubricant to the forefinger and middle finger on delivery of an overhand fast ball can produce some of the same effects as the split-finger fast ball: the ball will slide off the fingers, accumulating less backspin and then drop more than the usual fast ball thrown with backspin."[11] Grimes always maintained that it took him a matter of minutes to teach a pitcher how to throw a spitball, but that it took years to master the pitch. Even then, a pitcher could have it one inning and then completely lose it the next.

By the time he ended his tenure with the Red Jackets in the summer of 1907, Grimes had experimented with various lubricants for his spitball. Unable to stomach tobacco and disinclined to use messy licorice, he tried a number of substances before finally settling on the inner bark of the slippery elm tree, which thrived in the lush soil surrounding Polk County's lakes and riverbanks. White with a distinct smell, the slippery elm's inner bark had been used for

Clear Lake School Team, 1908. Grimes's successful spring led to a spot on the Yellow Jackets. Grimes (seated left) played every position except first base (Charles Clark Photo Collection).

a bevy of medicinal purposes over the centuries. When making contact with water, or in this case saliva, the bark's mucilage (a thick, sticky substance) oozed out, making it perfect for doctoring the ball.

The following spring Grimes had an impressive season for Clear Lake High School's ball team, where as a freshman he played every position but first base. Now maturing into his early teens, the combination of farm labor and numerous hours spent in the Wisconsin wilderness were showing on his sturdy frame. His spring performance landed him a spot on Nick Grimes's Clear Lake Yellow Jackets team, beating out William Nilssen, a 20-year-old regular who recalled that he "wept with chagrin, because I could never be as good as he was."[12]

Fans of the Clear Lake Yellow Jackets took their ball team seriously, and rightfully so. Not only was it for town bragging rights, but many invested their own money to bring in ringers from the Minneapolis–St. Paul area to pitch. After a 13–5 defeat at the hands of their fiercest rival, the New Richmond Tigers, these supporters let Nick Grimes know their displeasure with his choice

The Clear Lake Yellow Jackets. Manager Nick Grimes (back row, fourth from left, without a hat) never pitched Burleigh (front row, seated, far left) in Clear Lake after a disastrous first start. Elwyn Church (back row, second from left) helped young Burleigh develop his spitball (Charles Clark Photo Collection).

of pitchers. He abided by their wishes, but privately took umbrage over being told how to manage his roster. The result was that young Grimes rarely took the mound in Clear Lake during his nearly four years on the club, even when he was striking out teams by the dozen on the road. Years later Grimes quipped that he wondered if he was good enough yet to pitch in Clear Lake.

Much like Grimes's Red Jackets days, the Yellow Jackets traveled to away games via three-seater rigs. Again playing every position except first base, Grimes was getting a baseball education by playing against men substantially older than him. Long gone were the tears of his youth baseball days, now replaced by a broad smile and the occasional sneer when called for. Years later he recalled spinning his first cap during his early days on the Yellow Jackets. "There was a fellow playing left field for Clayton that had a derby on and he come up to the plate and Doc Campbell hollered 'You hit the derby and I'll give you a buck.'"[13] Grimes returned to the family farm a dollar richer.

Somewhere along the line Grimes told a tall tale about having to join the lumber trade at a young age to provide for his family after his father's premature death. The fib gained steam and has been repeated over the years in a number of biographical sketches of him. The truth is that Grimes did work as a lumberjack from an early age, but it wasn't because of his father's death. Due to economic reasons, Grimes quit high school after his second year. At the time Clear Lake only had a two-year high school, and then students traveled to nearby Amery or New Richmond to complete their schooling. Unable to afford both the travel and the loss of Burleigh's labor during the day, Nick Grimes decided that it would be better for the family if his eldest son ceased his education in favor of labor.

In late autumn 1908, after finishing up the fall harvest on the family farm, Grimes headed into the woods for his first winter as a lumberjack. With a reputation for exceptional horsemanship, he was given the job of "driver," sitting atop a pyramid of logs and guiding a team of horses. Like most lumberman jobs, death for a driver was just a misstep away, especially when perched on a load of logs that could weigh anywhere from five to twenty tons. That first winter he worked for Bert Horel, who two years later was shot in the shoulder by John Dietz, the infamous "Defender of the Cameron Dam."

When the ice broke on the rivers, Grimes headed back to the family farm to plant the spring crops and get ready for the upcoming baseball season. The winter gave him a new perspective on what he wanted out of life — to be a professional baseball player. This carried over into his mound persona, which showed a little more edge. Grimes recalled his new outlook: "I decided the best I could make back home was thirty-five dollars a month driving horses in a lumber camp. Baseball was my answer. And I'd say to myself: 'How do

I get more money?' The answer was simple. There was only one man standing between me and more money, and that was the guy with the bat. I knew I'd always have to fight that man with the bat as if he were trying to rob me in a dark alley."[14]

As early as 1911 Grimes was trying to break into organized ball. The winter leading up to the '11 season Nick Grimes contacted Fred Cooke, the new manager of the Red Wing Manufacturers of the Class C Minnesota–Wisconsin League, to see if he would give his seventeen-year-old son a tryout. Cooke didn't bite on the unproven youngster, so Burleigh once again found himself in a Clear Lake uniform.

Grimes continued to hone his skills against some fairly stiff competition. Every year the Yellow Jackets played games against two of the best teams from the Twin Cities area — the Minneapolis Keystones and the St. Paul Colored Gophers — two of the premier African American teams in the midwest. In 1910, the Gophers thumped Grimes

Grimes (left) and teammate Lincoln Holmes as members of the Clear Lake Yellow Jackets, 1908 (Charles Clark Photo Collection).

and the Jackets 12–2, but in 1911 the Gophers squeaked out a 3–2 victory. After the game the Gophers catcher approached Nick Grimes and declared: "That kid is ready to go!"[15]

2

From the Bottom to the Top, 1912–1916

Once again Burleigh Grimes emerged from his winter of driving lumber in 1912 with professional baseball on his mind. Although Nick Grimes could have used his son's strong back on the farm and his burgeoning skills on the baseball diamond, he remembered the advice of the catcher of the St. Paul Colored Gophers. Instead of trying to contact a team in hopes of earning a tryout, the elder Grimes encouraged his son to travel over to St. Paul to see if Mike Kelley, manager of the St. Paul Saints of the American Association, had an open spot for him.

With his five-dollar glove, an old pair of baseball shoes wrapped in newspaper and $15 that his father gave him, Grimes hopped a train for St. Paul. Upon arrival he went to Kelley, who turned away the youngster but encouraged him to start out at a lower level. "Go out and get some experience — show me what you can do," advised the Saints skipper.[1] Kelley directed Grimes toward Eau Claire, Wisconsin, where Russ Bailey, manager of the Eau Claire Commissioners of the Minnesota-Wisconsin League, was looking for talent to fill out his roster.

Entering its fourth year of existence after succeeding the old Northern League, the Minnesota-Wisconsin League was already in jeopardy of going under. The 1912 campaign saw the number of ball clubs cut in half from eight to four, with the surviving teams being Eau Claire and La Crosse on the Wisconsin side and Winona and Rochester from Minnesota. In addition, the league dropped down to class D status after spending its first three years at class C. As was common for floundering leagues, financial issues were at the forefront. With a strapped budget, Bailey, in his first year of managing, had little money to entice recruits. Even if players were interested in coming to Eau Claire to play ball, they had to pay their own way to the city, as well as their own living expenses, until the team was finalized.

The Minnesota-Wisconsin League was rarely a springboard to the major leagues, but once in a while a player was noticed. This had been the case with Dave Callahan, who terrorized league pitching with a .365 average in 1910. His torrid hitting caught the eye of the Cleveland Naps (soon to be known as the Indians) who signed him in September. Callahan found himself playing left field next to a recently called-up center fielder from the Southern Association's New Orleans Pelicans — Joe Jackson. While Callahan's career fizzled the following year, Jackson went on to become one of the game's premier players, before being banned from organize baseball for life as a result of the 1919 Black Sox Scandal.

Russ Bailey had been a teammate of Callahan in 1910 and in September of that year he too earned a promotion when he was acquired by the Milwaukee Brewers of the American Association. But Bailey's climb to the majors ended later that month when he suffered a gruesome ankle injury when sliding into a base. He returned to Eau Claire in 1911 and now found himself managing the Commissioners.

Grimes made a quick stop back in Clear Lake to throw a few innings for the hometown Yellow Jackets before boarding a southbound train to Eau Claire. He arrived in town and met with Bailey, who agreed to let him work out with the team, but emphasized that Grimes would have to pay his own expenses and that a roster spot was not guaranteed.

For the next three weeks, Grimes worked out with the Commissioners at the Eau Claire Driving Park, a multi-purpose complex located in the city's third ward. In addition to the baseball field, the complex housed "a horse racing track, football field, polo field and track and field facilities."[2] Grimes pitched batting practice, took grounders, shagged fly balls and fetched everything from foul balls to water for the team. Walking a mile and a half to and from the Driving Park to his downtown living quarters to save a dime wasn't enough to stretch his money, so he wrote to his father for another five dollars. Nick Grimes hesitantly sent the sum, but not without questioning "what the hell he was doing with all of his money."[3]

At the end of the tryouts, Bailey posted his roster. The name Burleigh Grimes was not on it. Many would have taken the rejection and headed home, but not Grimes. Showing the gumption that would one day make him legendary, he confronted the manager. "Mr. Bailey," he said, "I paid my own expenses. You ought to give me at least one shot anyway."[4] Surprisingly, Bailey put up little fight. He agreed to let Grimes stay on with the team, but didn't offer him a contract. After all, it didn't hurt to have an extra player who could play practically every position on the field. Burleigh went on throwing batting practice and helping out in any way possible, including shining shoes. Years later, he revealed his motivation: "I had to do it or I'd been back up in Clear Lake driving that team of horses."[5]

Bailey scheduled a game with a team made up of Eau Claire locals known as Big Jo's to help him assess his roster. In a 19–2 whitewashing of the Big Jo's, Grimes never saw the field, yet he remained undeterred. An interesting side note to the otherwise forgetful game was that the shortstop for the Commissioners that day was a 19-year-old from Milwaukee named Oscar Felsch. His name was erroneously recorded as "Falsh," and it was the only game he played for Eau Claire. Felsch, later given the moniker of "Happy," went on to be one of the American League's top hitters, before, like Jackson, being banned for life after his involvement in the Black Sox Scandal.

The Commissioners traveled to Winona, Minnesota, to open their season against the Winona Pirates. Getting a taste of a higher level of ball, Grimes spent the ride down in a train sleeper car. Still without a contract, he remained on the bench during the five-inning rain-shortened Eau Claire victory by a score of 5–1. After another day of rain, the two teams squared off and once again Grimes found himself on the bench. It appeared that the sleeper car was going to be the highlight of the trip until the Commissioners shortstop was hit by a pitch and unable to continue. Burleigh was called in to play and filled in nicely, playing error-free ball and contributing a run and a hit.

The next day the 2–0 Commissioners traveled to Rochester, Minnesota, home of the world-famous Mayo Clinic. The town's ball team was aptly nicknamed the Medics. For his solid play the previous day, Grimes was rewarded with a seat outside the park. As was customary at the time, a member of the visiting team was assigned to collect tickets, and he was lucky enough to be the one.

Grimes was still at the gates when one of his teammates came running out to tell him that manager Bailey needed him right away. Upon entering the park, Grimes saw that the Commissioners were already trailing 2–0 and they weren't even out of the first inning. Bailey told him to get ready to pitch. After a hasty warm-up in foul territory, he found himself on the mound with the bases loaded and nobody out. His first pitch was belted for a two-run single, increasing the deficit to 4–0. He didn't allow a run the rest of the game and contributed a double as Eau Claire plated three runs in the top of the ninth for a 5–4 victory.

As soon as the game ended Grimes's catcher, Elmer Benrud, came out to congratulate him. Pulling him in close the veteran said, "Kid he's going to offer you sixty dollars. Get eighty out of him." Walking to the dugout Burleigh saw a beaming manager Bailey, the same man who just weeks earlier had planned on cutting him. Bailey told him to follow him into the clubhouse.

"I'm signing you up for sixty a month," said a still smiling Bailey.

"I think I ought to get eighty," replied the stone-faced Grimes.

"Somebody told you that," said Bailey, his smile vanishing.

"That's right," said Grimes, not backing down.

"All right, I'll give you eighty," replied a reluctant Bailey.[6]

Grimes had just agreed to his first contract. Inexplicably, he decided on monthly payments rather than the standard weekly allowance — a decision that would come back to haunt him.

Little recognition was given to Grimes in the press. The next day, both the *Eau Claire Leader* and the *Winona Daily Republican-Herald* referred to him as "Bryan." His effort didn't go unnoticed by Bailey, however, who informed him that he would start the home opener against Rochester.

The first "official" game of the season was a big event in Eau Claire, the lumber boom town known as the "Sawdust City." Many of the shops and factories closed their doors early so that employees could attend the game. The team planned to parade from downtown to the Driving Park, where the mayor was to throw out the first pitch. Unfortunately, the weather for the home opener was horrible, as a brisk wind swept across the field. Compounded by a constant drizzle, the conditions weren't suitable for a pitcher with Grimes's repertoire, particularly his spitball. By the time he was pulled in the middle of the fifth inning, he had given up six runs.

Grimes's next two starts were more successful, as he earned complete-game victories in both games, while striking out eight and seven respectively. Back home, *The Clear Lake Star* gave frequent updates on his season. His father and brother were able to attend a game against Rochester that turned out to be his best all-around game in an Eau Claire uniform. In addition to the complete-game mound victory he also rapped three hits in the win.

Although the Commissioners were atop the standings with a 12–3 record, it was still hard to retain players because of rumors of the league dissolving. Grimes soon was playing in the field on days he wasn't pitching. Spending most of his time in the outfield, he played alongside Russ Bailey, who inserted himself into the lineup after a combination of player ineptitude and injury.

The rumors finally came to fruition on July 1 when the Minnesota-Wisconsin League disbanded. While it left all of the players without money and a place to play, Grimes was one of the hardest hit. Having chosen to receive his salary in one lump sum at the end of the month, Burleigh had no money and no immediate prospects for playing ball.

Using his baseball contacts, Bailey put Grimes in touch with Dutch Meaney, who played and managed a team in Austin, Minnesota. A member of the Southern Minnesota League, the Austin Bills had a doubleheader scheduled for July 4 and were short a pitcher. Bailey gave the penniless Grimes $5 and put him on a train bound for Austin on July 3. This act of kindness wouldn't be forgotten. Throughout his professional career, Grimes frequently stopped in Eau Claire to see Bailey on his trips back to Wisconsin to visit family. He even visited his old manager on his deathbed in 1951.

The train arrived in Austin in the early-morning hours of July 4. By the time Grimes lay down for bed it was nearly 4:30 in the morning and his money had dwindled to 15 cents by what he suspected was a case of people taking advantage of an out-of-towner. A few hours later he was awakened by a knock at his door. The visitor notified him that after breakfast he was to report to the park, because he would be pitching in the game that morning.

More than 1,000 people assembled at the Athletic Park to see the local squad take on rival Albert Lea. The large crowd didn't intimidate Grimes, who pitched Austin to a 5–2 victory. He also contributed a double and a triple at the plate. The local paper gushed about their new recruit: "He is a classy twirler, fields his position perfectly, and [is] some clouter. He is young, good natured and has a smile that at once won the hearts of the fans."[7]

Following an anticlimactic second game that ended in a 13–1 Austin walloping of Albert Lea, Grimes was given $50 for his services. Serious discussion was also given to him returning for the duration of the season. By the time he boarded the train for Clear Lake, Grimes had agreed on a monthly salary of $125 that included running a local pool hall. He was home long enough to throw for the town team, handing rival Osceola its first defeat of the season. In addition to his mound victory he also picked up a new suit and overcoat as part of a side bet. The new attire was perfect for his pool hall attendant job.

Grimes's next start for Austin was better than his first — a complete game, one-hit shutout. He also moved up in the batting order from ninth to fifth, where he contributed a double and four RBIs

Grimes came to the Austin (Minnesota) Bills in July 1912 after the Minnesota-Wisconsin League collapsed (Charles Clark Photo Collection).

in the 6–0 victory. The presence of Grimes on the mound and in the batter's box made Austin a top-flight team in the state. There was even some talk of an end-of-year match-up against Alexandria at Nicollet Park in Minneapolis, with the winner being crowned Minnesota state champions. Over the next month and a half, Grimes and his teammates rolled through the competition. While there would be no season climax at Nicollet Park, the team did defeat the Twin Cities champion North Side Athletics. The win was enough for the Bills to label themselves the champions of the state. By season's end Grimes had amassed more than just victories, recalling, "I won sixteen games and lost one and I went home with my three shirts, two cases of shells and a new automatic shotgun."[8]

Upon returning to Clear Lake in mid–September, Grimes put in plenty of hours working on the family farm during the fall harvest. He also logged a few more innings on the pitcher's rubber, the highlight being a game at the Polk County Fair between two teams made up of the best ballplayers in the area. Behind the plate umpiring Grimes's 6–4 victory was Roy Patterson who had gone 21–9 for the Minneapolis Millers. Patterson hailed from nearby St. Croix Falls, Wisconsin, and had come of age playing in the same circles as Nick Grimes. Known as the "Boy Wonder," Patterson's major league career spanned seven years for the White Sox. He threw the first pitch and won the first game in American League history in 1901.

Grimes had taken one step forward in his baseball path in 1912 by playing for the minor league team in Eau Claire, but it had been his play in Austin that caught the attention of another league. Shortly before heading into the woods for another winter of hauling loads of lumber, he received offers from teams in the Central Association of Iowa and Illinois, another Class "D" syndicate. In the fall the Galesburg (Illinois) Pavers had shown interest in Grimes, but early in 1913 the frontrunner became the defending league champions, the Ottumwa (Iowa) Packers.

The Packers were also known as the "Speed Boys" for the reliance on base-stealing in the offense implemented by Edward "Ned" Eagan, a highly respected manager who was a year away from graduating from medical school. Eagan had won everywhere he had managed, and within a few years would be regarded as the "Connie Mack of the minors."[9] He spent his playing days on diamonds all over the midwest and into Canada. One of those stops had included sharing the diamond with Nick Grimes. No sentimentality existed, however, as Eagan and the younger Grimes haggled over a salary. The two parties were $15 apart when Dutch Meaney offered Grimes $250 a month to return to the Austin Bills. Grimes was going to use that as bargaining leverage before his father stepped in and advised him to take the offer to get back into professional ball.

In early February Grimes arrived in Ottumwa, located in southeastern Iowa. There he found that nobody was aware of his performance the previous year as a member of the Austin ball club. "Who Guines [sic] is or what he is nobody in Ottumwa knows," said the *Ottumwa Daily Courier*.[10]

As one of seven pitchers in camp, Grimes did nothing to distinguish himself from the other five right-handers. In fact, Eagan was all set to send him to Centerville, Iowa, for a little more work when one of the Ottumwa players convinced their manager that Grimes was the fastest runner on the team. Knowing that speed was crucial to his game plan, Eagan set up a foot race between Grimes and another pitching prospect. Three times in a row Grimes beat him from centerfield to home plate; the last time he bet his competitor $10 he would win. The penniless Grimes won $10 and a spot on the Ottumwa roster.[11]

Grimes's feat ended up earning him a start in center field for the Packers' first exhibition game before settling into his place on the mound. Just a few weeks into the season, Grimes was already garnering attention for his pitching performances. After allowing

In 1913 Grimes's pitching for the Ottumwa (Iowa) Packers caught the eye of major league scouts (Charles Clark Photo Collection).

a run in an exhibition game against Des Moines, he went on a scoreless inning streak that caught the eye of big league clubs. He started with four hitless innings against the St. Paul Saints of the American Association, before striking out 13 in a 3–0 shutout of the Winnipeg Maroons, the eventual Northern League champions. He then pitched eight innings of two-hit relief against Keokuk (Indians), before coming within one out of throwing a no-hitter against Burlington (Pathfinders). All told he had pitched 29 consecutive scoreless innings.

By the end of May, scouts from the St. Louis Browns, Chicago White Sox, Chicago Cubs, Detroit Tigers and Pittsburgh Pirates were following the Speed Boys to different cities in the Central Association to see Ned Eagan's young hurler. Scout Jim McGuire, who said Grimes had "everything in the way of 'stuff' and unlimited nerve," convinced Tigers owner Frank Navin to sign the young pitcher and first baseman George Burns for a combined $4,000.[12]

Coming off a season in which the Tigers had finished in sixth place at their new ballpark, Navin Field, the Tigers were nearly 20 games back in the standings and needed all the help they could get in bringing fans out to the corner of Michigan and Trumbull. However, both players needed more work and were farmed out to different cities. Burns was sent to nearby Sioux City of the Western League, while Grimes was shipped some 700 miles southeast to play for the Chattanooga Lookouts of the Southern Association. He hoped a good showing would get him to Detroit by September or sooner.

Chattanooga is located in southeastern Tennessee on the banks of the Tennessee River. Like many early twentieth century Southern cities, Chattanooga boasted a booming iron and steel industry. It was a world away from the Grimes family farm in Wisconsin, and the next few months changed young Burleigh's life forever. Not yet out of his teens, he was introduced to Southern culture, played against a higher caliber of ballplayers than he had ever seen, wooed and married his first wife, and was influenced by a man who changed his in-game personality forever.

Named for nearby Lookout Mountain, the Chattanooga Lookouts had been a part of the eight-team Southern Association since that circuit succeeded the disbanded Southern League in 1901. The Lookouts never finished higher than fourth in that time and had finished in seventh the year before. They played their games at Andrews Field, built in 1910 by the team's owner, Chattanooga businessman Oliver Burnside (O.B.) Andrews. Located on East Third Street near the busy Southern Railway station, the field had a concrete foundation and drab, poorly constructed wooden bleachers that seated nearly 5,000. The bleachers had been so shoddily built that in January of 1914, carpenters who were doing their annual repairs "expressed surprise that they had not collapsed last season."[13]

Grimes arrived in Chattanooga on a rare off day. First-year Lookouts manager Norman Elberfeld had called off practice to give his depleted pitching staff some rest. Nicknamed "The Tabasco Kid" or "Kid" for his feisty demeanor, Elberfeld, who was playing shortstop in addition to his managerial duties, was beloved by his players and despised by seemingly everyone else. He was once described as "the dirtiest, scrappiest, most pestiferous, most rantankerous (sp), most rambunctious ball player that ever stood on spikes."[14]

In 1905 Elberfeld had given a Detroit Tigers rookie a rude welcome to the major leagues. While the youngster slid headfirst into second base, Elberfeld buried his knee into the ballplayer's neck, quickly cutting off his air supply. The rookie gasped for air as he struggled to get Elberfeld off him. The ballplayer's name was Ty Cobb and he never made the mistake of sliding headfirst again.

Elberfeld was said to have initiated Grimes into umpire baiting, bench jockeying and all-around intimidation on the diamond. Grimes's obedience to his manager earned him an immediate reputation that followed him into the professional game and made him a marked man at times. Years later, Grimes explained Elberfeld's influence on him. "I was an 18-year-old [sic] country boy. I'd been driving a four-horse team in a lumber camp for $35 a month, so when Elberfeld signed me for $150 per, I thought that was all the money in the world and that he was the greatest man. Being of such sentiments, I naturally did everything he told me to."[15]

With the Lookouts already having an established four-man rotation, Grimes was slated to serve as a reliever and spot starter in Chattanooga. His move to the Southern Association was an obvious step up in the level of competition, as a number of former and soon-to-be major leaguers graced the league's rosters. One of those players was the Lookouts' ace pitcher, Harry Coveleski, who was putting together one dominating performance after another. Nicknamed the "Giant Killer" for having defeated John McGraw's Giants three times in five days to keep them from winning the 1908 National League pennant, Coveleski had spent the past four seasons in the Southern Association trying to recapture that magic.

Elberfeld tabbed Grimes to start a June 12 home game against the Atlanta Crackers. After giving up a run in the top of the first, he cruised through until the fifth with the aid of his battery mate, Gabby Street, who threw out three would-be base stealers. In the sixth inning, Grimes lost his control and surrendered five runs on three hits, two walks, and a hit batsman before being removed from the game.

Grimes's next start was against the second-place Nashville Volunteers. He proved his worth to his teammates, giving up five hits in a 12-inning complete-game victory that leapfrogged the Lookouts into second place. He also caught the eye of a female admirer who had taken in the game. That evening, he and Gabby Street were dissecting the day's game while dining at their hotel when Grimes received a phone call. On the other end of the line was a fan from Atlanta by the name of Florence Ruth Patten. The two conversed for a while before deciding to get together for a date later that evening.

As the season progressed, it became apparent that a promotion to the Tigers wasn't going to happen. That didn't seem to matter, as Grimes soaked up life on and off the diamond. He visited his first ocean — the Atlantic — and enjoyed cookouts at the Elberfeld homestead in North Chattanooga. He mingled so easily among the locals that at times he was even mistaken for one. He developed a faux Southern drawl and concocted a family history in which his Grandfather Elias had come to Wisconsin as a youngster when "he traveled up the Mississippi River after contracting malaria while in Nashville."[16]

Elberfeld wasn't the only one who taught Grimes lessons about intimidation. He was sometimes the recipient of the opposition's tactics. At the time it was customary for all fielders, including the pitcher, to leave their gloves on the field while their team was at bat. Grimes followed suit, even going so far as to throwing his wad of slippery elm into his mitt when he retired to the bench. He had been doing this since his days on the Yellow Jackets, but soon encountered trouble: "I'd put the elm in my glove and drop the works between the mound and the dugout after each inning. But those guys on other teams would kick my glove and get my elm full of dirt."[17]

The Lookouts ended the season in fourth place at 70–64. Grimes finished with a pedestrian 6–7 record, but his defense was gaining rave reviews. In the bunt-heavy Dead Ball Era, a pitcher needed to know how to field his position, and Grimes did so impeccably. Going against the common practice of throwing with his right foot planted parallel to the rubber, Grimes "developed an unorthodox stance — he simply faced the plate squarely, planting his right foot at only a slight angle to the plate. Burleigh insisted he could throw harder and do more things about base runners than if he threw by pushing off in the conventional way."[18]

The highlight of Grimes's season took place off the field on the morning of August 9. Just nine days before his 20th birthday and some five weeks after their first date, Burleigh Grimes and Ruth Patten were married in front of teammates at Kid Elberfeld's home. It was the first of five marriages for Grimes and marked the beginning of an at times tumultuous seventeen-year union.

With only a verbal agreement that he would be back in Chattanooga in 1914, Grimes and his bride returned to his family's farm in Clear Lake. Once again, there were ballgames to be played and work to be done on the farm.

Only a few months into their marriage, problems were already arising between the newlyweds. A big-city Southern girl, Ruth had trouble adjusting to life on a Wisconsin farm: she didn't like living in Clear Lake and couldn't seem to get along with Grimes's parents or his siblings. Her frustration with the situation came to a head one day when she wanted to take a picture with Burleigh, who had been in the fields driving a grain wagon. Wearing overalls and a straw hat, he approached her on the porch. She urged him to remove the hat, but he refused and an argument ensued. Ruth ended it when she threw "the camera on the porch floor, stamped it to pieces and then kicked the pieces into the yard."[19]

When the fall harvest was finished, Grimes headed back into the woods for another winter of driving horses for $35 a month. Upon informing his fellow lumberjacks that he was set to receive $175 a month to play ball for Chattanooga in the spring, his bunkmates were indignant. Years later, he explained their incredulous reaction: "They don't mind a good liar up there, but they want him to use a little judgment in his lies. That was too raw for them to swallow."[20]

In late January of 1914, Grimes and a handful of his Lookout teammates were reported as "non-committal."[21] It wasn't that Grimes was weighing his options, but rather that he had yet to receive a contract. Detroit Tigers owner Frank Navin couldn't be blamed for not concerning himself with a little-known minor league pitcher when he was in jeopardy of losing Ty Cobb, his best player. While the Navin-Cobb contract haggling sessions had become a rite of spring, a suitor named James Gilmore, the new president of the Federal League, offered Cobb a five-year contract for $15,000 a year with the first year's salary paid in advance.[22] Cobb wasn't the only star being offered sizable raises by the upstart league, as Walter Johnson, Christy Mathewson, Sam Crawford and Tris Speaker were just a few of the big names said to be mulling substantial offers.

Formed in 1913, the Federal League had been a six-team independent circuit struggling to compete against not only the American and National League, but the International League as well. All that seemed to change when James Gilmore, a Chicago manufacturer, took over as league president on November 15, 1913. Gilmore enticed a number of wealthy investors, including Charles Weeghman of Chicago and Phil Ball of St. Louis, both of whom had been unsuccessful in earlier attempts to purchase major league clubs. Besides the Chicago Whales and St. Louis Terriers, the eight-team league included the Brooklyn Tip Tops, Pittsburgh Rebels, Kansas City Packers, Indianapolis Federals (Hoosiers), Buffalo BufFeds and the Baltimore Terrapins.

Grimes was still convinced that he would be pitching somewhere that summer and boldly wrote to Navin to inquire about the delay. In the meantime, he continued to haul lumber. In early February, Grimes and a close family friend, Louis Fitzer, were assigned to take a load of some 7,000 feet of timber from the Hall Lumber Camp near Rice Lake to the Hammond Spur. With Grimes leading a team of his father's horses and Fitzer acting as his watchman, they traversed the treacherous Wisconsin terrain. When they came to a steep embankment, Grimes and Fitzer cautiously navigated the team and its enormous parcel down the steep grade, with Fitzer throwing hay down as traction. As they descended, the sleigh was upended by a snow-covered rock. Fitzer was able to jump to safety, but Grimes was trapped in front of an avalanche of logs. Instinctively he jumped in front of the halted sleigh, the load rolling over the top of him. Miraculously, he landed in a position that saved his life, but was left unconscious with a broken left arm. After being rescued from his perilous position, Grimes was rushed to his parents' home to recover.

News of Grimes's injury reached Frank Navin. If there had been a sliver of hope of his return to Chattanooga or an invitation to train with the Tigers in Gulfport, Mississippi, the lumber accident put an end to those possibilities. Navin ended up retaining all his players from the previous season except for Grimes, who was put on waivers. He was soon signed by another team, the Southern Association Birmingham Barons, who had witnessed Grimes's potential the year before when he threw a ten-inning complete game and won it with an inside-the-park home run.

The Barons were owned by millionaire industrialist A.H. "Rick" Woodward, chairman of the Woodward Iron Company. Woodward had purchased the Barons in late 1909 and his first order of business had been a plan for a ballpark to replace the West End Park's "Slag Pile." Owned by the Tennessee Coal, Iron and Steel Company, the small ball field was known by that nickname because of the "mounds of slag beyond the outfield fence where fans could sit and watch games for free."[23] Woodward consulted part-owner and manager of the Philadelphia Athletics Connie Mack, who earlier in 1909 helped construct Shibe Park, the major leagues' first steel-and-concrete ballpark. Drawing from Shibe Park, as well as Cincinnati's Crosley Field and Pittsburgh's Forbes Field, Woodward also bucked the wooden bleacher norm and opened the minor leagues' first steel-and-concrete bleachers in August 1910. Its dimensions were 405 feet to the left field fence, 470 feet to center field, and 334 feet to right field. The new park's name was chosen in a newspaper poll: Rickwood Field.

Grimes delayed his arrival in Birmingham to let his immobilized arm heal, but in early March he removed the splint and made his way south. When

Grimes arrived, Barons manager Carleton Molesworth eased him into camp activities. Molesworth, whose career as a major league pitcher had spanned four games over a two-week period in late September 1895, had been manager of the Barons since 1908. Two years earlier, in 1912, his Birmingham squad had won a Southern Association title.

Nearly a month went by with minimal involvement in workouts, yet Grimes's previous laurels earned him a spot on the roster. Still suffering pain in his non-throwing arm, Grimes took to the Rickwood Field mound on April 17 against the Mobile Sea Gulls. He didn't make it out of the first inning, surrendering five runs on five walks, a balk, and just one hit. He lasted less than a month with the Barons, amassing a 0–2 record in four appearances and getting kicked out of the ballpark in Montgomery while coaching third base.

On May 5, with the Barons sitting in seventh place with a record of 5–11, Molesworth announced that the club was sending Grimes to the class C Richmond Colts of the Virginia League. He remained property of the Barons and was promised an invitation to spring training in 1915. Molesworth was encouraging, saying the demotion was essential to the young pitcher's growth. "Grimes has a world of stuff but he has much to learn in the pitching line. He should make us a winning pitcher next year," said the Birmingham manager.[24]

Once Grimes arrived in Richmond there seemed to be no signs of his early-season struggles. In his first five starts he went 3–1, with the other game being called a tie after 10 innings. He was also a standout at the plate, batting .500 (10 for 20) with two doubles and three triples. Local sportswriters, who had initially labeled him a malcontent, were surprised by the sunny disposition he displayed. "Mr. Grimes smiles, not a stingy, smirking smile, but the broad, encompassing variety that glows from ear to ear, and from eyelash to Adams apple."[25]

Grimes's record was 11–3 by the end of June and he established himself as the Colts' jack-of-all-trades. With a roster of just 14 players (including pitchers), he took on the role of bedrock starter, late-inning stopper, pinch-hitter, and pinch-runner. He started a game in right field and usually coached third base, enabling him to razz the pitcher.[26] He also showed that he hadn't lost any of his skills as a farmer, catching a well-greased pig that had been "turned loose among the players of both teams" as part of a post-game exhibition for Roanoke's Rotary Days.[27]

As the new star in town, Grimes could do little to distract Richmond baseball fans from the Baltimore Orioles of the International League. Jack Dunn's Orioles were struggling to compete with the Federal League's Baltimore entry, the Terrapins, despite being atop the International League standings.

The Richmond Business Men's Club was supportive of bringing a higher level of baseball to the city, but at the July 3 meeting of the directors of the Virginia League it was "decided Richmond was too important to the league and they would only permit the move of their Richmond club to another city if $15,000 was paid to the league in exchange for territorial rights to the city."[28] With no deal, Dunn was forced to sell off some of his young talent, including George Herman Ruth, who was packaged with Ernie Shore and Ben Egan to the Boston Red Sox for nearly $25,000.

At the same July 3 meeting, the Virginia league directors decided to split the season into two halves. The first half would end on August 1, while the second half would run into September. All games between July 2 and August 1 counted toward both halves of the season. The directors hoped "the arrangement would increase attendance by crafting two pennant races."[29]

Grimes continued his all-around consistency into the season's second half, winning five of his next six games and batting .500 (9-for-18) with three doubles, a triple and a home run.[30] Despite his efforts, the Colts finished second to the Norfolk Tars in both halves of the season. Grimes finished 23–13 on the mound and .331 at the plate, good enough for the batting title, having played in four games more than the 50-game requirement. He returned to the Birmingham Barons after the Colts ended their season, but did not see any action as the Barons wrapped up a Southern Association title.

With a professional baseball career in his sights, Grimes decided against risking life and limb by returning to the lumberjack trade. Instead he spent the winter months "rolling logs and clearing new ground on the family farm."[31] In late December, he wrote to Birmingham owner Rick Woodward to explain that his poor showing for the Barons the previous spring had been due to the logging accident that nearly took his life. He assured Woodward that "My arm is feeling fine and I am ready to go. I was unfortunate in getting a late start last season, but I honestly believe that I will make someone on the Baron club hustle for a berth next season."[32]

In January, Grimes received a contract with Birmingham and a ticket to Orlando for spring training. When he stepped off the train in Florida, he brashly declared that "he was a regular and didn't like to be called a rookie."[33] Despite unfavorable weather for much of the team's stay, the Barons took advantage of their surroundings by spending much of their off-time fishing or hiking around the beautiful lakes and orange groves. They also had open access to a nearby country club, where many players golfed or played tennis. After wrapping up their training the Barons arrived in Birmingham, where a few welcome-home celebrations were followed by a weeklong slate of games against major league teams, including the Cubs, Indians and Pirates.

Although Grimes had declared himself a "regular," he was still not guaranteed a spot on the roster. To test his mettle, manager Carleton Molesworth pegged him as a starter against the Cubs. Playing in front of a crowd that included the Pittsburgh Pirates, the Barons played shaky defense behind Grimes in a 7–4 loss, but his spitball was impressive and he struck out nine Cubs.

The next day Birmingham owner Rick Woodward, who often suited up and went through drills with the team, was out on the field when he was approached by Honus Wagner. Intimidated by the Pirates great, Woodward opted not to talk baseball; instead he brought up fishing, one of Wagner's passions away from the diamond. Woodward later recalled that Wagner "got all pepped up over that and we went into the bleachers and sat there until game time. He did not even take infield practice. As he got up to leave, he said, 'By the way, this boy Grimes you had in there yesterday looks pretty good to me. If I were you I would hold on to him.'"[34]

A week after receiving this high praise from Honus Wagner, Grimes was slotted as the Barons' fourth starter. The third pitcher was fellow Wisconsinite Art Johnson, an eccentric right-hander from the Madison area who was said to be "as big a 'nut' as any lefthander one ever saw," often entertaining fans with his spot-on Charlie Chapin gait.[35]

"Bertillion" or "Bertie," as Grimes was referred to by the local press, started out in midseason form and could have easily been 6–0 by early May if not for shoddy defense behind him. Instead he was 4–2, with his early success including two shutouts, a 12-strikeout performance and complete games in all six starts. He also was hot at the plate, batting .333 (7-for-21), including a pair of doubles and two triples.

In addition to his solid pitching, the press took notice that Grimes "is a clean liver, doesn't drink, smoke or chew. Never touched a cigarette in his life."[36] All of his clean living couldn't keep him from becoming ill. He came down with a case of the mumps in early May, leaving him with a swollen face as a result of enflamed glands. Grimes needed nearly two weeks to recover. Early-season maladies proved to be a problem that plagued Grimes throughout his playing days.

When Grimes finally returned to the mound after a two-week layoff, it took a while to get his legs back under him. The Barons' strong pitching staff was able to compensate for Grimes, who was unable to put together consecutive strong outings. Finally toward the end of July and early August he returned to full strength, winning four of five starts. Those victories didn't go without incident, however, as he nearly incited a brawl against his former team, the Chattanooga Lookouts, on July 31. After throwing a high and inside pitch to Frank Kitchens, the Lookouts catcher headed for the mound with his bat in hand. Both teams congregated there before "cooler heads prevailed on them not to start a free-for-all which seemed imminent."[37]

After regaining his health, Grimes put together a three-game stretch that had major league scouts once again taking note of the right-hander. On August 18 he pitched the Barons to a scoreless 11-inning tie with the Chattanooga Lookouts.[38] Three days later he shut the Lookouts out on three hits. He followed that up with a 14-inning 1–1 tie against the Memphis Chickasaws on August 26. In all, Grimes threw 34 innings, allowed 13 hits and gave up just one run over the three games.

A September call-up to the major leagues seemed inevitable, but on the next-to-last day of August Grimes ended his chances of playing in the majors that year by taking part in an ugly altercation with the Nashville Volunteers. In the top of the sixth inning, Grimes fielded a slow roller up the first base line by Monroe "Dolly" Stark, applying a firm tag to the Nashville shortstop. Stark, a fiery competitor in his own right took umbrage with the tag and lowered his shoulder, sending both players tumbling to the ground. Grimes hopped to his feet and fired the ball at Stark, who deflected the throw and charged at the hurler. Grimes's pugilistic instincts took over and he knocked the charging Stark to the ground with a vicious blow to the jaw. The incident set off a free-for-all, but when the dust settled, Grimes was the only player who was kicked out of the game.

Following the game Grimes said he was merely defending himself after Starks spiked him. "I did not intend to hit him with the ball, but I was mad good and plenty," said Grimes.[39] Having already been warned after the near brawl with Chattanooga a month earlier, league officials suspended Grimes for 10 days. The *Birmingham News* explained the situation with humor: "When Mr. Grimes hit Dolly Stark in the head with a baseball and came near ruining a perfectly good baseball he ruined his chances of entering the big leagues this Fall."[40] When Grimes returned from his suspension he went 3–2, finishing up at 17–13 for the second-place Barons.

Instead of returning to Wisconsin, Grimes and his wife wintered in Birmingham and Burleigh found work at the Tennessee Coal, Iron and Railroad (TCI) plant. The labor differed from his usual off-season regimen, but by the end of the winter he reported that working in the plant had made him "hard as nails."[41] There was no disputing his place as a regular on the Barons' roster as they headed into the 1916 season. With much of the starting rotation intact, a strong showing was expected.

Bothered by an unspecified injury to his side that required bandaging, Grimes's season got off to a disastrous start. He lost his first three decisions on embarrassing lapses: two of the losses came via a wild pitch (one of which sailed into the grandstand) that allowed the winning run to score, while the third came on a bases-loaded walk. While the injury surely affected his pitching, he was also distracted by an event off the field. Back home in Clear Lake, his beloved grandfather Elias had succumbed to bronchial pneumonia. Being unable to be with his family during this time weighed heavily on Grimes.

In light of the high expectations placed upon him, Grimes's first few months were a disappointment. A two-game winning streak brought his record to 7–7 heading into the last week of June, placing him in the middle of the pack for Southern Association pitching. He wasn't alone in underperforming, however. The other Barons pitchers weren't doing much better, leaving the club in fifth place on July 1 with a record of 32–39.

Much as he had the year before, Grimes then heated up and strung together a streak of games that again had scouts following him. From July 1 through August 3, he amassed a 5–2 record, and during the last five appearances he gave up a total of 15 base hits, only four of which left the infield.

Grimes's pitching as a member of the Birmingham Barons in 1915 and 1916 led to a contract with the Pittsburgh Pirates. Grimes is kneeling in the middle row, far right, in this 1915 team photograph (Charles Clark Photo Collection).

The *Birmingham News* raved that Grimes "has more stuff than any pitcher in the Southern Association and as strong an arm as any man in baseball."[42] Charlie "Boss" Schmidt, a former major league catcher who was managing and catching for the Mobile Sea Gulls, echoed the sentiment, but added the one caveat that plagued Grimes throughout his minor league tenure and continued into the first few years of his professional career. "That fellow Grimes has more stuff than any man I have ever faced, but he knows less how to use it," said Schmidt.[43]

On August 5 the Pittsburgh Pirates purchased Grimes's contract from Birmingham. Another club had also been interested in him, but Pirates scout William "Captain" Neal urged owner Barney Dreyfuss to sign Grimes immediately. The move was "the forerunner of an agreement between Barney Dreyfuss" and Birmingham Barons team president W.D. Smith "that the local club would get the best Pirates had to offer in the way of players next season."[44]

The Pirates agreed to a stipulation that allowed Grimes not to leave Birmingham until the completion of the Southern Association season. Vexed at the decision, Grimes vented about the possibility of having to return to Birmingham the following year. "If I can't make more money playing ball than the Southern League has to offer I can doing something else," he declared, before adding that he was "through with this circuit for good."[45] His frustration didn't show on the mound as he continued his blistering pace, accumulating a 6–1 record over the next five weeks. He finished with a record of 20–11, but it wasn't enough to push the Barons higher than a sixth-place finish.

After the Barons' final game, Grimes and his wife boarded a train out of the "Pittsburgh of the South" and headed for Chicago, where the Pirates were scheduled to play the Cubs. His ascension to the major leagues had taken four years.

3

Problems in Pittsburgh, 1916–1917

Sitting on a northbound train, Grimes knew little of the situation that he was being thrust into with the Pittsburgh Pirates. Team owner Barney Dreyfuss was cutting costs whenever and wherever he could, while manager Jimmy Callahan was said to have never been able gain control of the clubhouse. It was a less-than-glamorous introduction to the professional game for the young right-hander.

In 1883 German-born Barney Dreyfuss had immigrated to Paducah, Kentucky, where he worked as an accountant for the Bernheim Brothers Distillery, owned by his cousins. Dreyfuss diligently crunched numbers and studied English until long hours caused his health to suffer. On orders from his doctor, Dreyfuss began to spend more time outdoors exercising. He chose the game of baseball, playing on amateur teams in and around Paducah. When the Bernheim Brothers Distillery moved to Louisville in 1888, Dreyfuss moved with them and within two years he had purchased a share of the National League's Louisville Colonels. By 1899 he was sole owner.

Shortly after Dreyfuss obtained full title to the Colonels, the National League decided to contract from 12 to eight franchises. The four franchises that were eliminated were Louisville, Baltimore, Cleveland and Washington.[1] Ever the shrewd businessman, Dreyfuss "brokered a deal that allowed him to purchase a half interest in the Pittsburgh Pirates and by accepting a smaller settlement from the National League ($10,000), take 14 of his Louisville players with him."[2] Included in those 14 were: Deacon Phillippe, considered the greatest right-handed pitcher in Pirates history; Tommy Leach, who at 5-foot-6 and 140 pounds was one of the better power hitters of the first decade of 1900s; Fred Clarke, longtime player-manager and future Hall-of-Famer, and the immortal Honus Wagner.

In the decade and a half after moving to Pittsburgh, Dreyfuss became one of the game's most respected owners. He transformed the Pirates into one of the league's most consistent winners, earning the nickname "First Division Barney" after 13 years of prosperity that saw the club always finish at least seven games over .500.[3] Often a member of the rules committee and heavily involved in league scheduling, Dreyfuss worked diligently to better the game of baseball, most notably by helping organize the first World Series in 1903 (which the Pirates lost to the Boston Americans five games to three).

The Pirates faltered in 1914 and 1915, finishing 69–85 and 73–81, respectively. Most of the players who brought the franchise to prominence were either no longer on the team or past their prime. Now into his 40s and still the face of the franchise, the great Honus Wagner's skills had begun to erode. In addition, longtime manager Fred Clarke stepped down after the 1915 campaign after amassing a 1,602–1,181 record. He led the Pirates to two World Series, one of which they won in 1909 over the Detroit Tigers. In his place came Jimmy Callahan, who took over in 1916 after Wagner refused the job. A former pitcher-outfielder, his claim to fame as a pitcher was throwing the first no-hitter in American League history while with the Chicago White Sox. Most recently as manager he had led the White Sox on a barnstorming trip of Japan with the New York Giants.

The Pirates were in Chicago to start a 22-game road trip. Rain had put a strain on the club's schedule throughout the season, so they were making a one-day stop to make up a game from earlier in the season. Grimes and his wife arrived at Union Depot early Sunday morning, and made their way to the team's hotel to drop off luggage before heading over to Weeghman Park (later known as Wrigley Field).

Hours after arriving in the Windy City, Grimes found himself walking to the mound in relief in the bottom of the fifth inning, the Pirates losing, 5–0. He put in a solid first appearance in an apparent mop-up role, allowing two runs on three hits through the eighth. In the top of the ninth, Pittsburgh strung together six runs, making the score 8–7 Pirates. Grimes went back out for the ninth as the pitcher of record, but was removed with no outs as Al Mamaux came on to preserve the victory. It was the first of 270 major league victories for Grimes.

Two days later Grimes started against the first place and eventual pennant-winning Brooklyn Robins at Ebbets Field. It was a close game that the Pirates ended up losing 3–2, with Grimes being tagged with the tough loss. The key play of the game was an error by shortstop Honus Wagner in the sixth. With a runner on first base Wagner strode to the mound to offer a few words of encouragement. "Make him hit it to me kid," he said confidently before returning to his position. The next batter, Brooklyn right-fielder Casey Stengel, hit an easy double-play ground ball right at Wagner. The ball went through the Flying Dutchman's legs. Once again Wagner returned to the mound and wryly addressed Grimes, "Those damn big feet have always been in my way."[4]

The Pirates' pennant hopes had died months ago, so Callahan, looking ahead to the 1917 season, decided to give his younger players as many opportunities as possible for the duration of the season. He then feigned illness and went on a bender with friends in Philadelphia, forcing Wagner into managerial duties for the entire six-game series at the Polo Grounds against the Giants, winners of nine straight. After losing the first three games of the series, Grimes started the back end of a Monday doubleheader. He held New York to three hits in a 1–1 tie that was called after nine innings due to rain. The tie was significant because it was the only blemish in the Giants' major league-record 26-game winning streak.[5]

On September 30 the Pirates were finally able to showcase their new pitcher at Forbes Field. Pittsburgh's state-of-the-art steel and concrete ballpark was located in the Oakland suburb near Carnegie-Mellon University, some three miles away from the smog of downtown Pittsburgh. On June 30, 1909, it had replaced Exposition Park, whose proximity to the Allegheny River often led to the outfield being flooded. Initially, Dreyfuss was mocked for situating the new field so far from downtown. Instead, however, people flocked to the state-of-the-art stadium, which was equipped with a three-tiered grandstand and ramps and elevators to ease navigation throughout the multi-tiers.

Attendance at Forbes Field in 1916 was under 300,000 for the fourth year in a row, but Grimes's maiden appearance at Forbes Field was well attended. In the stands to cheer him on in the second game of a doubleheader against the Reds were his Birmingham Barons manager Carleton Molesworth and the man who helped bring him to Pittsburgh, scout "Captain" Neal. Both men boasted loudly of their protégé. Grimes pitched another solid game, but once again poor defense spelled disaster — four errors, including three from young second baseman Carson Bigbee, led to five runs, four of which were unearned. Although tagged with the loss, Grimes made an impression. "The Pirates surely have picked up a first-class boxman in this youngster," reported the *Pittsburgh Press*.[6] The setback put his record at two wins and three losses for the season.

The following day the Pirates closed out their season with a loss in Cincinnati. The defeat ran Pittsburgh's losing streak to a season-high ten games and meant that the team finished the season 28 games behind pennant-winning Brooklyn and 24 games under .500.

Within a week of the season's end, Grimes and his wife were back in Clear Lake, Wisconsin. Grimes worked on the family farm that winter and got reacquainted with friends and family. He also spent a lot of time in the woods hunting with his brother Shurleigh, who was becoming quite a pitcher in his own right. Several inches taller than his older brother, some said that Shurleigh was as good a pitcher as Burleigh, but lacked the gumption of his elder brother. Burleigh also was inducted into the local Masonic Chapter; he would remain a member (although not too active a one) for the rest of his life.

During the trip back home, Grimes began the practice of hoarding lush slippery elm from the Clear Lake area. He stocked up for the season, keeping his cache in an airtight pine box. Grimes had found out the hard way that store-bought slippery elm wasn't the same, because while sitting on the shelf of a drug store the elm absorbed the aroma of whatever was around it. The first time he encountered this phenomenon while in the minor leagues it made him physically sick.

The offseason was an unsettled one for the Pirates organization. Clubhouse turmoil became public when it was revealed that one of the team's few stars, outfielder Max Carey, had been at odds with Jimmy Callahan for much of the season. *Sporting Life* reported that, "For stages of two weeks plus the two parties at loggerheads failed to exchange words with each other."[7] Carey and his backers pushed for a trade to the Giants. It was rumored that "John McGraw will take Max off the Pirates' hands any old time the local outfit puts him on the block. Some assert that Mac has longed for the man and stands ready to fork over players and lucre for the fast mover."[8] Dreyfuss knew better than to part with one of the game's premier outfielders.

Max Carey had been called up to the Pirates as a shortstop in the last few days of the 1910 season. When he reported to the stadium for infield practice, he famously went out to shortstop and informed Honus Wagner "that he was here to be the team's new shortstop."[9] He moved to the outfield the next season, embarking on his Hall of Fame career. Carey's greatest asset was his legs, which on advice from Wagner he kept well conditioned in the offseason. Forbes Field fit his style of play, as he could track down balls in the cavernous outfield on defense and could turn singles into doubles and doubles into triples at the plate. An excellent base stealer, Carey ended his career with a total of 738 swipes. He also left his mark on baseball attire by wearing a new design of sliding pants (which he later patented) and flip-up sunglasses before they were popularized.

Carey wasn't the only person who had a problem with Callahan's managerial style. A contingent of fans, press and unnamed players were said to have questioned his managerial competency. Dreyfuss showed faith in his manager, however, even after he found out about the bender in Philadelphia. Instead of disciplining Callahan, Dreyfuss fired team secretary Peter Kelly, who along with members of the Pittsburgh press had tried to cover up the binge. "Peter was supposedly working for me, not Callahan," said the perturbed owner.[10]

None of the chaos within the Pittsburgh organization seemed to bother Grimes, who showed up early for his first major league spring training in Columbus, Georgia. Since taking over the Pirates, Dreyfuss had always sent his team to Hot Springs, Arkansas, being one of the first owners to do so. He was a proponent of the area's baths and spas, feeling that they were beneficial to his players' early-season conditioning. In recent years, however, Hot Springs had become a fashionable leisure resort, with golf taking precedence over baseball. Perhaps swayed by the new atmosphere or possibly driven by financial reasons, Dreyfuss decided to move training camp to Georgia.

Early in camp Callahan spoke highly of his young right-hander. "Grimes has a world of speed, quickly-breaking curves, and is a master of the change of pace," said the Pirates manager.[11] Grimes was projected to be one of a trio of pitchers who would make up for their shortcomings — namely every other aspect of the game. Beside Grimes was Al Mamaux, the right-handed Pittsburgh native who had had back-to-back 21-win seasons, and Wilbur Cooper, who appeared to be cut from the same cloth as Grimes. A sturdy lefty with a blazing fastball and a devastating curve, Cooper's disdain for defensive incompetence led him to openly berate teammates after a misplay. Of the three, Mamaux seemed to be the most talented, but the least interested in the game. Instead he indulged in libations, women and song, which would lead to the premature end to his professional playing days, but an extended stay on the vaudeville circuit.[12]

The emergence of the promising young pitching staff was overshadowed by the glaring absence of Honus Wagner. A hometown boy, Wagner was born February 24, 1874, in Chartiers, just outside of Pittsburgh. The local boy had returned in 1900, brought home from Louisville by Barney Dreyfuss, and became arguably the best player of the Dead Ball Era: he never batted lower than .300 from 1899–1913; fell just four extra-base hits short of 1,000 for his career; was quietly one of the best base stealers of all-time, swiping 723 for his career; and played a nimble shortstop, utilizing his powerful throwing arm.

A longtime bachelor, Wagner had quietly gotten married on the evening of December 30, 1916, to Bessie Baine Smith who was said to "be a good cook, liked baseball and the outdoors, could bait a hook and loved him despite his homeliness."[13] When Wagner was offered a contract for a reported $5,400 (down from $10,000), he declined the offer.

Following training camp, the Pirates had 10 exhibition games scheduled as they worked their way north for the April 11 regular season opener at Cincinnati. The docket included a pair of games at Birmingham's Rickwood Field against the Barons on April 6, allowing Grimes to return to his old stomping grounds in the Southern Association. It was an unfortunate sign of things to come, however, as he barely made it through the fourth inning with the Pirates managing just two hits in the 8–2 loss.

The loss was likely noticed by very few because the following day's headlines were dominated by the United States declaring war on Germany. The United States had remained a noncombatant since World War I had begun in the summer of 1914, but continuing threats to U.S. citizens, including the sinking of three American merchant ships in March, prompted President Woodrow Wilson to ask Congress for a declaration of war against Germany on April 2. The declaration was made public on April 6. In his war address, Wilson declared that the world "must be made safe for democracy."[14]

Heading into the 1917 season, the Pirates saw Grimes as one of stars of the future (Charles Clark Photo Collection).

With Dreyfuss having done nothing to better the team in the off-season, the Wagner-less Pirates struggled to start the season. Grimes excelled, however, putting together four strong starts in a row. Unfortunately, he was backed by a putrid offense and a shaky defense so his record was only 2–2. Both wins were 3-hitters against the Cubs (April 20) and the Reds (April 28).

Cincinnati Enquirer sportswriter and editor Jack Ryder, not usually one to give praise to those who weren't wearing a Reds uniform, raved to a member of the *Brooklyn Daily Eagle* about the Pirates rookie. Ryder "began to deliver a long dissertation upon a husky youngster on the Pirate roster named Burleigh Grimes. He borrowed a smoke and a match, but never interrupted his flow of conversation about this athlete, and we perforce became interested."[15]

On May 10 Grimes won his third game of the season by throwing 5⅔ innings of relief against the Boston Braves. It evened his record at 3–3, but he wouldn't win another game for the rest of the season.

In his next start on May 15 in Philadelphia, Grimes was cruising along, giving up two hits and striking out six through the first four innings. In the top of the fifth, however, he wrenched his knee sliding into home plate on a close play. When he took the mound in the fifth he couldn't put any weight on the knee and was quickly batted out of the box. Initial reports were that Grimes would "not be able to work for several days," but he was back on the mound three days later, losing to the Giants.[16] The loss put the Pirates' record at 8–18, dropping them into eighth place. It was a spot they held for the remainder of the season, which turned out to be one of the franchise's worst campaigns ever.

On May 21, President Woodrow Wilson ordered all males between the ages of 21 and 30 to register in their hometown by June 5. Unable to make it back to Polk County, Grimes filed papers in Pittsburgh on May 29. There were already several prominent baseball players serving in the military. Shortly after President Wilson's declaration of war, former New York Giants third baseman Eddie Grant had enlisted in the Army. The first active ballplayer to enter the service was Hank Gowdy, who joined the Ohio National Guard on June 1.

Despite his pitching woes and the possibility of being drafted, Grimes and his wife tried to have some type of normality in their lives. On June 3, Burleigh was baptized at a Baptist Church in the Oakland neighborhood, just a few blocks from Forbes Field.

In early June, after a few weeks of speculation, the Pirates got some good news when it was announced that Honus Wagner would be back in a Pittsburgh uniform. After Dreyfuss and Wagner reached an agreement, Wagner sent off a telegram to the chairman of the National Commission, August "Garry" Herrmann. "Finding the call of baseball too strong to resist, I desire to continue to play the game I love, and to which I owe all I possess, and I hereby petition the National Commission to grant my request for reinstatement, so that I may play with my old club tomorrow," said Wagner.[17]

It was evident that this would be Wagner's final year, and other National League teams planned an unofficial farewell tour when he came to their town. He actually played a serviceable first base and looked surprisingly sprightly at bat, but it did little to help Pittsburgh's cause. The losses also continued to mount for Grimes, whose record sunk to 2–8 after a loss to the Giants on June 13. Following the defeat, his fifth consecutive, Grimes was informed that he was being removed from the starting rotation in favor of lefty Bob Steele.

It's unclear who ordered the move, but Callahan and Dreyfuss had been at odds all year. The manager felt that the owner's miserly ways were affecting the ballclub's morale. To begin with, most Pittsburgh players were making less than their counterparts. Dreyfuss also skimped on road expenses, giving Pirates players only $2.50 for food (compared to $3 for other teams), while only reserving one sleeper car (compared to other teams' two). The Pittsburgh owner had started to agree with the sentiment that Callahan was doing a poor job of catering to the team's personalities, especially Al Mamaux, who was more concerned with what he was doing after the game.

On June 30 prior to a game against Cincinnati, Jimmy Callahan was dismissed by Dreyfuss with the club in eighth place at 20–40. Dreyfuss had to scramble to find a replacement after Honus Wagner once again declined the job. Considered to replace Callahan were Larry Doyle of the Chicago Cubs, Harry Wolverton of the Pacific Coast League's San Francisco Seals and Jack Hendricks of the American Association's Indianapolis Indians. Meanwhile, Callahan began airing his frustrations with Dreyfuss' tightfistedness to anyone with a pen. Pirates stockholders, some of whom hadn't been paid dividends in two years, called for Dreyfuss's resignation. Finally, after a great deal of cajoling, it was announced that Wagner would manage the club, but would be free of business duties, which were assigned to West Coast scout Hugo Bezdek.

Wagner's tenure as manager lasted all of five games, winning his first and losing the next four. Having never wanted to be manager in the first place, he stepped down on July 4 and Dreyfuss promptly named Bezdek manager. A former star fullback for Alonzo Stagg at the University of Chicago, he was currently the supervisor of physical instruction and head football coach at the University of Oregon. Bezdek's baseball experience was limited to playing for Stagg's ballclub in the spring, as well as coaching at the University of Arkansas, where he scrimmaged against the Pirates a few years earlier. He had impressed then-manager Fred Clarke so much that he suggested that Dreyfuss make Bezdek the team's West Coast scout.

Under Bezdek, the Pirates started off with three consecutive victories, but not without a cost as left fielder Bill Hinchman, who had been the offensive leader the year before, broke his leg sliding into home on a pointless double steal in the ninth inning. A week later, Wagner was inadvertently spiked by Brooklyn's Casey Stengel sliding into first base. The injury greatly affected Wagner's output for the remainder of the year. Wagner's heir apparent at shortstop, Chuck Ward, continued to struggle. The only consistent player was Wilbur Cooper, who won 17 games (the team's only pitcher with a winning record) and logged nearly 300 innings (297⅔). It didn't seem to matter who was managing. The Pirates were a dreadful ballclub.

On the morning of July 20, a blindfolded Secretary of War Newton Baker started the military draft by drawing a numbered capsule from a large glass bowl. Throughout the day and into the early-morning hours of the next, draft numbers continued to be drawn by clerks. One of those capsules was numbered 1769, belonging to Burleigh Arland Grimes.

Unaware that he had been drafted into the military, Grimes pitched the next day against the New York Giants. He was given his first start in nearly six weeks in favor of Al Mamaux, who had been suspended indefinitely for not returning to the team's hotel the night before. In addition to the game, a full military spectacle was planned, highlighted by the display of the flag, marching guardsmen, and the Naval Band playing between innings.

Since his last start Grimes had accumulated three more losses in relief appearances, but he looked sharp against the first-place Giants. After the Pirates squandered a no-out, bases-loaded situation in the top of the tenth inning, the Giants scored a run off Grimes in the bottom half of the frame on a pair of errors by catcher Walter Schmidt. The 4–3 loss put Grimes's losing steak at 12.

No team hit Grimes better during the 1917 season than the New York Giants. He lost all four of his starts against them and received no decision in a long relief appearance. In all he gave up 32 runs on 46 hits in 37⅔ innings. It is not surprising that a team that went on to win the National League pennant (before losing the World Series to the White Sox four games to two) was able to effectively hit a struggling rookie, but the Giants also had some help. Veteran shortstop Art Fletcher, who was often near the top of the leader board in being hit by a pitch, was an expert at picking up on a pitcher's idiosyncrasies. Early in the season, he noticed that Grimes was tipping his pitches. Years later, Grimes explained his mistake. "Instead of tucking my pinkie under the ball, I would stick it out to the side — you know, the way a woman daintily holds a teacup," recalled Grimes.[18]

Within a week of being inserted back into the starting rotation, Grimes received notice that he had been drafted into the military and was to report to Balsam Lake, Wisconsin, on August 6, to be given a physical. He immediately filed for an exemption on account of being the sole income provider for his wife. Meanwhile, President Wilson put to rest speculation that the rest of the season would be canceled. In response to an inquiry, his secretary replied: "The president sees no necessity at all for stopping or curtailing the Base Ball schedule."[19]

Although Grimes wasn't able to earn a victory with his arm, at least he was able to contribute to one with his legs. In a game on August 15 against Cincinnati, he pinch ran for slow-footed catcher William Fischer. Grimes reached third on a single by Wagner before scoring on a Walter Schmidt single to center.

Grimes somehow missed out on pitching in Pittsburgh's four consecutive extra-inning contests between August 19–23 in which they played a total of 60 innings —14 against the Phillies and 46 against the Robins. The final game against Brooklyn went 22 innings, ending in a 6–5 loss. That weekend the Pirates lost two of three games from the seventh-place Boston Braves (Grimes allowed only four hits but dropped a tough four-hit decision in the opening game). Following the last game the team traveled to New York, where they had an off day before a series against the first-place Giants. There would be no resting on that off day, however, as the Pirates were to travel across the Hudson to Paterson, New Jersey, where they were to play a local team as part of the ongoing Honus Wagner farewell tour. Wagner had started his career in Paterson 20 years earlier. A large crowd was expected and he was to be presented with a silver chest.

With the train traveled to New York, the Pittsburgh players tried to get what rest they could. It was late in the evening when several sailors boarded the team's private coach. Manager Bezdek explained to them that the car was chartered by the Pirates and was able to persuade most of them to leave. Three stuck around, however, and one of them pulled a large knife. Bezdek went after the seaman, but before he could reach him, "Grimes had seized the intruder from behind and the big pitcher shoved him bodily upon the platform."[20] After Bezdek escorted the other two men to another car, the team was able to laugh about the near fight. A week later it would be no laughing matter when Grimes and Bezdek came to blows in one of the most vicious player-manager fights of all time.

It had been another tough Saturday for the Pirates, having just lost both ends of a doubleheader to the Cardinals by identical 1–0 scores (also the score of the game they lost the day before). As the Pullman traveled toward Cincinnati, Grimes, who was scheduled to start the next day, congregated in a washroom with teammates Max Carey, Carson Bigbee, Bill Fischer, and Pirates beat writer Chilly Doyle. The group began to vent their frustrations about being on a last-place team. Much of their vitriol was aimed at management, in particular team president Dreyfuss. As the group conversed, Bezdek entered the cramped quarters. Everyone immediately quieted down except for Grimes, who continued his diatribe from his seat on the windowsill.

"You're getting paid every two weeks, aren't you?" snapped Bezdek, who had heard enough.

"Well, so are you," retorted Grimes. He wasn't particularly happy with Bezdek either, having been used sporadically since the manager had taken over.

Grimes then turned his anger toward Bezdek, demanding an answer for his perceived misuse. Bezdek's response implied that Grimes lacked the intestinal fortitude to succeed at the major league level. Soon the men were nose-to-nose and the argument continued until Bezdek had heard enough, reeled back and punched Grimes on the chin. Burleigh absorbed the powerful blow and pounced on his manager, who had several inches and nearly 50 pounds on him. The pair became locked in a tight embrace, crashing around the confined space. Bezdek got his fingers in the corner of Grimes's mouth and began to pull. Burleigh responded by nearly biting off his manager's finger.

Stunned members of the Pirates finally got them separated, moving the bloodied men to respective ends of the car. From his end, a still-enraged Bezdek wagered $1,000 that he could beat up Grimes. His fists full of money and his bloodied shirt in tatters, Grimes came storming down the aisle to meet the challenge. This time teammates were able to intervene before things escalated any further.

Once the fracas died down, Pirates road secretary Sam Walters asked Bezdek if they should drop Grimes off at the next station. "No," replied Bezdek, nursing his mangled finger. "If he shows the right spirit I'll pitch him tomorrow."[21]

Wearing his pajama coat, the only suitable piece of clothing that wasn't shredded, Grimes remained on the train. Bezdek did start him the next day, and although he didn't factor into the decision, the Pirates came through with an 8–7 victory. It was the last start of the season for Grimes, but the scuffle seemed to momentarily reenergize the Pirates, as they went on a season-high four-game win streak. A month later the Pirates' season mercifully ended with a record of 51–103. The team's only winning month was their 1–0 October.

Grimes ended the season with a 3–16 record, losing his last 13 decisions. He did finish 18 games in relief, good enough for second in the National League. A final insult was hurled at Grimes's losing streak when he and Mamaux, who had finished 2–11 in just 16 games, were named to *Baseball Magazine*'s "All-Star Cellar Champs," a tongue-in-cheek celebration of the most disastrous outputs of the season: "Grimes, although receiving great help from his cellar champ club, forced opponents to win from him 16 times and has 13 straight games in which he kept his club from the disgrace of winning."[22]

The winter once again brought out discussions of rule changes. Barney Dreyfuss championed the idea of banning the spitball and other doctored-ball pitches. Grimes spent the winter in Birmingham, working as the manager of the Birmingham Bowling Alley. In early January 1918, Dreyfus summoned Grimes and fellow spitballer Hal Carlson to Pittsburgh to inform them of the possible rule change. He urged them to take the opportunity to return to the minor leagues and develop another pitch to replace the spitter. Carlson took Dreyfuss up on the offer, but Grimes was defiant. Sealing his fate, he refused the offer, telling a flustered Dreyfuss, "I came to the big leagues with it and I'm gonna throw it."[23]

A few days after his meeting at Dreyfuss's office, Grimes got word that he had been traded. On January 9, 1918, Grimes, Al Mamaux and Chuck Ward were dealt to the Brooklyn Robins for George Cutshaw and fan-favorite Casey Stengel. Most sportswriters and fans viewed Grimes as a "throw-in" on the deal. Those involved in the game, however, believed that Grimes had tremendous potential. His former manager Jimmy Callahan spoke highly of him. Despite their knock-down-drag-out brawl, Hugo Bezdek saw a bright future for the youngster. "Grimes has the makings of a bang up right hander. With a man like [Brooklyn manager Wilbert] Robinson to put a fine edge on him and initiate him into the secrets of his art, he will be a corker, or I will be very much mistaken," said the Pirates manager.[24] Even Dreyfuss praised him: "I know we dealt away a fine young pitcher, but that Grimes just fights with everyone, friend or foe."[25] Brooklyn management also remembered the high praise of the *Cincinnati Enquirer*'s Jack Ryder early in the season. They felt that Grimes could turn out to be the jewel of the trade.

4

Boily in Brooklyn, 1918–1921

The trade of Grimes to the Dodgers coincided with the 20th anniversary of Brooklyn's membership as one of the five boroughs of New York City. The milestone was celebrated by few Brooklynites, many of whom referred to the merger as the Great Mistake of 1898. After two decades, many Brooklyn residents still felt they weren't accepted as part of the city. That seemed to suit them just fine, enabling them to thrive on the neighborhood atmosphere of the Borough of Trees.

Brooklyn's chip-on-the-shoulder attitude spilled over onto the baseball diamond where the Robins, who despite having reached the World Series in 1916, played in the shadow of the juggernaut New York Giants. The animosity between the two clubs was heightened by the strained relationship between the two managers. John McGraw and Wilbert Robinson had been close friends and teammates on the rough-and-tumble Baltimore Orioles of the 1890s, even going into business off the field.

A former catcher, Robinson joined the Giants coaching staff in 1910. According to author Alex Semchuk, "His main duties were keeping the club loose, jockeying the opposition, and developing the pitching staff."[1] Robinson and McGraw had an ugly falling out in 1913 at an Orioles reunion following New York's series-ending Game Five loss to the Philadelphia Athletics. A drunken McGraw loudly criticized Robinson's third base coaching, to which Robinson retorted with a critique of McGraw's managerial skills. McGraw kicked Robinson out of the get-together, but not before Robinson doused him with a glass of beer. To spite his former friend, Robinson signed to manage the Brooklyn club less than a month after their squabble.

Although formally known as the Brooklyn Dodgers, they were commonly referred to as the "Robins" in a nod to their manager. The Robins had finished in seventh place in 1917, ahead of the Pirates. Many of the core players remained from their World Series club of 1916, however, including two-time batting champion Jake Daubert at first base, utility man Jimmy Johnston, veteran catcher Otto Miller, fleet-footed centerfielder Hi Myers, reliable yet

much-maligned infielder Ivy
Olson and the venerable Zack
Wheat in the outfield. A solid
group of pitchers also remained,
with the likes of Leon Cadore,
Rube Marquard, Ed "Jeff" Pfeffer and Sherrod "Sherry" Smith.
Like all teams, the Robins were
unsure who would be on their
opening day roster because the
United States involvement in
the war had increased in the
months following the '17 season.
As a result, Grimes was one of a
dozen pitchers invited to spring
training by Brooklyn owner
Charles Ebbets.

Charles Hercules Ebbets
was a lifetime resident of New
York City, having been born in
Greenwich Village on October
29, 1859. By the age of 23 he
had already amassed a résumé
that included architect, book
publisher, and door-to-door
salesman. According to John

Manager Wilbert Robinson. When Grimes
came to Brooklyn, he said Robinson "got me
to believe in myself" (George Grantham
Bain Collection, Library of Congress).

Saccoman, "[A]n unsuccessful campaign for the New York Senate convinced
him to devote his considerable talents to baseball rather than politics."[2] He
started working for the club in 1883, being employed as a clerk, bookkeeper
and scorecard salesman during Brooklyn's inaugural season in the Interstate
League. He remained with the team and became president and manager of
the National League's Brooklyn Bridegrooms just days after Brooklyn became
one of the five boroughs in January 1898. Within five years he owned all but
a few stocks, which he bought out over the next decade.

For the second straight year the Robins traveled to Hot Springs, Arkansas,
for training at Whittington Park. Grimes's spring got off to a bad start before
he even took the field. Shortly after arriving he took ill with the grippe, leaving
him laid up for nearly two weeks at the team's hotel. He wasn't alone, as his
wife Ruth and several teammates were suffering the same malady. Compounded by various injuries including a Chuck Ward ankle injury and Al

Mamaux's sore arm, some wondered if bad luck from the previous season had carried over.

Grimes's illness was quite possibly part of the flu pandemic which ran rampant during the month the Robins arrived in the south. Over the next two years the influenza spread across the globe. "Total deaths were estimated at 50 million and arguably as high as 100 million," while nearly one-third of the world's population (500 million of 1.6 billion) was infected.[3] In total, the flu claimed more than twice as many lives as World War I.

Besides the rash of illnesses and injuries keeping players off the field, the most glaring absence from Brooklyn's camp was offensive leader and fan-favorite Zack Wheat, who remained on his farm in Polo, Missouri, in response to a proposed salary cut. Wheat had been limited to 109 games in 1917 due to ankle problems stemming from his dainty size-five feet, but when healthy he was one of the game's best all-around players. The contract squabble was similar to the one between Ebbets and Wheat one year earlier, when it took *Brooklyn Daily Eagle* sportswriter Abe Yeager forging a telegram from Ebbets to Wheat to get the two to meet in person to hash out a contract. This year, Ebbets was threatening to replace Wheat in the lineup with Napoleon Lajoie, who hadn't played in the major leagues since 1916, but had batted .380 and managed the Toronto Maple Leafs to the International League title in 1917.

There was a surplus of pitchers in camp, forcing Grimes to take the mound before he had fully recovered. In his weakened state, he performed surprisingly well over his first few appearances before completely losing command of his spitball. After a few more lackluster showings Ebbets took steps to send Grimes back to the minors, even going so far as to put him on waivers. However, Wilbert Robinson convinced the Brooklyn owner to rescind waivers and give Grimes one more try.

Unaware that his status was in jeopardy, Grimes took the mound against the Red Sox in Waco, Texas. Before the game Robinson urged him to abandon the spitball for the time being and instead focus on a fastball, changeup and nickel curve, which the two had been working on over the past week. The results were impressive, as Grimes held Boston to three hits and one run. He then caught wind of Ebbets's intentions and when Grimes confronted Robinson and Ebbets, who tried to placate him by telling him that it had all been a mistake and that waivers had actually been asked on Dan Griner, but "a misprint made it look like Grimes."[4]

If ever there were a coach who could help right Grimes's promising career it was Wilbert Robinson. Known as "Uncle Robbie" for his rapport with players, the former catcher had a knack for working well with pitchers, whether it meant reviving the careers of castoffs or mentoring youngsters. One of the best examples was Rube Marquard. The lefthander had floundered in his first few seasons as a New York Giant, but when Robinson joined the coaching staff Marquard ripped off three 20-win season from 1911–1913 (24, 26 and 23 respectively), including winning 19 in a row in 1912. After Robinson's dismissal in 1913, Marquard returned to earth, going 12–22 in 1914 and performing even worse to start the '15 season. In August of that year Marquard brokered his own sale to the Robins so that he could once again pitch under Robinson's tutelage. The results were impressive — he helped Brooklyn to the 1916 World Series with a career-best 1.53 ERA and led the team with 19 wins in 1917.

A few days before Grimes's near dismissal, team owners had agreed to cut spring training short and head north to start the season. When the Robins finally broke camp a few weeks later, the roster looked dramatically different than when spring training had begun. Pitchers Sherrod Smith, Leon Cadore, Johnny Miljus and pitcher/outfielder Clarence Mitchell all had or shortly would be enlisting. Pitchers Jeff Pfeffer and Al Mamaux had been drafted (although Mamaux ended up work-ing in the shipyards to avoid mili-tary commitment). Infielder Chuck Ward also enlisted, making Grimes the only player remaining from the Brooklyn–Pirates exchange.

Zack Wheat remained absent from the team, leaving first base-man Jake Daubert (still recovering from an injury) as the Robins' only left-handed batter and offensive threat. There would be more losses to the military as the season pro-gressed. The sudden shortage of hurlers secured spots for both Grimes and Griner when the team headed north to 55 Sullivan Place, home of Ebbets Field.

In 1908, Charles Ebbets had gone out on a walk in Pig Town, a neighborhood on the south side of Brooklyn bordering Flatbush, and strolled by "four and a half acres of as squalid a tract of land that ever disgraced a civilized community," a

Grimes was lucky to make it out of spring training with a spot on the Brook-lyn roster (Cleveland Public Library).

locale that "sent up stenches that must have reached further than Heaven."[5] While everyone else saw a garbage dump, Ebbets envisioned the sight of a new steel-and-concrete ballpark to replace the fire hazard that was Washington Park. Over the next three years he spent close to $200,000 acquiring 1,200 parcels of land from the more than 40 persons who held a claim.

After buying the land, Ebbets ran into financial difficulties when construction of the ballpark was delayed. In late August 1913 he sold 50 percent of the Dodgers to Stephen and Edward McKeever, well-to-do Brooklyn building and general contractors. The result of the collaboration was one of the most storied stadiums in major league history. Donning the name of the long-time owner, Ebbets Field opened on April 9, 1913, with a capacity of 25,000.

Grimes continued to pitch without his spitball, but his regular season woes continued. He dropped his first two decisions, running his losing streak to 15 games. With a depleted roster the Robins weren't faring well either, losing their first eight games. They finally defeated the Giants 5–3 on April 27, handing their intracity rival their first loss of the year.

With the Brooklyn's losing streak over, attention went back to Grimes's unfortunate run. Jack Nabors's major league record 19-game losing streak was in sight, but Grimes ended that talk when he threw a 3–0, three-hit shutout of the Phillies at Ebbets Field on May 4. As the game wore on Grimes worked at a rapid pace, overpowering Philadelphia and facing one batter over the minimum during the final five innings.

The Robins' offense got a boost when Zack Wheat finally came to terms and joined the club in early May. Wheat would eventually play the most games behind Grimes of any position player, starting 250 of Grimes's 287 starts in a Brooklyn uniform. Years later, Grimes reflected on the greatness of Wheat. "He won more ball games for me than any other individual," said Grimes. "He was just terrific. A great hitter in the pinch, particularly after the seventh inning."[6]

Over the next few months Grimes worked as a reliever and spot starter, pitching .500-ball while relying on his fastball, off-speed pitches and nickel curve. After a satisfying 2–0 shutout of the Pirates on June 10 that saw him collect one of the Robins' two hits — an eighth-inning double that plated both runs — Grimes was inserted into the starting rotation.

He should have been happy, but Grimes couldn't seem to shake a severe case of homesickness. Between the war, Ruth's illness and the many months since he had last seen family and friends back in Clear Lake, at times he struggled to keep it together. According to Grimes historian Charles Clark, his pining for the familiarity and comfort of northern Wisconsin often brought him to the New York City docks, where he "watched Wisconsin butter be loaded on to ships just so he could be closer to home."[7]

In late June, Provost Marshal General E.H. Crowder issued a work or fight order by which, "after July 1 all men of draft age, regardless of their classification, must engage in employment held to be productive or join the army."[8] On the status of baseball players Crowder's office said, "Baseball playing 'at present' was regarded as non-productive though there would be no ruling until an individual case had been appealed from a local board."[9]

A few days after the work or fight decree had taken effect, Grimes received notice from the Wisconsin draft board that he was "not in the quota," meaning that for the moment he wouldn't be called to duty.[10] He was given a status of 2-B, which deferred him due to his occupation, allowing him to stay in a Brooklyn Dodgers uniform for the duration of the season. However, he was given the option to enter the Marines or Navy over the next 10 days.

By July the Robins had lost 13 players to the military and another four to the shipyards or munitions factories. At one point Brooklyn's roster consisted of only 13 active players. With major league rosters becoming thinner, the military occasionally gave enlisted players a brief leave from their duties to play for their teams. The Robins took advantage when Leon Cadore and Jeff Pfeffer returned for abbreviated stints. Both players showed no signs of rust as Pfeffer two-hit the Cubs in his only appearance, while Cadore shut out the Cardinals and nearly did the same to the Pirates three days later. The pitching-depleted Robins ended up using 17 pitchers during the season.

On July 18, Grimes put an end to a nine-game losing streak that had dropped Brooklyn into last place. He also halted a three-game losing skid of his own that saw his record fall to 8–7. Grimes went the distance in the 16-inning, 3–2 victory over the first-place Chicago Cubs and their ace left-hander, 6'4", 220-pound James "Hippo" Vaughn. Vaughn went on to win the pitching Triple Crown (1.74 ERA, 22 wins, 148 strikeouts) and lead the Cubs to the World Series. It was the first of a nine-game winning streak for Grimes that lasted until August 20. During that stretch he defeated the Cardinals once and the Cubs, Reds, Phillies, and Pirates two times each.

Years later Grimes counted the victory over Vaughn and the Cubs as one of his favorites, recalling how he mainly relied on his fastball and off-speed pitches. Grimes also reintroduced the spitball into his arsenal after realizing that the reason for his control issues were due to his "fingernails were too long and were ticking the ball as it left his hand."[11] For years he had been breaking nails from the pressure applied during his "watermelon seed squeeze" delivery.

The time away from relying on the spitter had enabled him to work on other pitches, including a devastating change-up. Clark said that power-hitting Cy Williams, the first National Leaguer to hit 200 home runs, put

Grimes's change of pace in a class with that of Christy Mathewson. "Cy would always say 'Burleigh had the guts of a burglar with that change-up,'" Clark said, recalling how Grimes would throw it regardless of the count.[12]

One day after the marathon against the Cubs, Secretary of War Newton Baker announced that baseball was a non-essential occupation under General Crowder's "work or fight" decree. Baseball's brain trust had supplied Baker with a lengthy argument on behalf of classifying the sport as an essential occupation. They pointed out that "baseball is a business in which very large investments of money have been made." In addition, they maintained that "the occupation of a professional baseball player requires a very high degree of specialized training and skill procurable only by a substantially exclusive devotion." Finally, they noted that "baseball has been accepted as the national sport of the people of the United States, that it affords wholesome outdoor relaxation and enjoyment to large number of the American people."[13]

Baker listened to baseball's argument, but in the end decided that "the times are not normal; the demands of the army and of the country are such that we must all make sacrifices, and the nonproductive employment of able-bodied persons useful in the national defense, either as military men or in the industry and commerce of our country, cannot be justified."[14]

The decree set off a flurry of enlisting by ballplayers, including Grimes, who joined teammate Rube Marquard in stopping in at a military rally at a theater near the team's Chicago hotel. By the time they exited they were sworn into the Navy Reserves as machinists in the Mine Sweepers Division, but wouldn't have any military obligation until after the season ended. Roughly a week later, Baker exempted players from the "work or fight" order until September 1 and both leagues agreed to end the 1918 season on September 2, Labor Day.

With all of the uncertainty going on around the league Grimes was hitting his stride, as was Zack Wheat, who was in the midst of a 24-game hitting streak that was enough to earn him the National League batting title. Wheat would be the last National Leaguer to win the title without hitting a home run. Their combined efforts weren't enough to push the emaciated Brooklyn roster higher than a fifth-place finish with a record of 57–60.

Grimes led the National League in 1918 with 40 games pitched. He also placed in the top five in several pitching categories, including: second in shutouts (7); third in wins (19) and strikeouts (113); and fifth in ERA (2.13). Both the shutout and ERA totals turned out to be career bests. Showing that he was still finding his way as a pitcher he also set a career high with 11 wild pitches. A .500 pitcher on the road, Grimes excelled at Ebbets Field, where the Robins drew an estimated 84,000 for the season, ranking seventh of the eight National League teams. Grimes's sparkling 11–1 record and dour attitude on the mound endeared him to Brooklyn fans.

His Ebbets Field admirers bestowed Grimes with a bevy of sobriquets. The Brooklyn pronunciation of "Burleigh" came out "Boily," which was expanded into "Boiling Boily" because of his frequent outbursts. He also gained the moniker of "Lord Burleigh" for his steady mound presence. Finally, he was also known as "Wire Whiskers" and "Ol' Stubblebeard" as a result of his habit of not shaving a day prior to his starts.

In a time when the common man was clean-shaven, it was convenient to describe Grimes as the bad guy: snarling, unshaven and throwing at batters' heads if he didn't like the way they looked at him. The real reason for not shaving was actually due to his sensitive skin, which became easily irritated by both the slippery elm and the rosin that was on most of the towels in the dugout.

There was no postseason mockery made of Grimes's performance in 1918. Along with teammates Zack Wheat and Jack Daubert, he was named to *Baseball Magazine*'s All National League Team. F.C. Lane, editor-in-chief of the periodical, wrote, "In a season when the ball player encountered many things to divert him from his accustomed task Grimes gave the very best that was in him and toiled just as hard to win for Brooklyn as though every game he pitched were decisive of the pennant."[15] In subsequent years Grimes became a favorite topic of Lane and his magazine.

The season ended on September 2, followed by an abbreviated World Series in which Babe Ruth and the Red Sox defeated the Chicago Cubs four games to two. Many major leaguers obeyed the "work or fight" ordinance that was in place, but a number lingered in their team's city playing for semi-pro teams. Following the World Series, several Cubs players stuck around Chicago to put a few extra dollars in their pockets before getting out of town in mid–September. It was soon brought to light that despite having been assigned to run a Naval recruiting station in Chicago, both Grimes and Marquard were still in Brooklyn and set to pitch for the United States Navy Yard (also known as the Brooklyn Navy Yard) against an Army team. When Army officials caught wind of this, they made it known that Grimes and Marquard weren't where they were supposed to be. Grimes's official start date of service was October 7 and he was given orders to report to the Great Lakes Training Camp in Chicago.

In the first week of October baseball experienced its first casualty of the Great War when former New York Giant Eddie Grant died in combat. Grant, a captain in the 77th Infantry Division, had been the first former or current baseball player to enlist when he signed up in April of 1917. On October 5,

The Grimes family, fall 1918, after Burleigh returned to the midwest for training at Great Lakes in Chicago. Back row, from left: Hazel, Shurleigh, Burleigh. Front row: Nick and Ruth (Charles Clark Photo Collection).

1918, he was killed by an exploding shell as he led a troop of soldiers in search of the "Lost Battalion" after all of his superior officers had been killed during the Meuse-Argonne Offensive.

Just a few days before Grant's death, Louis Fitzer had been killed at the Second Battle of the Marne. Fitzer had been taken in by the Grimeses after a falling out with his own family as a teen and had been with Burleigh when he nearly lost his life in the lumber accident back in the winter of 1913. Fitzer thought of Mr. and Mrs. Grimes like parents and their children as siblings. It was a particularly difficult loss for the Grimes family.

By November, 144 major leaguers were serving in the military in some capacity, including 18 Brooklyn Robins players. Not all players were as fortunate as Grimes in being limited in their obligations. Several big-name players and executives had been sent over to Europe, including Ty Cobb, Christy Mathewson, Branch Rickey, Grover Cleveland Alexander and George Sisler. Cobb, Mathewson and Rickey all served in the same Chemical Warfare Division, where both Cobb and Mathewson were exposed to mustard gas during a drill when officers inadvertently failed to give the signal that they were using the real thing. The error led to several men's deaths and a dozen others suffered long-term effects. Cobb escaped relatively unscathed from the incident. Mathewson, who was suffering from a case of influenza, had inhaled a dose of gas that would greatly affect his health. He died a premature death in October 1925.

At eleven o'clock on November 11, 1918, Germany and the Allies signed an armistice to end military conflict on the Western Front. Many soldiers remained in Europe for the next few months before being relieved of the military obligations and returning home.

A day after the armistice was signed, Grimes and several major leaguers, including Brooklyn teammate Rube Marquard, were called back to New York City as part of their military obligation. Representing the third Naval District, the group split into four teams and took to the hardwood for a month-long series of basketball games to benefit the United War Work campaign. A joint fund raising drive for the Army and Navy, the campaign had been put in place by President Wilson, and involved several charitable organizations. Grimes helped his team, the Mine Sweepers, to a 4–0 record.

Burleigh and Ruth did not return to Birmingham in the off-season. Having been released from his military obligations on December 13, the couple planned on heading back to Clear Lake, but what was supposed to be a brief stopover in Kensington, Ohio, at teammate Hi Myers's farm turned into a winter-long stay. Grimes stayed in shape by working on the farm and playing toss with Myers.

Grimes's turnaround from 1917 to 1918 was a hot topic in the off-season. When Al Munro Elias, who along with his brother Walter would be appointed the league's official statisticians in 1919, wrote a piece on Grimes's month-long string of wins, he asked Grimes what caused his remarkable turnaround. "Wilbert Robinson did it," Grimes replied. "When I reported to him in the spring he studied my work closely. Then he made many helpful suggestions. He pointed out my faults and helped me to correct them. He got me to believe in myself—and the rest is history."[16]

There was no question about Grimes's status for the 1919 season. Newspapers reported that he had been pegged by Robinson to be the staff anchor for the upcoming season. If the Robins' ownership expected Grimes to be happy with simply the title of staff ace rather than being paid like one (he was scheduled to make roughly $1,800), they were mistaken. The two parties took part in fruitless negotiations that ended in the right-hander threatening to remain in Ohio for the summer. Charles Ebbets, Jr., secretary of the Brooklyn club fired back a salvo of his own: "As far as the Brooklyn club cares he can stay there for the remainder of his days. We have a few other pitchers besides Grimes."[17]

Besides not meeting Grimes's demands, Brooklyn management had done little to improve the Robins' roster. In fact, they got even weaker offensively when Ebbets traded Jake Daubert on February 1. Ebbets had been looking to peddle Daubert ever since he had threatened to jump to the Federal League in 1914, thereby strong-arming the Brooklyn owner into paying him a hefty salary of $9,000. The final straw came on February 1 when he won an out-of-court settlement for the balance of his war-shortened 1918 salary. The Robins paid him $2,150 and then promptly shipped the first baseman to the Cincinnati Reds for Tommy Griffith. The two-time batting champ's departure took away Brooklyn's main power threat and left the team with only one left-handed bat in Zack Wheat.

The Robins had been in their new spring home in Jacksonville, Florida, for a few days when Grimes arrived after signing a contract for an undisclosed amount. He immediately began training but had a scare when his wife became seriously ill and was laid up at the team hotel, the Hotel Seminole. She still hadn't fully recovered from her infirmity from the previous season. On the field there seemed to once again be an overabundance of quality pitchers as the team broke camp, including Grimes, Larry Cheney, Al Mamaux, Jeff Pfeffer, Rube Marquard, and Leon Cadore. Besides the departure of Daubert the offense remained intact, with Wheat having been given the title of captain.

A couple of new wrinkles were added to the baseball schedule in 1919. At the winter meetings the baseball owners worried about their patriotic image after having contested the "work or fight" decree one year earlier. As a result, they decided to cut the schedule to 140 games. Locally, New York City would see Sunday baseball after Governor Al Smith signed a bill on April 19.

The Robins began the season by sweeping an Opening Day doubleheader against the Braves in Boston. Grimes was tabbed to start the third game of the series, but first there was a three-day break in the schedule. In between games, the Robins were to travel back to New York City to take part in a two-game intracity exhibition with the Yankees. Before the club left Boston, however, Charles Ebbets purchased Braves first basemen Ed Konetchy who was holding out at his home in St. Louis.

After winning his first start of the season against the Braves, Grimes took to the mound against the Philadelphia Phillies on April 30 in what turned out to be the longest appearance of his career. Neither he nor his pitching counterpart Joe Oeschger were on the top of their game through the first nine innings with Brooklyn scoring a run in the top of the ninth to tie the game at six. Over the next nine innings, both were superb: neither pitcher gave up a run, and Grimes allowed just one hit. It looked as though Brooklyn had the game wrapped up in the top of the 19th when Hy Myers hit a three-run home run, but the Phillies again solved Grimes, scoring three of their own in the bottom half. The 20th inning brought another scoreless frame before umpire Bill Klem called the four-hour affair a tie due to darkness.

A week later the two pitchers squared off again. Oeschger had nothing on his pitches, obviously affected by the marathon session. He pitched in just two more games before being shelved for the season. Grimes, on the other hand, continued to take the ball when called upon and showed no ill effects; tallying five wins over the next month.

It looked as though Grimes was going to repeat his iron-man performance of 1918 until he fell ill a week into the team's three-week road trip while in Pittsburgh. He was in agony for three days with a severe case of tonsillitis. Unable to eat and barely able to get down liquids he dropped nearly 20 pounds, leaving him extremely gaunt. The club left Grimes in Pittsburgh to undergo a tonsillectomy; he didn't pitch again for nearly a month.

The road trip brought about a season-worst 10-game losing streak that saw Brooklyn fall from third to sixth in the standings. Grimes wasn't the pitching staff's only casualty during that stretch. Rube Marquard's season ended when he broke his leg trying to stretch a double into a triple in Cincinnati. In addition, hurlers Sherrod Smith and Jeff Pfeffer complained of sore arms and Larry Cheney was still weak from a bout of pneumonia. For good measure among the list of maladies the *Daily Eagle* listed Leon Cadore as "a democrat."[18] The only thing keeping the club out of last place was the hot hitting of Hi Myers, Zack Wheat and Ed Konetchy.

On July 4, Grimes returned to the mound with a few innings of relief in Boston. He started two days later against the Braves and didn't make it out of the first inning. Still recovering his strength Grimes was unable to string wins together during the ensuing weeks. Just when he was starting to show signs that he was healthy, Grimes's disappointing season came to an end with a gruesome injury on August 31 against the New York Giants.

With the Giants visiting Ebbets Field for the last time of the 1919 season, more than 17,000 saw Grimes and Jesse Barnes — who was leading the league with 21 wins — engage in a pitcher's duel. The Robins had been out of the pennant race for months, but the *Brooklyn Daily Eagle* had been stoking the flames of controversy by accusing the Giants of trying to buy their way back into the pennant race. Things got testy in the seventh inning after a close play at third on a triple by the Giants' George Burns, breaking up the 1–1 tie. The Brooklyn bench jumped all over home plate umpire Bill Klem, who in turn cleared the Dodgers bench.

The next inning, brash Giants rookie Frankie Frisch came to the plate. In his autobiography, *Frank Frisch: The Fordham Flash*, Frisch recalled the incident that not only ended Grimes's season but nearly his career and led to a decade-long series of run-ins between the fierce competitors:

> Burleigh, if he wanted to throw at you, didn't abide by the usual rules. He didn't care what the count was. I know he scared the daylights out of me one time by firing one at my head with the count three and one. Imagine that. I always thought you were fairly safe and could dig in at the plate when the pitcher was behind you like that. But that wasn't true with Burleigh. That pitch not only scared me, it made me as angry as I ever was at another ballplayer. So I decided I'd do something about it.
>
> I couldn't fight Grimes. He was too big and I never was a fighter. But the next time I went to bat I bunted toward the first baseman to force Grimes to cover and accidentally on purpose my right foot, spikes and all, landed on one of Burleigh's feet. I didn't want to hurt him that bad and felt deeply sorry when I learned that the spike had cut his foot so severely that the Achilles tendon was hanging by a shred. It almost ended Burleigh's career.[19]

The feisty Grimes attempted to retaliate, but his Achilles tendon had been shredded and he couldn't get off the ground. Carried off the field to a round of applause, he didn't return to the mound for the remainder of the season, finishing with 10 wins and 11 losses. Brooklyn limped to another fifth-place finish at 69–71, 27 1/2 games behind the eventual World Series champion Cincinnati Reds and former Robins first baseman Jake Daubert.

In the second week of February 1920 a major league rules committee made up of Barney Dreyfuss, Connie Mack, Clark Griffith and William Veeck met in Chicago to examine changes to the game for the upcoming season. Also in attendance were the two league presidents (John Heydler and Ban Johnson) and two umpires (Bill Klem and Hank O'Day). The group discussed whether to eliminate the intentional walk, argued at length about what constituted a balk, and gave umpires the power to call or resume a game delayed due to rain (previously the home team manager's decision).

The longest and most heated discussion, spanning two days, concerned the abolition of "freak deliveries." Not surprisingly, Dreyfuss headed the movement to outlaw such pitches and was backed strongly by Mack and Griffith. Veeck was the only rules committee member who remained undecided. At first it seemed as though all pitches of this nature including the spitball were going to be banished, but eventually National League President John Heydler put forth the following tentative agreement on behalf of the committee:

> I think we shall give the old-time pitchers who are recognized as spitball throwers, a certain period to develop something to take the place of this delivery. He might be granted a year or possibly only about two months or so. Every club would have to register with the league the names of the recognized spitball pitchers. No others would be granted that extra time. No newcomers of this year would be permitted to throw the spitter.[20]

The American League had yet to agree to the stipulation, but the National League went forward with the decree. The final proclamation stated that each team was allowed two pitchers to throw the spitball for the duration of the 1920 season, after which they would have to abandon it or face a fine and possible suspension. Ebbets submitted the names of Grimes and Clarence Mitchell, the outfielder-pitcher who was the only left-handed pitcher named. Dreyfuss showed his disdain by declining to file the names of any Pirates pitchers. When the American League adopted the ban, Mack and Griffith also declined to file any names.

Grimes explained years later why the spitter was banned: "The real reason the spitter was barred was because pitchers were roughing the ball with pop bottle caps, sandpaper, emery and whatnot, ripping a stitch or two of the seam with razor blades and such, and discoloring the ball with tobacco, licorice, coffee and in other ways."[21]

Zack Wheat and Hy Myers arrived in Jacksonville, Florida, on the fifth day of training camp, making Grimes the last player to report. He told the club that he was waiting to hire a manager to run his new business venture — an auto garage. When Myers showed up he reported that, "Burleigh has two cars for which he has prospects. He refuses to report until he lands the said prospects or they sidestep."[22]

On March 18 Grimes finally reported. He was underweight and had to deal with questions about whether he could succeed without a spitball, as well as rumors that he was being shopped over the winter to the St. Louis Cardinals and Boston Braves. "Nothing doing," he replied. The *Brooklyn Daily Eagle* expounded on his two-word answer: "He likes not the St. Louis climate and he wants not any close companionship with George Stallings [the manager of the Braves]."[23]

Grimes was kept out of live activity except for an intrasquad game nearly two weeks after his arrival. Almost two more weeks passed before his first official appearance on the mound in the Robins' last game of the spring against the New York Yankees. In the middle of the Yankees lineup was their big off-season acquisition, Babe Ruth, who singled and struck out on a quick-pitch fastball by Grimes. Ruth had come to the Yankees five days into the new year from the Boston Red Sox for the hefty sum of $125,000. He had come into the league as a strong-armed pitcher, but was transitioning to a full-time outfielder for the Yankees. Ruth's arrival in the Big Apple brought new attention to the home run and also pushed Brooklyn down in the city's baseball hierarchy. Much of the focus would henceforth go to the Polo Grounds where the Yankees and Giants played their home games.

After winning his first two starts of the season, Grimes dropped a 13-

inning, 4–3 contest to the Philadelphia Phillies at Ebbets Field. It came a day after the Robins had battled in Boston against the Braves in what the *New York Times* described as a "prolonged, heartbreaking struggle."[24] For 26 innings Brooklyn's Leon Cadore and the Braves Joe Oeschger (who had thrown 19 innings against Grimes the year before) battled until the game was called due to darkness, resulting in a 1–1 tie. Following the loss to the Phillies in Brooklyn, the Robins traveled back to Braves Field where they lost 2–1 in 19 innings. In all Brooklyn played 58 innings over the three days, going 0–2 with a tie and dropping a slot in the early-season standings from second to third.

Still continuing to learn his craft, at times Grimes pitched without thinking about the game situation. He was, however, starting to notice the subtle nuances of the game. One such observation was that the Forbes Field pitcher's mound seemed different on days that Pirates ace Wilbur Cooper was pitching. According to Grimes, Bill Fogarty, the Pirates groundkeeper, added a few inches to the mound on days when it was Cooper's turn to start. Since he was roughly the same height as Cooper, Grimes implored his manager to let him start against Cooper. Despite struggling at Forbes during his days in a Brooklyn uniform (9–11 in 26 appearances), Grimes performed exceptionally well there against Cooper. For his career, Grimes had a 3–1 record against the Pirates' lefthander at Forbes, including a 4–1 victory on May 22.

At the end of May, Grimes's record was 6–2, and the Robins were a half-game behind the first-place Cubs. It was becoming more apparent that he was Brooklyn's number one pitcher. He still hadn't completely won the affections of the Brooklyn fans, however. When the *Brooklyn Daily Eagle* posed the question "Who do you consider the best pitcher on the Brooklyn Baseball Club?" as part of their "Inquisitive Scribe" column, Grimes was merely an afterthought. The most common response was Al Mamaux, who after going 0–1 in 1918 went 10–12 with a 2.66 ERA in 1919. Not only were his pitching skills were lauded, but so were his singing abilities. "He's a good tenor singer and consequently a good singer," said one respondent.[25] Also gaining votes were Pfeffer, Leon Cadore and Sherry Smith. One person did say Grimes was "doing the best work," but still declared that Mamaux was "the best."[26]

Brooklyn spent 10 days in first place during June, then slipped all the way to fourth before making it back to second by the final day of the month. The nasty temper of "Boiling Boily" bubbled to the surface during the last week of June with his anger being directed toward teammates. Catcher Otto Miller was his first target on June 22 against the Philadelphia Phillies.

A well-respected receiver with a strong arm, Miller was in his tenth year and enjoying the best season of his career. On a hit to the outfield Grimes cut off a throw to home that likely would have erased the runner because of receiving no directive from Miller. Already peeved that the scoring runner had reached base on an error, Grimes dressed down his good-natured catcher at home plate. According to the *Brooklyn Daily Eagle*, "Grimes reproved Miller violently for not giving the cry to let the ball go through to the plate. They continued the squabble on the bench and Grimes threw his hat at Miller."[27] The altercation changed the two men's relationship for the remainder of their days as teammates.

In his next outing on June 26 in Boston versus the Braves, Grimes went after recent acquisition Bill McCabe, who was filling in for injured shortstop Ivy Olson. With runners on first and second Grimes fielded a come-backer to the mound. He whirled to throw to second to start a double play, but McCabe was late covering the bag and all runners were safe. Grimes went ballistic, throwing his glove to the ground and chastising the shortstop. Teammates Ed Konetchy and Jimmy Johnston had to restrain Grimes from physically attacking McCabe.

Known for having zero tolerance for defensive miscues behind him, Grimes seldom seemed to take responsibility for his own. In both of these incidents, some believed that Grimes was at least partially at fault. It wasn't the last time that he put undue blame on a teammate, and in particular his actions toward the well-liked Miller weren't forgotten.

Grimes was finally able to enact revenge on Frank Frisch for nearly ending his career the previous September. Frisch had been out of the lineup since late April with appendicitis, so he was not in the lineup for Grimes's first four appearances against the Giants. Frisch thought he had made amends, but when he stepped into the box on June 30 Grimes had different ideas. Frisch ended up on his back on four straight pitches, his quick reflexes keeping him from being hit. On his way to first base he incredulously said to Grimes, "Damn it Burleigh, I apologized!" "Yes," said Grimes matter-of-factly, "but you didn't smile."[28]

At the season's midway point Brooklyn was in first place. With no Robins batter putting up huge numbers, the club seemed to be scoffing at the offensive explosion that was going on around them. Instead, the veteran team continued to rely on their Dead Ball Era sensibilities. Robinson also was at his best, once again "showing an ability to put together a pitching staff whose depth made up for its lack of singular brilliance."[29]

If there was a pitcher who raced ahead of the pack in the Robinson's six-man rotation it was Grimes. In the six weeks following his explosions he remained tight-lipped, letting his right arm do the talking. Grimes not only took the ball every fifth day but also threw in relief, going 10–2 over that span (July 4 through August 15) as Brooklyn began a tug-of-war for first place with Cincinnati. July was Grimes's best month of the season, going 6–1 in eight appearances. Heading into August his batting average also sat at a robust .354.

Brooklyn moved into a tie for first place with the Reds on July 8, when Grimes picked up his twelfth victory of the season in a 14–2 drubbing of the Cardinals at St. Louis's Robison Field. The last three innings of the game were caught by a young catcher named James "Zach" Taylor. Although the Robins already had a trio of catchers who split games (Otto Miller [90], Ernie Krueger [52], and Rowdy Elliot [41]), Robinson thought enough of the youngster to keep him on the roster. Taylor only played in nine games, but he made an impression on the Robins manager and two of its stars. "Uncle Wilbert, Wheat and Grimes tell all comers that Taylor is the best looking catching product that they have seen come up in years," reported the *Brooklyn Daily Eagle*.[30] Within a few years, Taylor became Grimes's personal catcher.

Brooklyn held tightly to first place for much of July and into August, but the lead never rose to more than four games. Grimes put the Robins up one game in the standings on August 15 by throwing the last four-and-two-

Half of Brooklyn's 1920 six-man rotation. From left: Jeff Pfeffer, Burleigh Grimes and Sherry Smith (Charles Clark Photo Collection).

thirds innings of a 6–5, 12-inning victory over the Phillies. Hot on their trail were the Reds and the resurgent Giants, who just a month earlier had been 10 games back in seventh place. Invigorated by the reemergence of Frank Frisch, who finally returned to full strength after his appendectomy, the Giants pulled within just two-and-a-half games of the Robins. The next day the pennant race was momentarily forgotten when tragedy struck the baseball world across town at the Polo Grounds, where the New York Yankees were taking on the first place Cleveland Indians.

On an overcast afternoon Cleveland's star shortstop Ray Chapman stepped to the plate with one out in the top of the fifth inning. On the mound for the Yankees was the surly Carl Mays, whose penchant for throwing inside and extreme submarine-style delivery kept batters on their toes. When Mays noticed Chapman's back foot shifting to take the ball to right field he didn't hesitate to throw one inside. Chapman didn't move, the ball hitting him flush in the temple with what sportswriter Fred Lieb described as a "sickening thud."[31] The ball bounced out to the pitcher's mound where Mays fielded it thinking that it had hit Chapman's bat and threw it to first baseman Wally Pipp. Only when he turned around did he see Chapman on his knees, blood flowing from his left ear. Chapman momentarily regained enough strength to attempt to walk to the clubhouse, but collapsed on the way. After surgery was performed to relieve the pressure in his skull, the initial prognosis was that he would recover. Instead Chapman died the next morning at St. Lawrence Hospital.

The same fate had nearly befallen the Yankees' young third base prospect Chick Fewster five months earlier during a spring training game against the Robins. By coincidence, Carl Mays had just retired Brooklyn in order in the top of the first when Fewster came to bat in the bottom half against hard-throwing Jeff Pfeffer. A 2–1 fastball from the big right-hander struck Fewster in the temple, the impact sounding "like a cocoanut shell cracking."[32] Like Mays, Pfeffer's intentions were unclear, but he was regarded as "an intense competitor who let no one get an edge."[33] He led the league in hit batsmen in 1916 and '17. Fewster suffered a fractured skull and concussion and his initial condition was grave, but he was back on the field by July 5. Unfortunately, he was never the same again.

Following the Fewster incident, the Robins had tried to trade Pfeffer to the St. Louis Cardinals, but the deal never materialized. The big righty had never been a favorite of Charles Ebbets due to contract squabbles. Nor was Wilbert Robinson particularly fond of him, evident by the fact that despite winning 25 games for the 1916 World Series club, Pfeffer had pitched out of the bullpen for the first four games versus the Red Sox. With the series on the line in Game Five he was given the start, only to lose a tough 4–1 decision. Now with the National League race heating up Grimes had a running mate as Pfeffer went undefeated for nearly two months, snapping off nine consecutive victories from July 2 through August 31.

As the season progressed and pennant fever struck Brooklyn, the fans' rabidity for their team grew. They felt a kinship with the Robins that extended beyond the Ebbets Field grounds. Not only were they rooting for their favorite ball club, they were also cheering on their neighbors. Many of the ballplayers lived in the neighborhood adjacent to Ebbets Field, including Manager Robinson and his wife, known as "Ma." Baseball historian Harold Seymour, a native of Brooklyn who was a batboy for the Robins in the 1920s, recalled how Grimes was a familiar face around the neighborhood: "Burleigh Grimes sometimes passed by on his evening stroll with a great black cigar in his mouth while youngsters were playing punch ball in the street. It was a thrill to be able to recognize him and say 'Hiya Burleigh!' and have him reply 'Having a workout son?' This simple exchange imparted the feeling that we, too, belonged to the wonderful world of baseball, even though on a different level."[34]

Zack Wheat was the subject of the greatest adulation. During the season, crowds waited outside the team's clubhouse at Ebbets Field to ask for an autograph, shake his hand or simply to see him up close. It got to the point where the throng followed him home. When the crowds got too much for him, Wheat escaped through the clubhouse's side door, walked under the stands and ended up in the outfield: "He cut a hole in the far corner of the right-field fence, and he escaped through it whenever he didn't feel up to the attention of the inevitable mob."[35]

A logjam atop the National League over the last two weeks of August and into much of September kept Brooklyn fans checking the standings in the newspaper each morning. The Robins roared on, winning 20 of 24 games. They were aided by off-the-field issues that distracted both the Giants and Reds, hindering their pennant hopes.

The Giants were stymied by John McGraw's legal problems, stemming from a brawl at the Lamb's Club, of which McGraw was a part owner. At the heart of the case was McGraw's possession of multiple bottles of whiskey, a serious offense during Prohibition. The passing of the Eighteenth Amendment in January 1919 greatly changed the way many baseball players spent their off-field hours, forcing them to seek out speakeasies such as the Lamb's Club. McGraw wound up expending an exorbitant amount of time and energy trying to clear his name, sidetracking him from his managerial efforts.

The Reds were being affected by what was being said in a Cook County,

Illinois, courtroom. What was supposed to be a trial about the alleged fix of a game between the Chicago Cubs and Philadelphia Phillies on August 31 instead led to the incendiary revelation that the 1919 World Series had been fixed. Gambling had always been baseball's dirty secret, but the game's dirty laundry had never been aired in public to this extent. The case was to become known as the Black Sox Scandal.

The Robins finally clinched their second pennant of the World Series Era and fifth overall on an off day when the Boston Braves beat the Giants. The Braves had done the same favor for Brooklyn in 1916 when they swept the second-place Philadelphia Phillies. Now all the Robins had to do was wait to see who they would be playing.

While waiting for an opponent Brooklyn, the local press giddily clamored for any story it could about the pennant-winning club. Grimes was increasingly becoming one of the sportswriters' favorite subjects, evident by the six paragraphs the *Brooklyn Daily Eagle* dedicated to a story about how he had lost his wife's handbag while at the Parkside Theater in Flatbush. The contents included a good luck charm of Grimes: a hundred dollar bill that Charles Ebbets had given to each player as a reward after their brutal western road trip in July that saw them play 22 games in 19 days, of which they won 16. Showing the simpler times, the *Eagle* ended the article by asking, "If the finder will call up B.A. Grimes on his phone, Flatbush 6969, he will make glad the heart of the finder."[36]

In spite of the trial in Cook County, the Chicago White Sox had battled the Cleveland Indians down to the wire, bowing out on the next-to-last day when the Indians defeated the Detroit Tigers. Cleveland was led by the great Tris Speaker, who had rallied the Indians after the shocking death of Ray Chapman.

In his first full season as player-manager, Speaker was ahead of his time in creating what would become known as the platoon system. He also had some late-season acquisitions who helped propel the club to the postseason, including Chapman's replacement Joe Sewell and pitcher John "Duster" Mails, a Brooklyn castoff who posted a 7–0 record for Cleveland down the stretch. As a team the Indians hit .303 and had a three-headed pitching attack, consisting of 31-game winner Jim Bagby and spitballers Stan Coveleski and Ray Caldwell, who finished with 24 and 20 wins respectively.

For the second year in a row the World Series was a best-of-nine series, with the first three to be played in Cleveland, the next four in Brooklyn and then back to Cleveland for two more if necessary. In a move that ended up benefiting his club, Indians owner Jack Dunn asked for the Series to start in Brooklyn to enable his staff to better prepare Dunn Park. Charles Ebbets also gave them an advantage when he graciously allowed Sewell to participate in the Series despite joining the club after the August 30 deadline for eligibility.

The Indians were also the beneficiaries of Wilbert Robinson's peculiar decision to let Grimes start against the Giants on the next-to-last day of the season even though with the Robins having already clinched. Perhaps it was a chance for a jab at his former friend John McGraw, or maybe he just wanted Grimes to get some work after not pitching in a week. One could also surmise that it enabled Robinson to start his "favorite and protégé" Rube Marquard in the World Series opener. The veteran lefty had gone 10–7 for the year and may have been the sixth best starter on the staff.[37]

Statistically speaking, there was no comparison between the two pitchers as Marquard failed to reach the top ten in any National League pitching category, while Grimes was third in wins (23), ERA (2.22), complete games (25) and innings pitched (303⅔). He tied Hippo Vaughn for second in strikeouts (131). Grimes also batted .306, becoming the first 20-game winner to bat .300 since the Pirates' Claude Hendrix won 24 and batted .322 in 1912.

On Tuesday, October 5, the 1920 World Series commenced in Brooklyn on a bone-chilling fall day. Speaker used his platoon system deftly, inserting right-handed hitters Joe Wood and Joe Evans into the lineup. A surprisingly quiet Brooklyn crowd watched Cleveland score two runs off Marquard in the second inning and one more in the fourth, before his day ended after six innings. The Robins scored one in the seventh, but it wasn't enough as spitballer Stanley Coveleski controlled Brooklyn's bats during a 3–1 Cleveland victory. In addition to the Chapman tragedy, "Covey" as he was known had suffered his own personal heartbreak when his wife passed away in late May after a lengthy illness.

Back in Wisconsin, Clear Lake prepared for their hometown hero's Game Two mound appearance. A Western Union wire was extended from the train depot to the town's new moving picture venue, the Elburta Theatre. Those interested could pay 35 cents to listen to the results of every play. Grimes's parents, brother and two of his uncles made the four-mile trip into town to "listen" to the game.

From his first pitch, a strike to Cleveland's Charlie Jamieson, Grimes looked to be in top form. Speaker had instructed his players to take the first pitch, but they repeatedly found themselves down a strike to start their at-bats. Brooklyn scored in the bottom half of the inning when Zach Wheat drove in Jimmy Johnston with a double to center field to take a 1–0 lead.

Grimes helped his own cause when he led off the top of the third with a crisp single to center field. A sacrifice by the next batter, Ivy Olson, was fielded by Cleveland pitcher Jim Bagby, whose attempt to force Grimes at second pulled Joe Sewell to the first base side of the bag. In an effort to avoid the shortstop, Grimes catapulted over him. In the process the ball hit Grimes directly in the ankle, which immediately swelled up. He hobbled home two batters later on a Tommy Griffith double. There were no signs of the ankle injury bothering him as Grimes ended up allowing just one Cleveland runner past second, which came during an eighth inning, bases-loaded jam that he escaped from unscathed.

As Grimes's 3–0 gem was nearing its end, Cleveland scout Jack McCallister supposedly noticed that catcher Otto Miller "invariably picked up a handful of dust and tossed it away, sometimes in front of him and sometimes to the rear."[38] Now aware of Miller's alleged tendency, the Indians quickly determined that, "Each time he tossed dirt forward a spitball was delivered, the fast balls coming when he threw dirt between his legs to the rear."[39]

After the series, when the scouting tip was made public, several Brooklyn players came to the defense of Miller. Among them was Grimes, who said that the catcher, "Never has any trouble with my spitter and seldom 'goes into the dirt' as we call giving signals."[40] Years later the real culprit was fingered. Second baseman Pete Kilduff was actually the one picking up sand and putting it in his glove before each pitch. If it was a spitball he kept it in, if not he dumped it out, all in perfect view of the batter.[41]

Sherry Smith put the Robins in front two games to one by throwing a three-hitter in Game Three. From there the two clubs headed to Cleveland, where fans were clamoring to see a game. Robinson once again looked to Rube Marquard rather than one of his three better-rested starters. Instead, Marquard found himself at police headquarters facing possible jail time for scalping tickets.

On the evening before Game Four, several members of the Robins were lounging in the Winton Hotel lobby. When the topic of what people were paying for tickets came up, some players began joking about what they could get for their allotted tickets. Marquard quipped to Al Mamaux that he would give him "$50 if he sold the box for more than $400."[42] Overhearing the conversation, a reporter subsequently tipped off police to the player's scheme. The next morning when Marquard went to sell his tickets, the buyer was an undercover officer who immediately arrested him. He was released under his own recognizance with an arraignment scheduled for the next day.

In Marquard's place Robinson started Leon Cadore, who failed to make it out of the second inning after giving up a pair of runs. He was replaced by Mamaux, who in turn was relieved by the shamed Marquard in the third. He held the Indians scoreless for the next three innings, but Brooklyn was no match for Cleveland's Coveleski, who once again pitched brilliantly, winning 5–1. With the series tied at two games apiece, Robinson turned to his workhorse Grimes, who had dominated the Indians in Game Two.

From the start it was apparent that Grimes wasn't fooling the Cleveland batters. Leadoff batter Charlie Jamieson singled to right, followed by a Bill Wambsganss single to center. Tris Speaker laid a bunt down the first base line, which the usually nimble Grimes fielded and promptly fell on his backside, tweaking his tender ankle in the process. With the bases loaded lefthander Elmer Smith, who was 1 for 7 in the Series, including 0-for-4 against Grimes in Game Two, stepped to the plate. After a first pitch ball, Grimes threw two perfect spitballs that Smith let pass for strikes. When Grimes tried to throw a high fastball past him, Smith deposited the ball over the right field wall for the first grand slam in World Series history.

Grimes was able to hold the Indians scoreless over the next two innings, but in the bottom of the fourth World Series history was made once again. After a single by Doc Johnston, Joe Sewell grounded out. Grimes, Miller and Robinson conferred and decided to walk the number eight hitter, Steve O'Neill, to bring up pitcher Jim Bagby, hoping to induce a double play. Bagby, Grimes's old foe from their Southern Association days, watched the first pitch go by for a ball. The next one was a spitter that didn't break. Bagby hit it into the center field bleachers to put the Indians up, 7–0. It was the first home run by a pitcher in World Series history. Grimes was relieved by Clarence Mitchell after allowing a single to the next batter.

Mitchell allowed one more run in the 8–1 Cleveland victory but couldn't escape getting into the record books for a dubious accomplishment of his own. In the fifth inning, he came to bat with Kilduff on second and Miller on first. Mitchell connected for what looked like a hard single into right center. Cleveland second baseman Bill Wambsganss, who had been playing him to pull, "took the three steps toward second on the run, leaped as high as he could and caught the ball squarely in his glove."[43] He staggered for a moment, but his momentum took him toward second base, which he touched easily. When he twirled to throw the ball to first he saw that Otto Miller was no less than ten feet away and pulling up his stride. Wambsganss dashed toward him and tagged Miller to complete the only unassisted triple play in World Series history. For good measure, Mitchell grounded into one of Brooklyn's other three double plays in his other at bat.

After the game, Grimes blamed an ineffective spitball for his problems. "My spitter just wouldn't work right and therein lies the story in a nutshell of my inability to stop the Indians," said Grimes. "I was not right, that's all there is to it. If I had been right the Indians would not have hit me so hard."[44]

It was a humiliating couple of days in Cleveland for the whole Brooklyn team. On the day after the Grimes thrashing, Marquard had his day in court, where he was assessed a one-dollar fine (plus costs). Now a pariah, fingers were being wagged at Marquard from all baseball circles, including Charles Ebbets and the McKeever brothers. National League president John Heydler put forth an empty threat for the next season. "Baseball doesn't want men of his caliber and I don't think he'll be back in the league next season," said Heydler.[45]

In Game Six, the team suffered another embarrassment when former Brooklyn pitcher John Mails put together possibly the finest pitching performance of the Series in a 1–0 victory that put the Indians ahead, four games to two. With the Series in the balance Robinson turned to Grimes over Marquard. Although Grimes had been routed just two days earlier, at least he had faced only 19 batters.

Grimes and fellow spitballer Stan Coveleski hooked up in what had the makings of a pitchers' duel. Both hurlers had their spitball working as neither team scored during the first few innings, but in the bottom of the third Grimes suffered an injury to his throwing hand. With one out, Charlie Jamieson hit a hard one-hopper back through the pitcher's box. Grimes stuck his bare hand up to knock it down and throw it to first. Though he got the out, the play left his hand throbbing. The game was "delayed two minutes while players massaged the injury."[46] His swollen hand made it difficult for Grimes to grip the ball, so throwing the spitball was nearly impossible.

Cleveland finally got a run in the bottom of the fourth on a pair of singles followed by a Grimes error on a double steal. The runners had gotten such a good break that Otto Miller simply returned the ball to Grimes without a throw to a base. When Grimes turned around he saw that the runner from first, Doc Johnston, was about ten feet from second base. Grimes made a quick throw to second base that went between the second baseman and shortstop (Kilduff and Olson) and trickled into center field allowing Larry Gardner, the runner on third, to score.

The Indians tacked on one more in the fifth on a run-scoring triple by Speaker and one in the seventh on a single by Jamieson that drove in Coveleski for a 3–0 lead. Grimes escaped further damage in the seventh, getting out of a bases-loaded jam, but was relieved by Al Mamaux in the eighth inning after throwing 120 pitches. The Brooklyn bats never put up a challenge to Coveleski, who threw 90 pitches to complete the 3–0 victory and wrap up Cleveland's first World Series title. "Covey" put together one of the best pitching performances in World Series history, allowing two runs on 15 hits in three complete-game victories.

Following the game, Charles Ebbets and the McKeever brothers congratulated the Indians at home plate. Ebbets said in his speech that the better club had won, which was met by a rousing round of applause by Cleveland fans appreciative of the act of sportsmanship.

Wilbert Robinson wasn't as gracious. He had no issue with Speaker and was pleased that the Series passed without incident between the two teams and the umpires. He did, however, disagree that the better team won, instead blaming the Robins' cold bats. "Cleveland played great ball and deserves all the credit in the world. When I say we have better pitching in the National League I don't mean to detract from its achievement. The Indians outbatted us and that's all there is to it. However, I still insist that Brooklyn is the better club," expounded Robinson."[47]

The World Series loss bothered Grimes for the rest of his life and he couldn't seem to escape the infamy of Game Five. Nearly six decades later he entered a bait shop near his Wisconsin home on Lake Holcombe. The owner and a few customers were conversing at the checkout counter. Knowing Grimes as a former major leaguer, the men stopped their conversation and directed their attention to the Hall of Famer. "Just the man that would know this one," said the owner, pointing to a daily trivia question on a beer sign.

Grimes focused his attention on the sign as the man read it aloud. "Who hit the first grand slam in World Series history?" he inquired, not knowing Grimes's affiliation to the feat.

Grimes spit out the answer before the man had finished reading the question. "Elmer Smith."

"I knew he'd know it," said the owner proudly as Grimes paid for his bait.

As Grimes was about to exit the shop, he stopped at the door and turned toward the group at the counter. "And do you know who surrendered that home run?" The men responded that they didn't. "One Burleigh A. Grimes," replied Grimes, leaving the shop before the men could react.[48]

Following the World Series, some wondered whether Wilbert Robinson would be back Brooklyn. Abe Yeager of the *Brooklyn Daily Eagle* reported that the Yankees were courting him. "Ever since 1916 when Your Uncle Robbie won the pennant and his pal Col. Til Huston became part owner of the New York Americans, the rotund leader of the Superbas has been each winter signed up for the Yankees."[49] Rumored to take his place was Dodgers player Ivy Olson, Yankees manager Miller Huggins or Hughey Jennings.

Another named tossed around was a familiar one to Grimes: Mike Kelley, who had just led the St. Paul Saints to an American Association crown. Those rumors were put to rest before the end of October, however, when Robinson signed a three-year contract for $15,000 a year.

There had been minimal discussions about the fate of spitball pitchers during the regular season, but with three starters who effectively utilized the pitch during the World Series, the topic of revisiting abolition began to be discussed. In an interview with John J. Ward for *Baseball Magazine* before the Series, Grimes was candid about his trepidation about having to dispense with a major pitch in his repertoire. "Without it I doubt I could make good," said Grimes. "At a time of life when I ought to have several more good seasons and perhaps my very best seasons ahead of me, I should have to look to the minors for a job."[50]

With the season now over and the owners' meeting looming, members of the spitball fraternity went into full campaign mode. Grimes pleaded his case to the *Brooklyn Daily Eagle*. "In all fairness both to the players who use the delivery and those magnates and managers who wish the spitter done away with, I maintain that it is extremely illogical and also ethically unsound to force a number of players out of baseball at one time by arbitrary legislation," explained Grimes. "Why should the spitter be killed off in one or two seasons?"[51]

When the National League owners congregated at New York City's Waldorf-Astoria in mid–December, much of the chatter in the lobby before the session concerned the recent appointment of federal judge Kenesaw Mountain Landis as baseball's first commissioner. Replacing the three-man National Commission that had ruled over the game since 1903, Landis's judicial instincts brought stability to the game when it needed it most. His decisions were not always popular, but he helped stabilize the sport in the eyes of the fans following the Black Sox Scandal.

Once the meeting convened, the spitball was the hot topic of debate. St. Louis Cardinals spitballer Bill Doak wrote a letter to senior circuit owners on behalf of his brethren, arguing that barring the spitter would "deprive all these pitchers of their greatest power as pitchers."[52] Not surprisingly, Barney Dreyfuss spent a good amount of time explaining the virtues of doing away with the pitch, but when it came time to vote only he and William Veeck of the Cubs were in favor of a complete ban. Instead, by a 6–2 margin, registered spitball pitchers of the National League were given the right to use the pitch for the duration of their career. After some initial resistance, the American League adopted the same rule.

When it came time for teams to designate their spitball pitchers, the Pittsburgh Pirates and Chicago Cubs in the National League and the American League's Philadelphia Athletics and Washington Senators declined to submit any names. That left 17 players eligible to use the pitch for the duration of their career. They were:

National League
Boston Braves — Dana Fillingim and Dick Rudolph
Brooklyn Robins — Burleigh Grimes and Clarence Mitchell
Cincinnati Reds — Ray Fisher
New York Giants — Phil Douglas
St. Louis Cardinals — Bill Doak and Marv Goodwin

American League
Boston Red Sox — Allan Russell
Chicago White Sox — Red Faber
Cleveland Indians — Ray Caldwell and Stan Coveleski
Detroit Tigers — Doc Ayers and Dutch Leonard
New York Yankees — Jack Quinn
St. Louis Browns — Urban Shocker and Allen Sothoron

Coming off of their 1920 World Series appearance, several of the Robins felt that their contracts should reflect their status as defending National League champions. Grimes, Zach Wheat, Hi Myers, Sherrod Smith and Dutch Ruether, acquired from the Reds for Rube Marquard in December, all held out. Grimes was the only one who didn't sign within a few weeks of the start of training camp, holding steady to his belief that he should be making more money.

Threatening to sit out the 1921 season, Grimes claimed to be perfectly content living on his farm outside of Minerva, Ohio, and working at his new automobile business. He had expanded from the small private garage of a few years earlier and was now running a large public garage and rapidly becoming "a rising young salesman of autos and auto trucks."[53]

Charles Ebbets, whose health was beginning to fail, was becoming more difficult to deal with, particularly around contract time. Ebbets curtly responded, "Very well. Stay there!"[54]

Grimes mulled other options outside of organized baseball. An independent team from Chicago offered him $150 a game, and a semi-pro team from Canton, Ohio, a short distance from Minerva, proclaimed that it would "meet any proposal in the event that Grimes doesn't heal the breach with Brooklyn."[55] The Canton offer intrigued Grimes more than the Chicago bid, since it would allow him to live at home, draw more salary and save on paying two people to do his work at the garage and as a salesman.

With less than two weeks to go before the opener in Boston, Grimes had yet to appear at the team's new spring training site at Heinemann Park in New Orleans. He ignored all correspondences from Ebbets and Robinson and returned their contract offer unsigned (a reported "$7,500 contract and a $1,500 bonus provided he pitches as well as he did last year."[56]). Both owner and manager were perturbed by Grimes's response to *Brooklyn Daily Eagle*'s sportswriter Abe Yeager's telegram inquiring why he hadn't signed: "When Robbie and Ebbets wire they are ready to meet me, I will report at once."[57] The two parties were still a few thousand dollars apart, with Grimes demanding a salary of $12,000.

Publicly, Robinson took a diplomatic approach to the Grimes situation, telling reporters, "We could go along without Grimes of course, but not with the confidence his presence would inspire."[58] Privately, Uncle Robbie was infuriated that Brooklyn management had yet to negotiate a contract with one of the league's best pitchers. Finally, with opening day just days away he demanded that Grimes be signed. "I don't care how you get him. All I say is get him," said Robinson.[59]

The day before the opener, Grimes appeared at Ebbets Field while the club was working out. He had decided to concede, agreeing to a $9,000 contract, some $3,000 dollars less than his asking price. He did so with two contract stipulations: one that said he "would not be sold, traded, or released in the year without the athlete's consent" and a second that paid a $1,000 bonus for winning 25 games.[60]

Although always well conditioned, Brooklyn planned to give Grimes a few weeks of training before he was to pitch. The Robins sputtered to a 2–4 start and Grimes became anxious to pitch. He convinced Robinson to start him ahead of schedule against the Braves on April 21 at Ebbets Field. He didn't disappoint, going all

Contract squabbles between Grimes and Charles Ebbets, pictured, were commonplace during Grimes's tenure with the Robins (George Grantham Bain Collection, Library of Congress).

nine innings for a 4–2 win. The victory was the second of a season-high 11-game winning streak for Brooklyn. Having done minimal throwing in the offseason, the complete game left Grimes with a sore arm.

When he returned to the mound ten days later, Grimes seemed to pick up where he had left off in 1920, accumulating a 5–2 record by the end of May. On June 5, Grimes logged another complete-game victory, defeating the Cubs 5–3 in Chicago. He didn't escape the game unscathed, however, suffering a severely sprained thumb on his pitching hand after protecting his face from a line drive hit back through the box by Cubs center fielder Turner Barber in the ninth inning. He was able to finish the game, but missed his next start with a heavily bandaged thumb. During his absence the Robins went 2–7, dropping from third to fifth place.

Grimes feared that the bone in his thumb might have cracked. When he returned his thumb was still swollen and tender, but he didn't miss a beat, rattling off six straight victories, starting with a complete game on the extra-high mound in Pittsburgh versus Wilbur Cooper on June 15. Dating back to May 31, Grimes had won eight straight.

Although Grimes's record stood at 12–2 following the winning streak, it was evident that he was battling through his injury. Either doctors misdiagnosed the severity of the injury or he simply chose to overlook it, pitching through the rest of the 1921 season and the entire 1922 campaign with what later was diagnosed as a fractured thumb. The injury made throwing the spitball excruciating due to his "pinched watermelon seed" style of delivering the pitch. He persevered through the pain, but compensating for the injured thumb led to trouble the following year.

Grimes also overcame the livelier baseballs that were being used in 1921. During World War I, the quality of the baseballs had been poor because most quality wool was being used for the war effort. Now the ball seemed livelier than ever, affecting not only the way pitchers approached batters but how fielders positioned themselves. According to Zack Wheat, outfielders were "lying back 30 to 40 feet further than they ever did. They have to do that if they do not want the ball knocked over their heads. It goes with such a swift flight that if they stood where they stood last year they would be chasing extra base hits all the time."[61]

Adding to pitchers' difficulties was a new practice implemented in 1920 as part of the elimination of trick pitches. Umpires were now directed to replace any baseball that became even the least bit discolored. Previously the same few baseballs might be used for the game's entirety, but pitchers now regularly had to deal with a slick, shiny ball that they were unable to doctor in any way. The outcry by pitchers pushed major league officials to instruct umpires to rub down all game-ready balls with mud prior to the game.

Brooklyn struggled to remain in the first division, due in part to a mediocre offense. Robinson's tactics had helped push the team to the pennant in 1920 but now they seemed archaic and uninspired. The Robins finished in the bottom half of the National League in all major offensive categories.

Although Wheat was hitting for more power, his average wasn't seeing the same spike in hitting as some of the game's premier hitters. The team's top offensive player was fleet-footed third baseman Jimmy Johnston, who put up the best numbers of his career: 41 doubles, 14 triples and five home runs, while stealing 28 bases — all career highs. He also set a career high by batting .325 (which he matched two years later), recording 203 hits (which he also equaled two years later) and having the first of three consecutive 100-run seasons.

On June 18, Ebbets decided to shake up the Robins' aging roster by trading pitcher Jeff Pfeffer to the Cardinals for Ferdie Schupp and Hal Janvrin, both of whom ended up having minimal impact in a Brooklyn uniform. Pfeffer had been suffering from an ankle injury, but after the trade he recovered and won three of four starts against Brooklyn during the remainder of the year. A few weeks later the Robins cut first baseman Ed Konetchy, who had sprained his wrist while in Cincinnati in mid–June. That opened a spot for Ray Schmandt, a player whom Ebbets had been urging Robinson to start for a couple of years. Konetchy caught on with the Phillies to finish the 1921 season, but that was the end of his major league career.

Following his eight-game winning streak, Grimes lost three in a row. He then won eight of his next 11, including perhaps his best performance of the season on July 26 in Chicago when he scattered five singles in a 3–0 shutout of Grover Alexander and the Cubs. Grimes respected all of his opponents, but seldom was he in awe of them — except for Alexander. "If anybody was ever a better pitcher than that guy, I wouldn't know what his name was. It was just a pleasure to watch him work, even though he was beating your brains out most of the time," remarked Grimes. "Smooth and easy — always smooth and easy. I used more effort winding up than he did in pitching nine innings."[62] The two pitchers met seven more times over the next seven years, with Grimes mustering only one win compared with five Alexander victories.

Not only had Grimes found his pitching groove, he also had one of the more impressive offensive games of his career at the Polo Grounds during his streak. On July 6, he pounded four hits off Giants pitching, falling a triple shy of the cycle. His first of two career home runs came in the eighth inning, a line drive into the right field bleachers. He had nearly hit a homer in the fifth when he slammed one off the left field wall. The batting explosion added 56 points to his average, bumping it to an even .300. Everything seemed to be going his way.

In addition, Grimes was becoming a Brooklyn fan favorite. Long gone was the 1920 straw poll that saw Mamaux as the superior pitching talent. Grimes's new status allowed him and his wife to enjoy the spoils of fame: dapper clothing, jewelry and hobnobbing with celebrities of the day.

Always a fan of boxing, Grimes became close friends with heavyweights Jack Corbett and Jack Dempsey. Often referred to as the "Jack Dempsey of the pitcher's mound" for his pugnacious approach, Grimes and the heavyweight champ were often dinner companions. On one such occasion leading up to the Dempsey–Georges Carpentier fight, billed as the "Fight of the Century," Grimes and Dempsey were dining at an upscale restaurant in Manhattan. While the pair sat and talked, Grimes noticed a waiter who seemed to be hovering around their table instead of serving. Suddenly, he recognized the man as James Kilgallen, a reporter for the Hearst newspapers, hoping to get a scoop for the upcoming bout. When Grimes told Dempsey what was going on, they let Kilgallen get close to the table before grabbing the diminutive reporter and sticking him headfirst in a large plant holder. According to sportswriter Bob Broeg, the incident so infuriated Kilgallen (who became one of the nation's premier newspaper writers) that he contemplated having Grimes "rubbed out by the Big Guy (Al Capone)."[63]

After winning his first two decisions in September, Grimes went on a five-game losing streak. In four of the five defeats, he pitched well enough to earn victories as the Robins lost by scores of 3–1, 2–1, 1–0 and 3–1. Grimes picked up his 22nd victory over the pennant-winning Giants on the last day of the season. Despite slipping back into the second division with a fifth-place finish, the Robins were the only team to have a winning record against the Giants, finishing with 12 victories (of which Grimes had 5) versus 10 defeats.

Despite the thumb injury and his September slide, Grimes's 22 wins tied him with Wilbur Cooper for most in the National League. He also led the senior circuit with 30 complete games (including 17 of his last 18 starts) and 136 strikeouts. Although he failed to reach the 25-win plateau specified in his contract, Ebbets still awarded Grimes a bonus for his gritty performance.

Grimes and several of his Brooklyn teammates didn't wait around to see the first intracity World Series taking place at the Polo Grounds between the Yankees and Giants. Instead, Grimes put together an ambitious schedule of games that extended into December. The group planned on cashing in on the increasingly popular fall barnstorming tours that more major leaguers were participating in to supplement their salaries.

Teaming up with a squad made up of several members of the St. Louis Cardinals, the ballplayers planned to play a week's worth of games as they traveled west. After splitting up, the Robins scheduled contests against several town teams, including a homecoming for Grimes that saw him return to northern Wisconsin, followed by a game in Austin, Minnesota. Then they were to go to Cuba for nearly two months of baseball as part of the island's annual American Series.

The barnstorming trip encountered nasty fall weather that forced the cancellation of games in Pennsylvania and Illinois. The teams were finally able to play a few games, including a 2–1 Brooklyn victory in front of the "greatest crowd in the history of Columbia County Fair" in Portage, Wisconsin.[64] After the teams parted ways, the Robins had games scheduled in a few towns, but once again weather played a factor and they were only able to play once, an 8–1 victory in Oshkosh.

Grimes had handled the scheduling of the northern Wisconsin leg of the trip. He took particular interest in a game to be held at the Chippewa Falls Fair Grounds on October 10 against a team from nearby Augusta. Because of Chippewa Falls' proximity to Clear Lake, numerous family and friends planned to be in attendance. Following the game a banquet was planned.

If the idea of a professional ball team playing against locals wasn't incentive enough to draw a crowd, an error in a local paper added to the level of interest in the game. The *Eau Claire Leader* carried a large ad stating that the battery for the Augusta squad would be "Rube Marquard and Emanuel."[65] Perhaps it was done to drum up a crowd, giving locals an opportunity to see Grimes face off against his former teammate who was coming off a 19-win season for the Reds. It was actually supposed to read "Rube Marquardt," a pitcher from nearby Colby who was turning heads in the Three-I League and was set to join St. Paul of the American Association the following summer. Neither Rube Marquard nor Rube Marquardt were able to take the mound because the day scheduled for the game once again brought showers.

The Chippewa Falls Elks Club still went through with the banquet at the Hotel Northern. Local resident William F. Kirk, a writer who had covered the New York Giants for over a decade and still wired articles to the Hearst papers, started things off by reading a poem from his book *Right Off the Bat: Baseball Ballads*. Grimes then expressed his gratitude at being able to spend the night with family and friends, while Tommy Griffith and Leon Cadore shared humorous anecdotes from their barnstorming tour. Before the evening ended, the team had promised to return to the city later in the week.

Many of the fans who had hoped to see Grimes in Chippewa Falls made the trip to Rice Lake, where they saw Grimes throw five innings and hit a home run in a 9–7 extra-inning victory by the Brooklyn squad in front of an estimated crowd of 2,000. That same day the Giants were wrapping up their second consecutive World Series title with a 1–0 defeat of the Yankees. The series ended up 5–3 and was the last best-of-nine World Series.

When the Dodgers players returned to Chippewa Falls to fulfill their obligation, Grimes saw a familiar face warming up to pitch at the Fair Grounds. Art Johnson, his zany teammate from his Birmingham Barons days, was pitching for Augusta. The right hander had just returned to his home state after splitting time between Suffolk and Norfolk of the Virginia League in what proved to be the last year of his minor league career. Johnson was brilliant, striking out 14 Robins and getting big outs en route to a 5–4 Augusta victory.

Following the game, the Brooklyn players hopped on the Chicago, Milwaukee & St. Paul train and headed for Austin, Minnesota, where Grimes had played in 1912. For weeks the game had been advertised as a homecoming for Grimes, who was scheduled to be honored before the game and to pitch for the hometown team. Over 1,800 jammed into the Austin Ball Park, where the pregame ceremonies consisted of presenting Ruth Grimes with a chest of silverware and Burleigh with an undisclosed purse (later found to contain $200). When it became apparent that the crowd wouldn't cease their applause until Grimes said a few words, he obliged with a simple "I hope that I am all that you think I am."[66] Even with Brooklyn's regular battery of Grimes and Otto Miller, the Austin team wasn't much of a match for the Robins, who hopped out to a 6–0 lead after one inning and ended up winning 9–1.

Up until the Austin game the barnstorming trip had repaired relationships that had been damaged during the disappointing regular season. However, events following this game did away with what good the trip had done and deepened the schism between Grimes and several of his teammates. Grimes had reportedly pocketed not only his portion of the gate receipt, but also the entire purse, greatly perturbing his teammates who thought he would split the $200.

Grimes had a different version of what he did with the purse. "I gave $50 of that to the man who arranged the game and $75 to Otto Miller, who caught me," explained Grimes. "Otto divided his share among the Brooklyn players but I felt the remainder of the purse belonged to me."[67] The rift prompted several of the players to withdraw before the trip to Cuba, causing Grimes to scramble to fill the roster with players from other teams.

It was the third time that a Brooklyn team had played in Cuba's American

Series, and the first since 1913 (the other was in 1900). With a schedule of games alternating between the Almendares and Habana ballclubs, Grimes split pitching duties with Robins teammates Sherry Smith and Johnny Miljus as well as Philadelphia Phillies pitcher Lee Meadows, one of the first players to wear glasses, earning him the nickname "Specs."

The team played well against the two Cuban clubs, posting a 4–3 record against Almendares and 5–2 against Habana. Both of the Cuban squads had some of the island's best players of the day, including future Hall of Famer Cristobal Torriente, who was starring for Rube Foster's Chicago American Giants, and Adolfo Luque, whose light skin enabled him to pitch for the Cincinnati Reds. When the series against Almendares and Habana ended, the two island teams combined for an All-Star Cuban team. Once again the Robins held their own, going 5–2. Grimes was the most consistent pitcher on the trip, tallying a 5–1 record, including a 2–0 mark against the All-Star squad. Even so, there was more trouble during the trip, as the divide between Grimes and Otto Miller grew deeper for reasons unknown.

5

Burleigh and the Dazzler,
1922–1926

A few months after the American Series ended, the full Robins squad began to congregate in a new spring home in Jacksonville, Florida. The scenery may have changed, but for the second year in a row Grimes was a holdout. This didn't sit well with his teammates, who were perturbed by his actions during the barnstorming trip and Cuban excursion. Coming off a solid year, Grimes believed that a modest raise of $1,000 was in order, but Ebbets again balked at the proposal. Grimes called the Brooklyn owner's bluff by threatening to sign a five-year contract with a Chicago semi-pro team for $9,000 a season, even taking his plan to Commissioner Landis to learn whether he would be able to return to organized baseball.

The idea of joining a semi-pro team may have been a ploy to conceal that Grimes's ailing thumb had not recovered over his abbreviated winter. He continued to push for more stipulations in his contract, including a request for a 10-day notice clause to leave the club. "I want the same right to leave the club as the club has to release me on ten days notice, thus making the rights equal," said Grimes. He explained his motivation by saying, "I might have the opportunity to go into business that would net me more than I can get by pitching."[1]

With the Robins in desperate need of pitchers, a 31-year-old minor league journeyman showed himself to be a reliable arm in camp. Charles Arthur "Dazzy" Vance had had brief stints with the Pirates and Yankees in 1915 and again with the Yankees in 1918. In between he kicked around the minor leagues, with so many stops that he once insisted that, "I'll bet a hundred bucks that if I dropped in on every minor league club in the country — and I wouldn't care how small the league was — I would know at least three men on every one of them."[2]

Vance finally found his way back to the majors when Brooklyn signed catcher Hank DeBerry [sometimes recorded as De Berry] in early 1922.

DeBerry insisted that they sign Vance or else he wouldn't agree to play for the Robins. Ebbets was well aware of the pitcher, having passed on him numerous times. He initially scoffed at the minor leaguer's proposal, but finally conceded. It would be one of the greatest moves he ever made.

Without a signed contract, Grimes arrived at downtown Jacksonville's Hotel Burbridge, where the Robins were staying. He continued to talk about his supposed business plans. Within a few days he had a multi-year deal worked out with Ebbets. Grimes's salary was again $9,000 a year, with similar clauses, including the $1,000 bonus for 25 wins. Another clause specified that "he be sent to Hot Springs, Arkansas several weeks before spring training season before next year begins in order to get in the best possible condition."[3]

Grimes's first time on the mound was throwing batting practice to teammates in New Orleans. He immediately felt discomfort in his shoulder, but pitched through it. The next day he couldn't lift his arm above his shoulder. Grimes met with Robinson and the two hashed out a plan by which he issued a statement explaining that he was already in shape and therefore was not going to throw again until the regular season. "I believe in giving the young pitchers a chance at this time of year," Grimes said. "Robbie has plenty to go around — young fellows just aching to show what they can do, and this is the time for them to do it."[4]

On top of the injuries to his thumb and shoulder, Grimes was also showing signs of appendicitis, an ailment that would flare up on him on and off for the next decade, causing him considerable pain. After two weeks, Grimes became anxious to see how his arm was progressing when the team reached Richmond, Virginia, where he had played minor league ball in 1914. There was no greater test than the New York Yankees, the opponent of the Robins in a series of games being played as the two teams headed north to New York City. It was evident that something was wrong when Grimes threw with a sidearm delivery and served up a mammoth home run to Babe Ruth.

When the Robins arrived in Brooklyn, Grimes's ailments were made public. Robinson reported that, "Grimes has a sore thumb that is causing trouble in his arm and shoulder, but he should be ready for business in a few days."[5] The competitive Grimes was ready for business, but the injuries hadn't gotten any better. He persevered, throwing with a sidearm sling in his first start of the season a 5–3 complete game victory over the Giants at Ebbets Field. Grimes followed that up with unimpressive starts against the Phillies and the Pirates. He was so frustrated by the lingering injuries that he began dropping hints about a position change. The *Brooklyn Daily Eagle* reported, "Burleigh has visions of becoming an outfielder when his pitching arm begins to fail."[6]

Something needed to be done before Grimes's arm was permanently damaged. Ebbets and Robinson decided that he should skip his next start and travel to Youngstown, Ohio, where baseball's top "physician" John "Bonesetter" Reese, practiced medicine. In addition to his layperson clients, Reese, who had limited medical training, had a who's who clientele list of athletes, including some of the day's top baseball players. In all Reese treated 28 future Hall-of-Famers over the years.[7]

Grimes's trip to Reese revealed that a ligament in his shoulder was out of place, which the doctor slipped back into the proper position. After the adjustment Reese advised Grimes to "work gradually and then to pitch as hard as he please, but to be careful and not jerk the arm backward in winding up."[8] Grimes heeded the doctor's warning and returned to the mound after a nine-day hiatus. The struggles continued, however, as he lasted four innings in back-to-back starts in St. Louis before another shellacking at the hands of the lowly Phillies.

Each of these outings caused concern for the Robins, but they began to look to other reasons for his poor performance. They decided to focus on his two losses to the bottom-dwelling Phillies. In each game the normally soft-hitting Phillies pounded out 13 hits, looking as if they knew what every pitch was. Grimes had tried going to his mouth as a decoy for the spitter, but still they sat on the fastball. When he did throw the wet one, the batters weren't fooled by that pitch either.

The Robins were at a loss to account for Grimes's struggles against Philadelphia. After the first Phillies victory, which took place in Brooklyn they thought that new catcher Hank DeBerry was tipping pitches. Going into the second game at Philadelphia's Baker Bowl, DeBerry was told to act in the same way no matter what pitch was coming and advised to hide his signs to the best of his abilities. He hid them so well that even Grimes had problems seeing them. It was the same result, however, as the Phillies battered him out of the box in the seventh. The Robins were incensed, claiming that the Phillies had a spy with binoculars in the scoreboard relaying what pitch was coming. Although it was a practice that did go on, the Robins were wrong on all accounts. In fact, Grimes was the one giving away what pitch was coming.

It turned out that veteran Phillies shortstop Art Fletcher, who had spotted Grimes's extended pinkie when delivering a spitter a few years ago, had noticed another dead giveaway by the pitcher. It was well known that Grimes brought the ball and glove to his mouth before every pitch regardless of what he was throwing. Fletcher noticed that Grimes's cap wiggled from the flexing of his facial muscles when he lubricated the ball and tipped off his teammates. This fact remained unnoticed in Brooklyn for the rest of the year. Robinson even made sure Grimes's spot in the rotation didn't come around when they were taking on the Phillies. It wasn't until early 1923 that a bat boy finally noticed Grimes's cap moving when he threw the spitball. The pitcher switched to a larger hat and the problem was solved.

Grimes worked his way back into shape and Dazzy Vance started to show signs of the star that he would become, mixing his blazing fastball and devastating curveball. He had started off the season slowly, but in Pittsburgh on May 11 (a game he lost) he started his climb to baseball immortality. Grimes recalled the event years later:

> On this day in Pittsburgh, it was his turn to pitch, and because of a rain delay or something he went down to warm up in front of the Pittsburgh clubhouse. Some of the Pirates came out to watch him and he made their eyes pop. You never saw a ball do such tricks. Not only did he have that blazer, but he had a curveball that came in their like a scared snake. One of the Pirates said "For Christ's sake, if you threw that way in a game, nobody could touch you." Vance believed him, I guess, because from then on he went and became a great pitcher. Finally made it to shore.[9]

The May road trip where Vance had begun to blossom helped bring the Robins closer together and moved them up in the standings. After losing nine of its first 11 games and falling to seventh place, the team finished the western swing by winning nine of its last 10 and moving up to fourth in the standings. A week later Brooklyn had climbed into third. Much of the team's demeanor changed, thanks in part to the free-spirited Vance. The camaraderie blooming on and off the field was the genesis of the "Daffiness Boys," a period in Brooklyn history dominated by oddball characters and occurrences.

With most of the team growing closer, Grimes grew distant from many of his teammates, most notably Otto Miller. As the gap between the pitcher and catcher widened, it left the two in a precarious position on days that Grimes pitched. He even took to having a man from the Flatbush neighborhood named Mathias Schroeder warm him up before games rather than Miller.

Other teammates were still peeved with Grimes over the barnstorming tour, while still others did not care for his tyrannical mound antics directed at them. Yet another problem was his wife Ruth, who had supposedly made disparaging remarks about the wives of a few of Grimes's teammates, including Zack Wheat, Sherrod Smith and Bernie Neis. That left Grimes with few allies on the team, the most notable one being Ivy Olson.

No one could question Grimes's commitment to putting forth his best effort whenever he stepped onto the field. He fought through his travails and continued to develop into a heady pitcher. "In 1920 I led the league while chucking for Brooklyn," Grimes said. "The papers credited me then with being a pretty smart hombre on the mound but actually I was a dumb-O with a strong arm. It wasn't until a couple of seasons later that I really got wised up and from then on I feel I doubled my pitching knowledge every year."[10]

With the team prospering, a 5–2 June evened Grimes's record at 7–7. When July began, the Robins were still within four-and-a-half games of the first-place Giants, but a dreadful western swing sealed their fate. They played 18 of 19 on the road during that stretch, losing 14 and dropping into sixth place. After that, the team never came closer than 10½ games of first place. The long season wore on the aging ballclub, which was plagued by injuries to Grimes, Hank DeBerry, Tommy Griffith, Jimmy Johnston and Clarence Mitchell, each of whom spent extended time watching from the stands.

After his resurgence in June, Grimes spent the next two months at or near the .500 mark. After winning four of five decisions, Grimes threw another tantrum on August 6 at Ebbets Field against Cincinnati. Just three days earlier he had four-hit the Reds, and he looked likely to do it again when he sailed through the first three-and-one-third innings. Cincinnati finally got to him in the fourth inning, scoring six runs, the last two on former teammate Jake Daubert's inside-the-park home run. Grimes was incensed that some plays weren't made behind him and grew more enraged when Wilbert Robinson emerged from the dugout.

Years later, Grimes described the incident to the *Milwaukee Journal*'s Sam Levy: "When Daubert reached third, I heard the phone ringing in our dugout. I knew Charlie Ebbets was calling Robinson with orders to yank me. Uncle Robbie then came out to get me to leave."[11] Grimes refused to leave the mound. When he finally did, instead of handing the ball to his manager he hurled it against the grandstand. The two men returned to the dugout, where they engaged in a shouting match. When several of his teammates sided with Robinson, Grimes berated them too, before retiring to the clubhouse.

After an off day, Grimes was back on the bench against the Cubs. Brooklyn fans were exasperated that no action had been taken by Ebbets. Some openly suggested that Grimes "had the president buffaloed."[12] The owner issued a statement revealing that Grimes had in fact been immediately fined $200 and suspended without pay (although allowed to remain on the bench), but said that "the punishment he chose to inflict upon a player who committed his offense in the presence of 10,000 of his patrons was strictly a club affair and did not concern the public."[13] Despite numerous run-ins with management and teammates, it was the first time any punishment had been levied on Grimes during his tenure with Brooklyn.

In a letter to his suspended pitcher, Ebbets laid out a five-point plan for his reinstatement to the team:

1. That you will discontinue the use of insulting language direct or indirect to the manager and to the president of the Brooklyn club.

2. That you will curb your temper when in the discharge of your duties on the ball field or in the clubhouse.

3. That you will pitch as Manager Robinson advises or directs through the player he may assign to catch you.

4. That you will quit using intemperate, insinuating remarks relative to your winning and losing games.

5. That you will quit playing indifferently, and at all times give the Brooklyn club your best efforts in the discharge of your duties as we have the right to demand, consistent and to conformity with the terms of your contract.[14]

Grimes agreed to the plan and returned to the club a week after his suspension. He pitched the rest of the season without incident and had a solid September, highlighted by a game against the St. Louis Cardinals on September 20. Grimes threw a complete-game 3-hitter, in the process putting an end to Rogers Hornsby's 33-game hitting streak by inducing two groundouts, a strikeout and a fielder's choice.

In the spring Grimes had told the *Brooklyn Eagle*'s Abe Yeager that it was easy to tell Hornsby's intentions at the plate, adding that Cincinnati's Edd Roush was the toughest batter to face in the league:

> I can tell almost exactly what Hornsby is going to do by the position he takes at the plate, but Roush never. Once Rogers takes his position, he doesn't change it. If he crowds the plate I know he is going to try to place a hit in right field; if he stands back from the pan, it's the tip off for a left field swing. Hornsby always hits them for a drive over the infield; he never tries to dump them down.
>
> Roush on the other hand, almost invariably takes the same position at the bat, but has a pitcher guessing all the time. He makes his shifts with the old wagon tongue, pulling the unexpected by choking his bat while the ball is on the way or stepping back or into it for a long swing. He has fooled me lots of times by getting into position for one of his famous drives and then dumping the ball to the infield to advance the runner.
>
> Believe me, both Hornsby and Roush are great hitters, but Roush to my mind is the harder to pitch to.[15]

The Robins finished the 1922 season in sixth place at 76–78. Plagued by an anemic offense that ranked fourth or lower in most offensive categories, the league-wide power explosion had yet to make its way to Flatbush. Charles Ebbets was feeling the heat to bring a power bat to Brooklyn. The club's biggest power threat was once again Zack Wheat, who had 29 doubles, 12 triples, 16 home runs and 112 RBIs (the home runs and RBIs were career highs).

The pitching staff hadn't fared much better — wear and tear and time were catching up with more than one hurler, including Leon Cadore, Al Mamaux and Sherry Smith. Smith was put on waivers and claimed by Cleveland in September. There were bright spots on the staff, however, including the emergence of Dazzy Vance (18–12), who wrapped up the first of seven consecutive strikeout titles. Dutch Reuther also had his best year in a Brooklyn uniform compiling a 21–12 record.

The club had gotten solid performances out of a few of its newcomers. In addition to Vance and DeBerry, third baseman Andy High had enjoyed a good rookie campaign. Originally brought into camp when Jimmy Johnston held out, he moved to shortstop once Johnston signed. Soon High was playing third again on a full-time basis, while Johnston and Ivy Olson split time at shortstop. The 5-foot-5-inch High provided solid defense and was a contact hitter, playing in all but two of the team's games. His approach to the game impressed Grimes and the two became fast friends.

Grimes salvaged his season with a strong September, going 4–1. The month included one of the more bizarre outings of his career on September 9 in a game against the Boston Braves. The game got off to an odd start when the Braves arrived at Ebbets Field without their uniforms or equipment. The train carrying Boston's goods had derailed near the Woodlawn depot, delaying its arrival, forcing the Braves to wear the Robins' road uniforms and wield Brooklyn bats for the first two innings before changing into their own jerseys.

To add to the odd ambience, threatening weather meant that barely 2,000 were in attendance. Those who showed up saw Grimes pitch all 12 innings in the 6–5 Brooklyn victory. He was aided by two Zack Wheat home runs and a game-winning blast by Andy High in the bottom of the 12th. Grimes matched a career high by giving up 18 hits. He also struck out 10 batters, the first of only two times in his career that he reached double-digit strikeouts in a game.

Grimes ended the 1922 season with a record of 17–14, but his ERA ballooned to 4.76. It had been a few years since his name appeared in trade rumors, but his injury and the emergence of Dazzy Vance made it easier for Ebbets to put Grimes on the block. Before the new year, his name was mentioned in potential deals with the Giants, Reds and Cubs. Grimes headed into the off-season looking to get healthy and recover his form of 1920.

Charles Ebbets's heart problems had worsened during the trying 1922 season, so shortly after it ended he decided to get out of Brooklyn to recuperate. Ebbets headed to Clearwater, Florida, which was in the midst of a major real estate boom. After seeing how many people were flocking there,

Ebbets decided to move the Robins' spring training site to Clearwater. Over the next two decades the club spent all but a few seasons there. According to Frank Graham, author of *The Brooklyn Dodgers: an Informal History*, "so many Brooklyn fans trekked down every year to watch them that after a while the town took on the aspects of a little Brooklyn, and many of the sights and sounds of Ebbets Field were duplicated in the Clearwater ball park."[16]

There was no salary wrangling over the winter for Grimes since he was entering the second year of his two-year contract. The offseason didn't go without incident, however. In January 1923, X-rays showed that Grimes's aching thumb had actually been broken two years earlier in a game against the Cubs. For the past year-and-a-half he had been pitching with a piece of splintered bone floating around his thumb. A date for surgery was set for early February, but when it was learned that recovery time would be a minimum of three months, Grimes and Brooklyn management agreed to wait and see how things went to start the year. Instead, he traveled to Hot Springs to meet up with Dazzy Vance for some preliminary conditioning before heading to Florida to begin training camp.

When Grimes and Vance arrived in Clearwater, several of the usual faces were absent from camp. Besides Zack Wheat and Dutch Ruether — who were holding out — Ebbets had traded away a few veterans. Over a five-day period in February, the owner had dealt pitcher-outfielder Clarence Mitchell to the Philadelphia Phillies for George Smith and then swapped Hy Myers and first basemen Ray Schmandt to the St. Louis Cardinals for first baseman Jack Fournier.

Fournier had been a serviceable player during much of his decade-long career, but had struggled in 1922, even being pulled from the lineup down the stretch as the Cardinals battled for the pennant. Some felt Ebbets had ulterior motives for the trade, possibly fearing that, "Fournier, the only remaining nominee for the Players' Union Presidency might slip into the minors."[17] The plan seemed to backfire on the day after the trade was completed, when Fournier announced that he was asking Commissioner Landis to place him on the voluntary retired list in order to work full-time as an insurance salesman in St. Louis. His decision to retire left Brooklyn with nothing to show from the trade.

With team captain Zack Wheat absent and the Fournier trade a disaster, Grimes and Vance slipped into leadership roles. Feeling better than he had in a few years, Grimes rapped balls off the outfield fence in batting practice and pulled double duty in an intrasquad scrimmage, playing third base for one team and pitching for the other. The pitching tandem also made sure that there was camaraderie off the field, with Vance leading several of his teammates on a deep water fishing expedition. Grimes and his wife led others on a tour of local orchards, one of which they were considering as an investment. Charles Ebbets publicly lauded Grimes for the vigor with which he was going about his training.

Otto Miller had retired to take over as manager of the Southern Association's Atlanta Crackers, so Grimes's icy relationship with his catcher was no longer a problem. In Clearwater, Grimes worked closely with Zach Taylor and Hank DeBerry, who under the guidance of Robinson formed one of the best catching tandems in the league. Of the two, Taylor proved to be more adept at pouncing in front of Grimes's spitters, which when working properly was likely to end up in the dirt.

Although he had been touted as an excellent receiver as a rookie in 1920, Taylor had played sparingly in his first three seasons with Brooklyn before being sent to the Southern Association halfway through the 1922 season. His two months playing for Spencer Abbott and the Memphis Chickasaws had a wonderful effect on Taylor's play and by early May he was Grimes's personal catcher. Taylor was behind the plate for 95 of Grimes's next 102 starts in a Brooklyn uniform.

All things considered, the Robins had a successful spring training, and things were starting to come together when they headed north to Brooklyn for the season opener against the Phillies. Both Zack Wheat and Dutch Reuther had come to terms and Jack Fournier — who had signed on to manage a semi-pro team in Centralia, Illinois — was beginning to have a change of heart. He reached out to Brooklyn officials, reporting that he had been working out frequently and was interested in entering contract negotiations.

After an Opening Day tie with Philadelphia that ended 5–5 after 14 innings, Grimes hoped to end his recent struggles against the Phillies the next day. Even with the proper-sized hat on it, was the same story as the Robins found themselves trailing 5–1 heading into the bottom of the ninth. Already in the clubhouse, Grimes was surprised to hear cheering in the grandstands above him. He hastily made his way back to the dugout to see his teammates score five runs in the bottom of the ninth inning and give him his first victory of the season and his first against the Phillies since September 1921.

The early-season heroics didn't last long and after another slow start the Robins found themselves in last place by May 1. Over the next month the team went 18–9 to climb out of the cellar and work its way up the standings. Dazzy Vance started slow, but solid pitching from Grimes and rookie Leo Dickerman accounted for 10 of the victories. The ascension was aided by sound defense and the hitting of Jimmy Johnston, Zach Wheat (who had hit safely in 33 of the 35 games he had played in) and Jack Fournier, who came out of "retirement" to spark the offense with his prodigious power. There was no hotter trio of hitters in the game during the Robins' climb.

Brooklyn jumped into second place on June 4, eight games behind the Giants, when Grimes tossed a 5–3 victory over the Pirates. Seeing his team a notch below the Giants prompted Charles Ebbets to arrange a meeting with Pittsburgh owner Barney Dreyfuss, who was always open to a deal. Ebbets proposed a trade that would send infielder Andy High and pitcher Dutch Reuther (who had drawn the ire of his teammates for not hustling) in exchange for veteran pitcher Babe Adams, utility infielder Jewel Ens and star third baseman Pie Traynor. No one would have been more pleased with the trade than Grimes, who Traynor had always hit well. Alas, nothing came of what would have been a steal for the Robins.

The June 4 victory turned out to be Brooklyn's sole day in second place and the closest they came to McGraw's Giants, who stood atop the league standings for the entire 1923 season. Both Grimes and the Robins cooled off as June progressed; after being on the road for much of the month, they sunk into the second division, where they sat for the remainder of the season. As a result, crowds dwindled at Ebbets Field.

Feeling the effects of a collision with Taylor during the June 4 Pirates game that left his throwing arm tender, Grimes lost his next three starts. He didn't get much help from his fielders, who committed 12 errors over that span. Grimes's season got even worse in July and early August, when he was on the losing end in eight of nine decisions. He slipped below .500 (12–13) on August 4, but things started to turn around when he pitched shutouts in back-to-back games on August 12 and August 16 against the Pirates and Cardinals, respectively.

Twenty losses seemed to be a certainty when Grimes entered September with a 14–17 record. The previous two months of mediocrity were forgotten when Grimes tallied a 6–1 September record, turning around what could have been a very disappointing season and reestablishing his iron-man status. One more win on October 2 over the Boston Braves moved his record to 21–18. He led the National League in starts (38) and innings pitched (327), and his 33 complete games (including his last fifteen starts of the season) topped both leagues. He also led the National League in assists (101) and errors (10), evidence that Grimes's spitball was once again back to form and inducing groundballs. His 11 hit batsmen was a career high and also led the league. However, Grimes did struggle at Ebbets Field, which had always been a haven for him. He sputtered to a 9–8 mark in Flatbush, failing to reach double-digits in victories for the first time since his injury-shortened 1919 season.

A decade-and-a-half later in 1938, after his first year as manager of the

Dodgers, Grimes sat down with *Sporting News* publisher J.G. Taylor Spink and reflected on a number of topics, including the '23 season. "I consider 1923 my best season in the nine years I served with the Dodgers. You may be surprised at that, because in that year my record was only fair, as shown by the averages — 21 and 18," said Grimes. "I had everything except luck and batting support."[18] There were a number of close games that could have gone Grimes's way during the 1923 season but ended up in the loss column, including five one-run losses and seven shutouts.

Grimes's July and August struggles were mirrored by Dazzy Vance's success. Vance, who had come within an out of a no-hitter against the Reds on June 17, tore off a 10-game win streak from June 30 to August 12. While Grimes turned it around in September, Vance struggled to a 3–4 record to end the year, finishing at 18–15. Dutch Ruether was the only other Robin with double-digit victories (15), leading to the second consecutive sixth-place finish for Brooklyn. Once the guru of handling pitchers, Robinson's magic seemed to have departed.

Offensively, Zach Wheat ended up batting .375, but lost the batting title to Rogers Hornsby due to playing just 98 games as a result of another ankle injury, which left him relegated to pinch-hitting duties for over six weeks. An aching knee hadn't kept Jimmy Johnston out of the lineup (151 games), but caused him to tail off from his hot start and marked the last big season of his career in a Brooklyn uniform (.325, 29 doubles). Jack Fournier fell into a slump during the team's three-week home stand in July, but it wasn't enough to keep him from establishing himself as Brooklyn's first true power hitter. At 33 years old, Fournier enjoyed a renaissance, blending power (30 doubles, 22 home runs) with average (.351) and one of his most underappreciated attributes, speed (13 triples).

For all he did offensively, Fournier's defense was at best suspect, driving Grimes to fits. Once following an error by Fournier, Grimes fielded the next ball hit to him and instead of throwing it to the first baseman took it to the base himself, intentionally stepping on Fournier's foot in the process. At times, the two clashed and Fournier, like Grimes, never backed down from a confrontation. When the two were at odds it could get vicious. One time the two men had an argument on the 18th green of a golf course that led to a fistfight. Showing that they still respected each other, after the fight they finished the round and had lunch.

Brooklyn's struggles had taken their toll on Charles Ebbets and before the 1923 season was over he was ordered by a physician to return to Florida. The doctor even suggested living there year-round, which would force him to give up the management of the Robins. From his home in the gated community of Harbor Oaks, Ebbets wrote to several of his fellow owners mapping out a plan for his exit from baseball. His importance to the game was evident when the other owners "so urgently asked him to remain in baseball if it were at all compatible with his health that he immediately felt better and gave up all thoughts of quitting."[19]

Much of Grimes's off-season was spent in Ohio, where he worked at his garage, tended to his growing stable of racehorses and spent a great deal of time hunting foxes. Even in what was supposed to be a light-hearted correspondence with F.M. Lane for *Baseball Magazine*'s "Letters from the Firing Line," a column devoted to ballplayers' off-season pursuits, Grimes's perfectionism shone through. When describing a picture of him and his dogs with a fox they had caught, Grimes said it was "a poor snapshot taken in indifferent light by a rank amateur."[20]

Contract negotiations between Grimes and Brooklyn management went well during the winter, with the two parties coming to terms by late February, 1924. That didn't stop Grimes from showing up late to training in Clearwater.

Grimes (left) and Dazzy Vance (right) in spring training of 1926. They were one of the league's best pitching tandems during their time together in a Brooklyn uniform (Charles Clark Photo Collection).

He took his time straightening out matters for his garage in Minerva before traveling to Hot Springs, Arkansas, for a week of conditioning. Grimes arrived to a very loose camp where golf seemed to be the main source of training. With much of the same roster that had finished in sixth place the year before, Robinson boldly proclaimed, "Give me three fellows who can pitch that ball and four that can hit and I'll win the pennant."[21]

There was some extra motivation for National Leaguers going into the 1924 season. A $1,000 purse and title of League Most Valuable Player had been established in the senior circuit, following the American League's implementation of the same award in 1922. Dazzy Vance bet teammate Jacques Fournier an undisclosed amount that he would not only win the award, but would win more games than Fournier hit home runs.

For the third straight year Robinson had Grimes, Vance and Reuther at the top of his rotation, with a piecemeal staff behind them. Both Grimes and Vance lost their first starts, but followed with solid performances in May. On the other hand, Reuther struggled: something seemed to be amiss with the once-brash left-hander. A Grimes victory on May 23 closed out a 7–5 western road trip and moved the Robins to within a game-and-a-half of the first-place Giants, who were percentage points ahead of the Cubs. Behind the standout tandem and a 10–6 record to close out the month, the Robins dug their heels into third place on May 31, and held it for the next 45 games.

By the second week of June it was apparent that the current roster couldn't sustain Brooklyn's pennant hopes. Charles Ebbets made a few shrewd moves, first picking up outfielder Eddie Brown from the Indianapolis Indians on June 4. Brown, a New York Giants castoff, had been tearing up the American Association for the past three years as he tried to make it back to the big leagues. Ten days later Ebbets swapped pitchers with the Cardinals — Leo Dickerman, one of Grimes's few friends on the team, was traded for spitballer Bill Doak. Doak, a crafty veteran whose performance had been in decline over the past two seasons, was rejuvenated after being able to work with Grimes to shore up his spitball delivery. The acquisitions were crucial to Brooklyn's magical 1924 season.

A four-game winning streak to close out June made it Grimes's best month of the season with a 5–1 record and a stingy 2.16 ERA. He regressed in July, however, slipping to 4–3 and more than doubling his ERA (4.43). As Grimes's production fell, Vance and Doak began winning streaks that not only kept Brooklyn's pennant hopes alive, but helped propel the team toward the top of the National League standings. Beginning in mid–July, Vance chalked up 15 consecutive victories and Doak won 10 straight.

Unable to string together victories like Vance and Doak, Grimes's workmanlike 10–7 record over that time complemented the streaking pitchers. At the end of July Grimes put together two of his best performances of the year, striking out 10 Cincinnati Reds on July 26, followed four days later by his sole shutout of the season, scattering five Chicago Cubs singles. Both games were played at Ebbets Field, once again a beacon of success for Grimes. He ended the season with a career-high 14 home victories versus only 4 defeats.

Brooklyn was in fourth place on July 28, and by August 9 had fallen 13 games behind the Giants. The next day the team started an improbable climb up the standings with a doubleheader sweep of the Cardinals at Ebbets Field. On August 14, the Robins began a brutal stretch of games, playing 25 of the next 28 games on the road. The reprieve was three home games against the Giants.

On August 18, Grimes started on his birthday for the only time in his career. He nabbed a 7–4 complete-game victory over the Pirates, rapping a season-high four hits of his own, all singles. It was the seventh of his nine multi-hit games on the year. Grimes and Vance each compiled a 5–1 record against their former ballclub, greatly hindering the Pirates pennant hopes. It was the second year in a row that Grimes had achieved that record against Pittsburgh.

The western road trip started off well as the Robins won eight of their first 10 and moved two-and-a-half games closer to first place. Brooklyn looked to continue its winning ways when it rolled into St. Louis to take on the sixth-place Cardinals. After losing the first game of a Sunday doubleheader, 7–6, the Robins were embarrassed in the second game, 17–0. The sweep easily could have been the season's backbreaker, but Bill Doak came back the next day and won, 5–3, his fifth consecutive win. Like Grimes and Vance, Doak was especially hard on his former team, achieving a perfect 5–0 mark for the season against the Cardinals.

Meanwhile, an offensive surge was going on around the league. As a whole, the National League batted .283 and, for the first time since the end of the Dead Ball Era, Brooklyn had some of the league's top offensive threats. Once again healthy, Zack Wheat trailed only Rogers Hornsby (who hit .424) for the batting title, matching his .375 mark from the year before. Jacques Fournier was second only to Babe Ruth in the power department, leading the National League with 27 home runs. Andy High batted .328 and struck out just 16 times in 654 plate appearances.

Like any pennant run, players who had struggled in the past either had career years or came into their own. Highly touted Bernie Neis had been a disappointment since coming to the Robins in 1920, but he found his stroke in '24, batting .303. He platooned with Eddie Brown, the American Association pickup, who batted .308.

There was more to Dutch Reuther's problems than his attitude. After he finally was sent to Bonesetter Reese at mid-season, he contributed only three victories over the last three months. Other pitchers stepped up their production, including Art Decatur, who chipped in 10 wins working as a starter and out of the bullpen, and Rube Ehrhardt, who threw some crucial innings after being signed out of the Florida State League in July. His 5–3 record didn't do justice to how well he pitched down the stretch.

Grimes won the team's final game at Sportsman's Park before it headed back to Ebbets Field to take on the struggling Giants. Three weeks earlier the Giants had been nine games ahead of the Pittsburgh Pirates, but in the last two weeks they had losing streaks of five and three games and had seen their lead drop to four. The Robins swept the crucial series as Vance, Doak and then Grimes each won a game. The Giants' lead was down to two over Pittsburgh. Brooklyn, winners of five straight and 19 of its last 24, was within four games.

The team hopped the Sunday evening train to Philadelphia, where the schedule called for three doubleheaders in three days (September 1–3) at the Baker Bowl to make up rainouts. Three days later, when the Robins boarded a Pullman at Broad Street Station headed for Boston they had added six more games to their win column and were now a game-and-a-half behind the Giants (Grimes's 7–6 win was the closest game of the series, as Brooklyn scored a run in each of the last three innings to complete the comeback). There was no time to rest, however. The Robins were set to play five games in three days before heading back to New York for a home-and-home series against the Giants.

The hot streak continued. Brooklyn swept the September 4 doubleheader behind Vance (his 12th straight) and Dutch Reuther, who won his first game in nearly two months. The two wins leapfrogged the Robins over the Pirates into a first-place tie with the Giants, who lost 10–6 to the Phillies in 10 innings. It was the first time since May 25 that the Giants did not have sole possession of first place. The next day Rube Ehrhardt shut out the Braves 4–0 on five singles, but a the Giants beat Philadelphia to remain even.

On September 6, Bill Doak threw his second consecutive two-hitter in the first game of a doubleheader, beating the Braves, 1–0. In Philadelphia, the Phillies eked out an 8–7 win over the Giants. For a few hours the Robins stood alone in first place, but by the end of the night New York was back on top by percentage points after edging the Phillies in a 16–14 slugfest. Brooklyn's heartbreaking 5–4 loss was the result of a two-run error in the bottom of the tenth on pitcher Art Decatur's bad throw.

Of the whirlwind day, Thomas Rice of the *Brooklyn Daily Eagle* later wrote, "At 4:00 P.M., Saturday September 6, 1924, those Brooklyn Superbas led the National League. At 7 P.M. those said Superbas were third in the National League. 'Twas better to have led then lost than never led at all.'"[22] The Robins' winning streak had finally come to a halt at 15. Overall, Brooklyn had won 29 of its last 35, gaining a dozen games and moving up three spots in the standings. The Robins had no time to dwell on the streak, however, as Grimes and his teammates looked to regain their fleeting hold on first place the next day (September 7) at Ebbets Field.

It was a wild scene in Flatbush in the hours leading up to the game. Ed McKeever had requested a large police detail, but only 20–30 officers were dispatched, not nearly enough to contain the rambunctious crowd that was forming. Problems were compounded by the ballclub overselling tickets, which meant that thousands who had paid for a seat were in jeopardy of not getting in. The large crowd made it difficult for players and umpires to even make it into the stadium. According to the *Brooklyn Daily Eagle*, once the gates opened, mobs "climbed the walls and fences, crashed the turnstiles and gate and streamed into the baseball park," leaving hundreds "who had bought seats but could not enter the park, or entered and could not reach their seats."[23] To try to accommodate the throng, spectators lined the outfield wall. Reserve players were dispatched to line the rim of the outfield in hopes of grabbing foul balls so that there would be enough to complete the game.

The game was anticlimactic after the pre-game proceedings. Neither Grimes nor his mound adversary, Jack Bentley, were particularly sharp. With the close quarters in the outfield, doubles were abundant, as anything that made it to the spectators was a ground — rule double; in all, 11 were hit. Every starter, including the pitchers, recorded a hit, for a total of 33 for the game. Grimes allowed 17 of them, as well as six walks, but he kept the Robins in the game until five Giants hits. A crucial error by shortstop Johnny Mitchell and a walk led to five runs in the top of the eighth, breaking open a 3–3 tie. Brooklyn scored once in the bottom half of the eighth. In the bottom of the ninth the home team rallied for three more and had the tying run on third in the form of Grimes before pinch-hitter Dutch Reuther struck out. Despite the loss, the Robins remained in second place when the Pirates split a doubleheader at home to the Cubs.

Vance beat the Giants the next day at the Polo Grounds for his 13th straight victory. The two teams were once again in a virtual dead heat. The Robins, who played the remainder of their schedule (15 games) at Ebbets Field, looked to be in a good position to overcome the Giants, who were also benefiting from rounding out their schedule at the Polo Grounds. Contrary to past years, however, Ebbets Field wasn't much of an advantage to the Robins (they ended the year 46–31 at home and 46–31 on the road) and it showed as they posted a 6–4 record over their next 10 games, including Vance's 15-game winning streak coming to an end against the Pirates on September 20.

The Robins pulled back into a tie with the idle Giants on September 22, but slipped a game behind the next day, losing a 5–4 heartbreaker in 10 innings to the Cubs. Vance allowed only four hits, but three were home runs, two to George Grantham and one to Gabby Hartnett. Brooklyn desperately needed a win, and Grimes was called upon to do just that.

No doubt still stewing from his failure in the Giants loss, Grimes called an impromptu meeting before his start on September 24. "I only want the fellows who are to play in today's game," he announced, clearing out the Ebbets Field clubhouse but for the other eight Robins in the lineup that day.[24] "This will be the toughest game you ever played in! Anybody who can't take it can get out now! Is that clear?" he shouted as he prowled up and down in front of his teammates, whose guttural responses assured him that they understood. "You'll be thrown at, you'll be knocked down and they'll try to spike you! It's up to you to be ready!"[25]

In front of a small but full-throated crowd of 10,000, including some 250 members of the Brooklyn Chamber of Commerce, Grimes was at his fiercest. He set the tone for the game and backed up his pregame speech by throwing at leadoff batter Sparky Adams. The first pitch sailed past his head, sending the Cubs shortstop sprawling to the dirt. The beanball shouldn't have taken catcher Zach Taylor by surprise, but it did: "I had a hunch what was coming, but I never thought it was going to be that rough. I figured Burleigh might throw at Grantham and at Hartnett because of the homers they had hit the day before, but I wasn't prepared when Grimes cut loose with the first pitch at the first Chicago hitter."[26]

No Cubs were hit by pitches, but over the first two innings six batters found themselves dusting off their uniforms after a Grimes offering, including pitcher Grover Cleveland Alexander. After narrowly avoiding a pitch that sailed behind his neck and sent him lunging toward the Brooklyn dugout, the 37-year-old Alexander gave a look of terror. "Like a person who finds himself locked in a room with a madman," commented Taylor.[27] George Grantham finally had had enough and after being brushed back he walked halfway to the mound to let Grimes know how he felt. When the Cubs third baseman walked back to the plate he was showered with epithets from the stands.

In the fifth inning, with the Robins leading 4–2, Grimes made the play of the game and one of the most spectacular plays of his career. With rookie Al Weis on third base and Cliff Heathcote batting, Grimes bounced a spitball off catcher Zack Taylor's chest that bounded back toward the mound. Grimes scooped up the ball and, instead of flipping it back to Taylor, he dove headfirst toward the plate, blocking it from Weis, who came barreling down the line. Narrowly avoided a serious maiming, Grimes tagged out Weis. The Cubs finally strung some hits together in the seventh, tying the score at four. Brooklyn replied with two in the bottom half of the inning and, after a scoreless eighth, Grimes held the Cubs to one in the top of the ninth to earn a 6–5 victory.

The game went down as one of the signature performances of Grimes's career, epitomizing his mound demeanor. Members of both teams never forgot the way Grimes terrorized batters that day. A few years later when returning from St. Louis in the early morning hours, Hartnett stepped off the train at Chicago's Union Station. A Pullman porter offered to dust off his jacket, but Hartnett knew that he would be facing Grimes (by then with the Giants) later that day. The Cubs catcher replied straight-faced to the porter's offer, "Never mind boy, Grimes will dust me off this afternoon."[28] Hartnett avoided being hit by Grimes that day, but took the collar, going 0-for-4.

Following the victory, the Robins players were escorted via automobile to the Chamber of Commerce building, where a banquet took place honoring their pennant run. After the meal and some rousing speeches, the players were escorted to the 160th Armory at Bedford and Atlantic Avenue to receive an unspecified gift from the citizens of Brooklyn. In response to insufficient police presence at the Giants game, 70 officers were dispatched to make sure that order was kept. The number was still too small to handle the estimated 30,000 who crammed into the drill hall to catch a glimpse of the Robins as they received watches for their amazing late-season surge. In addition to the players' initials engraved into the back of the gift, the inscription read, "From the citizens of Brooklyn to the Brooklyn Baseball Club of 1924." Receiving the largest applause was Grimes, who according to the *New York Times* "actually blushed at the demonstration that greeted pronouncement of his name."[29]

The Robins had three days to sit around and think about their two-game series against the Boston Braves. Little time was spent on different scenarios needed to win the pennant, however: the Robins had to win both games and the Giants had to lose both games to the Phillies. The Braves, who had assisted Brooklyn in its previous two World Series in '16 and '20, were now in the spoiler role.

September 27 was declared Jimmy Johnston Day at Ebbets Field, with the longtime Robin receiving a car presented by his "legion of friends and admirers."[30] Even with the multi-day layoff in between games, Robinson stuck to his rotation of Grimes, Doak and Vance, this time sending Doak to the mound with a 10-game winning streak. It was an inopportune time for Doak's run to end. He lasted six innings, exiting with a score of 3–1 in favor of the Braves. Brooklyn scored one more in the bottom of the eighth, but that was as close as it got, losing 3–2. Across town the Giants clinched the pennant with a 5–1 victory. The next day behind Vance, the Robins wrapped up second place with a 5–1 victory to finish out one of the most exciting pennant races in the history of the game.

Statistically, Grimes's name was listed among the league leaders in several categories. He topped the National League in innings pitched (310⅔) and games started (36) and tied teammate Dazzy Vance for the major league lead with 30 complete games. He also trailed only Vance for the National League lead in wins (28 to 22) and strikeouts (262 to 135). Unlike Vance, who tried to strike out every batter, Grimes approached each hitter with the intent of simply recording an out. As a result of the number of innings he threw and batters he faced (1,345), Grimes also led the majors in hits allowed (351) and earned runs (132).

For the first time since 1921, several current and former Robins decided to take to the road for a fall barnstorming tour. With Jack Fournier leading the team, the tour took them back to Wisconsin, before embarking west. This time, the team played in Eau Claire, where Grimes had begun his career a dozen years earlier. Several players who had played on the team that had defeated the makeshift Robins squad in Chippewa Falls in 1921 suited up for the Eau Claire Moose nine, including Grimes's former Birmingham Barons teammate Art Johnson, who had twirled the victory three years earlier. This time Grimes and Johnson faced off in an uneventful 11–6 Brooklyn win, giving up 15 and 13 hits respectively.

With Vance and Grimes pitching, the undefeated club continued its barnstorming west, where it was scheduled to finish up with three games in Seattle. The trip to the Pacific Northwest was marred when four of the Robins landed in jail.

On October 19, Bernie Neis, Johnny Mitchell, Eddie Brown and Milt Stock were drinking in their room at the Elham Hotel in Wenatchee, Washington. A member of the party called down for ice and when bellboy William Weaver was tardy with the delivery, he was verbally assailed and then punched by an unspecified member of the group. All four players were arrested and put in jail. Split up into pairs in two different cells, three of them protested loudly, demanding that the jailer call Fournier to bail them out. When that didn't work, they demanded a lawyer. While all of this was going on, the fourth man "simply took off his coat, rolled it neatly, and placed it as a pillow on the upper bunk in his cell. Then he removed his pants, folded them as neatly, and carefully placed them under the thin mattress. He took off his shoes and socks, placed the socks in the shoes; climbed into the bunk and lay there quietly, composing himself for sleep." When the other three saw this they were flabbergasted, with one of the yelling at him, "You ain't fooling me you son of a bitch! You've been in jail before!"[31]

The next morning Charles Ebbets paid each of their $200 fines, reimbursed the hotel $100 and paid $750 for Weaver's medical bill and personal damages. The group was late making it to the depot, missing the train to Everett. With a makeshift team, Grimes took the only loss of the tour, a 15–3 drubbing by the semi-pro Everett Seagulls.

A month-and-a-half later, on December 1, the Washington incident was forgotten when Dazzy Vance was named the league's Most Valuable Player. He drew 74 points, 12 more than runner-up Rogers Hornsby. Besides Vance, six Robins landed in the top 22 vote getters, including Zach Wheat (fourth place, 40 points), Jack Fournier (ninth place, 21 points), Andy High (12th place, 9 points), Burleigh Grimes (15th place, 5 points), Jimmy Johnston (18th place, three points) and Hank DeBerry (22nd place, one point). The committee also named an all-star team that included Vance, Grimes and Wheat.

When the calendar turned to 1925, Grimes and Charles Ebbets once again were at odds about a contract. Aiding Grimes's cause was a large *Washington Post* article in January about how underappreciated he was by Brooklyn management. Conceding that Dazzy Vance was the superior pitcher, the *Post* suggested that Vance and the Robins wouldn't have been nearly as successful had it not been for the pitching of Grimes: "They say that Vance pitched the Brooklyn team to within a gnat's heel of the National League championship. And when they say this, they speak true. But at that, if it had not been for the cunning and courage of Burleigh Grimes, second fiddler in this pennant contending orchestra, Brooklyn would not have been within many games of that final pennant grapple."[32]

All contract issues were overshadowed by health issues facing the men that ran the team. Charles Ebbets continued his slide and Wilbert Robinson wound up in the hospital shortly before Christmas. Overweight and having trouble breathing, major chest pain landed Robinson in Baltimore's Union Memorial Hospital. He was found to be suffering from an attack of pleurisy that required surgery. A lesion was removed from his lung and after an extended stay he was released just in time to head south to Florida with his wife.

When camp opened in Clearwater, Grimes, wasn't the only no-show. Dazzy Vance, Dutch Henry and Zach Taylor were all holding out for a higher salary. Bill Doak decided to retire to go into the booming real estate business

in Florida. Within a few weeks, Vance, Henry and Taylor had all signed contracts, but Grimes again held steadfast to his asking price of a two-year,
$30,000 contract. Grimes claimed that Ebbets had made him that offer via
telegram shortly after the 1924 season, but was now reneging.

Ebbets and Grimes continued a volley of fruitless telegrams that had
been going on since the previous fall. When the Brooklyn owner abandoned
the charade, the members of the press made their own attempt. Sportswriter
Roscoe McGowen, who was making his first trip to spring training for the
New York News, later recalled how, "Somebody from one of the afternoon
papers got the bright idea of sending Grimes a wire asking when and if he
would sign and report, Burleigh's reply, sent collect, was several hundred well-
chosen words. It told us virtually nothing and it cost us about five bucks."[33]

It finally took the intervention of Commissioner Landis for the contract
negotiations to get resolved. After he had "delved into about three and a half
pounds of letters and telegrams in the course of the investigation," Landis
came to the conclusion that Grimes and Ebbets had agreed to a $14,000 salary
for two years rather than the $15,000 that Grimes claimed they had agreed
to the previous fall.[34]

On the last day of March, Grimes was once again a member of the
Robins, grudgingly agreeing to the lower sum of $14,000. He was then dis-
patched to Bradenton, Florida, to try to convince Bill Doak to resign, but his
pleas were to no avail. Doak was still perturbed over a $250 sum that was not
paid to him following the 1924 season. When Grimes returned to training
camp, he continued to voice his disapproval with Judge Landis's ruling and
promised to have it out with Charles Ebbets when the Robins arrived in
Brooklyn.

Grimes never got the opportunity to discuss the matter face-to-face with
the Brooklyn owner. On the early morning hours of Saturday, April 18, just
three games into the new season, Charles Ebbets died. He had been quarantined
in his suite at the Waldorf-Astoria since late March and finally succumbed to
the heart disease that had plagued him for years. Shortly after learning of
Ebbets's death, National League President John Heydler eulogized him:

> Mr. Ebbets was probably the best beloved man in baseball, not only in his
> own league, but in other leagues as well. He was highly regarded, and always
> stood for the best interest of the game. He was ever a constructive force, and
> took the keenest interest in the development of the smaller leagues. Mr.
> Ebbets always stood behind the work of the umpire. He felt that if they were
> not supported the game would suffer.[35]

Initially, the day's game against the Giants was canceled, but Heydler
and the McKeever brothers decided to play it. Instead, all games scheduled

for the day of Ebbets's funeral were called off. The Robins were flat in that day's 7–1 loss to the Giants. The next morning it was announced that Edward McKeever would succeed Ebbets as team president.

Tuesday, April 21 was a miserable, rainy day, but thousands filled the blocks surrounding the Holy Trinity Episcopal Church to pay their respects to Ebbets. Two thousand people packed the church, including the entire Brooklyn team and several other baseball notables. Commissioner Landis, Heydler and the other National League owners served as honorary pall bearers. Led by a police escort, the funeral procession made its way to the Green-Wood Cemetery, where Ebbets was laid to rest near Henry Chadwick, known as the "Father of Baseball." It was Ebbets's custom to lay flowers upon Chadwick's grave every April 20, the day of his death. It was on one of these occasions that Ebbets had picked out the adjacent plot.

Nine days later, with flags around the league still flying at half-mast in honor of Ebbets, the Robins were dealt another blow when new owner Ed McKeever died of influenza, which he had contracted during Ebbets's funeral proceedings. The second death in as many weeks left the Brooklyn chain of command in a state of flux. Initially, Steve McKeever was expected to be named team president, but following the deaths of Ebbets and Ed McKeever the team's shares were divided among a number of heirs in a manner that seemed to have no rhyme or reason. That left Steve McKeever's fate up to a shareholders' meeting in May.

With Brooklyn's front office still in flux, some of the Robins' more free-spirited members took advantage. While traveling from Philadelphia to Boston after a Sunday afternoon game, Vance and Fournier found out that the Braves were also on the train. The pair recruited Grimes to play a prank on their upcoming opponents. Donning pillow cases with eyeholes cut out, they charged into the sleeping car where most of the Braves were slumbering. Pulling several members from their beds, the three focused their attention on Boston catcher Mickey O'Neil. They pinned the now wide-eyed catcher to the ground, threatening him with his life if he didn't reveal the Braves' signals. When O'Neil finally disclosed them, the group departed from the car as quickly as they had come.

That was the extent of Grimes's involvement in debauchery as Vance and Fournier took newcomer Dick Cox under their wing. A stout former boxer with 150 bouts under his belt, Cox fit in nicely with Vance and Fournier — the trio drank, gambled and stayed out past curfew. Fournier took it upon himself to be the team's bookie. It was the true beginning of the "Daffiness Boys."

During this chaotic period, the Robins played loose, jumping from fifth place all the way to second during an 11–5 mid–May home stand. Brooklyn succeeded in spite of slow starts from Vance, who was suffering from a sore arm, and Grimes, who was struggling with control issues. After losing his first two starts of the season (including one to the Phillies that snapped an 11-game winning streak against Philadelphia dating back to the start of 1923), Grimes won two in a row on May 5 and May 9. The back-to-back victories turned out to be Grimes's only consecutive wins all season. The ace of the staff during May was Rube Ehrhardt, who boasted a 6–1 record by the end of the month.

On May 11, Grimes was called into the game to pinch hit for Dazzy Vance in the bottom of the 10th. With one out and Hank DeBerry on first, Grimes rapped a single and took second on a groundout by Andy High. Jimmy Johnston blooped a two-out single to right. Grimes hesitated and then was held up at third by base coach Ben Egan while right fielder Elmer Smith's throw home sailed up the third base line. If Grimes had run on contact, he would have scored easily. Zach Wheat was intentionally walked to load the bases and then forced at second to end the game, leaving Grimes stranded at third.

Before Grimes even reached the dugout, Robinson had begun chastising him for not scoring on Johnston's base hit. Grimes retorted that he shouldn't have been on the bases in the first place, a pinch runner being the obvious managerial move to make in that situation. The two argued for over an hour in the clubhouse about what had happened.

The incident proved to be the tipping point in Grimes and Robinson's volatile relationship. Robinson, who harbored fears of Grimes's managerial ambitions had had enough of his pitcher publicly second-guessing his moves while rarely taking blame for his own mistakes. Grimes, who had already garnered interest from other clubs for managerial posts, was tired of what he saw as managing miscues on Robinson's part.

Grimes was simply too valuable a pitcher to trade off, however. According to Tom Meany, author of *Baseball's Greatest Pitchers,* the two parties came to an agreement that when it was Grimes's turn to pitch he would be given a "note by Babe Hamberger, the clubhouse boy, or by one of the players."[36]

Before Brooklyn's successful May homestand ended, it had been decided that Robinson would forgo his uniform for a three-piece suit and the title of team president. Steve McKeever was outraged, voicing his displeasure that he had been passed up in favor of "a bumbling manager who'd blown two World Series and hadn't even shown he could get his team to the park on time."[37] The move greatly damaged the relationship between the two men. A thrilled Robinson named Zack Wheat "assistant manager," while Jacques Fournier was given Wheat's title as captain and Jimmy Johnston was given the title of strategist. For the time being everyone seemed to be pleased with the arrangement.

Grimes, whose record stood at 4–5, took the mound on a scorching afternoon at Cubs Park on June 6. Once again Grimes was wild, giving up seven free passes. Despite that, an eight-run sixth inning and a home run by Grimes into the left field bleachers in the seventh gave the Robins an 11–4 lead heading into the bottom of the eighth. During that frame, Grimes tried to field a line drive back through the box with his bare hand. He finished the inning and the Robins ended up winning 12–9, but he came away with a badly wounded index finger on his throwing hand. The injury came nearly four years to the day (June 5, 1921) after he had fractured his thumb in the same ballpark on a similar play.

Zach Wheat, who Grimes said "won more ball games for me than any other individual," took over as assistant manager and then interim manager during the chaotic 1925 season (George Grantham Bain Collection, Library of Congress).

With the Robins now in fourth place, struggling acting manager Zach Wheat badly wanted Grimes to return. When he did 11 days later in Pittsburgh, he was still not fully healed and thus unable to throw his spitball. He lasted just five innings in the 8–3 defeat. After the game, Grimes greatly angered team president Robinson by taking an unexcused hiatus to his Minerva farm. When he returned a week later, his injured digit had yet to heal.

Even with his above-average fastball and off-speed pitches, opponents' knowledge of Grimes's inability to throw his out pitch was evident. Grimes went 1–4 in his next five starts, giving up double-digit hits in each game. Frustrated with his performance and needing every break that he could get, Grimes was ready to explode on any call that did not go his way.

On July 5, Grimes finally had had enough of second-year umpire Peter McLaughlin's unfavorable strike zone. Heading toward the plate while "saying six words for every step of the journey," Grimes was soon ejected, but not before going nose-to-nose with the umpire and trading barbs. McLaughlin was met by a barrage of tossed pop bottles and a few fire crackers, none of which reached him. The incident earned Grimes an undisclosed fine and a suspension that caused him to miss a start.

It was an inopportune time for Grimes to be without his spitter. Offense was again booming around the league (batters hit a combined .292) and full swings at pitches was taking precedence over traditional strategies such as bunting and place hitting. Many players were vocal about their disapproval of the lively ball, even those who were benefiting from it.

Dazzy Vance ended up being the only Brooklyn pitcher to have much success on the mound during 1925. He recovered from his early-season arm problems to go 10–2 during June and July. Besides Vance, none of the Robins hurlers were able to take advantage of the gaudy numbers being put up by the Brooklyn offense. As a team the Robins hit .296, good enough for third in the league, with six regulars batting over .300: Wheat (.359), Fournier (.350), Dick Cox (.329), Milt Stock (.328), Zach Taylor (.310) and Eddie Brown (.306). Even with the trying managerial situation, Wheat put together his last great season (42 doubles, 14 triples, 14 home runs and 103 RBIs). Jacques Fournier had arguably the best campaign of his career (21 doubles, 16 triples, 22 home runs and 130 RBIs) all the while playing under intense scrutiny from fans at Ebbets Field, for his poor fielding. Milt Stock was the surprise of the lot. After batting .242 for the Robins in 1924, Stock was among the league leaders for the first four months of the '25 campaign and collected four straight four-hit games from June 30 to July 3.

Grimes again drew the attention of the National League office when he brawled with former teammate Max Carey on August 7 in Pittsburgh. Heading into the seventh inning, Grimes and the Robins were clinging to a 5–4 lead against the first-place Pirates. After Carey opened the bottom half of the frame with a single to left, George Grantham followed with a screaming line drive off the shin of Grimes that ricocheted to within a few feet of the Brooklyn dugout. Grimes collapsed to the ground, writhing in pain, but quickly jumped to his feet to take part in a rundown.

Grimes's injured leg didn't allow him to get out of the way of the speedy Carey, who was making his way to third base. According to the *Brooklyn Daily Eagle,* Carey "drove straight at Grimes with the fingers of his right hand spread open. He caught Grimes under the chin with the heel of his hand and in the nose and eyes with his fingers."[38] Enraged, Grimes countered Carey's move with a blow to the bridge of his former teammate's nose, which blackened both of the Pirates outfielder's eyes. Carey went reeling backward but then came at Grimes again, who landed another jab to the jaw. From there the skirmish was broken up and Grimes was ejected from the game, but he needed assistance to leave the field.

With a badly bruised leg Grimes retreated to his Minerva farm where he was informed that he had been suspended for three games and fined $200.

Still in fourth place and clinging to the first division, the Robins's struggles were compounded by a confusing managerial situation. Robinson was giving suggestions to Wheat from the box seats, but when the team struggled during the June road trip Robinson began to get the urge to return to the dugout. From then on, he sat on the bench in his suit, second-guessing every move Wheat made.

Privately, Robinson had begun to worry that Wheat's popularity with fans and players would push the club's board of directors to instruct him to permanently hand over the managerial reigns to Wheat. When Robinson heard rumors of the Cubs wanting Wheat to manage the club in 1926, he appeased the masses by announcing that Wheat would succeed him as manager when his contract expired following the 1926 season.

The managerial turmoil led to a loss of team discipline. Already partaking in the night life, Vance, Cox and Fournier made themselves charter members of an after-hours club known as the "4 for 0 club," a play on the 0–4 they would have at the plate after a particularly eventful evening. The club also included backup infielder Cotton Tierney and pitchers Jesse Petty and Rube Ehrhardt. The increase in numbers only upped the group's penchant for fast living. Vance, the self-appointed president of the club, wrote up by-laws including the all important, "Raise all the hell you want but don't get caught."[39]

History remembers this group fondly as the Daffiness Boys for their zany antics, but at the time they weren't looked at as favorably. The Brooklyn club as a whole began to gain a reputation as malcontents. The *Sporting News* described them as "peevish kids soured by losing a half holiday." Grimes was the subject of pointed criticism. After the brawl in Pittsburgh, Grimes was said to have become "[P]ermeated with the idea that he is a bigger slice of the team than anybody else." As a result, he "had to run amuck and swat Carey in Pittsburgh."[40]

Grimes continued the course, pitching .500 ball through July and August (6–6), but there was no September rejuvenation as in years past. His only victory of the month was a painful 10-inning affair against the Phillies at Ebbets Field on September 8 in the second game of a doubleheader. After narrowly avoiding another hand injury while knocking down a sure hit through the box by Freddy Leach with his bare hand, the next batter, Cy Williams, lined one off Grimes's shin that sent him to the ground in a heap and delayed the game for five minutes. Grimes pitched the next seven innings on the hobbled leg. When the two teams met five days later, Williams stepped to the plate in the first inning and was greeted with a fastball to the ribs by Grimes.

The fast living of the "4–0" club didn't faze Vance, who was at his best in September, winning his 20th decision on September 5. Three days later against the Phillies he allowed only one hit, a single in the second inning. He followed that up with a no-hitter against the Phillies on September 13. Only two batters reached base — a walk to lead off the game and a dropped fly ball in the second inning that led to a run in a 10–1 victory. Vance's 22 wins led both leagues, as did his 221 strikeouts, 81 more than runner-up Dolph Luque of the Reds.

Grimes's season of frustration and futility was encapsulated on September 22 in Chicago. Going up against Grover Alexander, Grimes allowed 16 hits and 7 walks, yet somehow extended the game into the twelfth inning before the Cubs scored to win, 3–2. Grimes's season was epitomized at the plate during the game. As Clarence Mitchell had done in the 1920 World Series, Grimes made seven outs in his first three at-bats. He ended the third and sixth innings with double plays and put an end to the eighth by grounding into a triple play. In his fourth at-bat he struck out. The feat earned him a spot in *Ripley's Believe it or Not*.

A week later Grimes started his last game of the season. He lasted all of four innings against the Phillies, allowing 10 runs (eight of them earned) on nine hits and four walks. Grimes's 1–5 September mark dropped his record to 12–19. Nineteen losses led the league and were the most of his career. His ERA also went over five (5.04) for the first and only time in his career, but he had plenty of company — no Brooklyn starter other than Vance had an ERA below 4.88. The lack of pitching led to a 68–85, sixth-place finish for the Robins. In the club's desperation to find a rhythm, 35 players suited up in a Brooklyn uniform, matching the total used when scrambling to fill the roster in the war-torn 1918 season.

The *New York Times* claimed that Grimes's season was an anomaly, blaming his 12–19 record on "poor fielding and languid base running."[41] Thomas Rice of *The Sporting News* stated that Grimes "had more ill luck in the way of losing through misplays behind him than any Brooklyn pitcher of the past decade."[42] There were indeed close games amid the 19 defeats, which included 6 one-run losses and three games in which the Robins were shut out.

Robinson had other theories, namely that Grimes threw from too many different angles during the '25 season. "I have maintained he is more effective pitching overhand and have ordered him to change his style he commented. He has agreed and we are sure success will mark our plans."[43]

Three days after the season ended, Brooklyn traded Jimmy Johnston, Zach Taylor and Eddie Brown to the Boston Braves for Jesse Barnes, Mickey O'Neil and Gus Felix. The departure of Johnston meant that Grimes and Wheat were the only remaining players from the 1920 pennant winners. Their spots on the roster weren't secure either, as Robinson tried dealing Grimes at the winter meetings in New York City. Sitting in the lobby of the Waldorf-Astoria the Brooklyn president-manager nearly dealt Grimes to the Cardinals, but at the last minute Cardinals president Sam Breadon was scared off by the $14,000 owed Grimes in 1926. When that fell through, Robinson tried swapping Wheat to the Cardinals in exchange for pitching, but again Breadon balked at the price.

Grimes and his wife were in northern Wisconsin within a week of the season's end. They had recently purchased a cottage on the north shore of Yellow Lake near the village of Webster. Located in sparsely populated and heavily wooded Burnett County, the spot was a place to which Grimes would retreat often over the ensuing decades. The cabin's proximity to Clear Lake enabled Grimes to split time between the two destinations.

During the first off-season at Yellow Lake, Grimes spent much of his time resting and recuperating. When he felt like it, he hunted, fished, or trudged through the woods in snowshoes. With Wisconsin's famed deer-hunting season in an off year of its every-other-year schedule, Grimes bagged his fair share of ducks. In his winter correspondence with F.C. Lane of *Baseball Magazine*, Grimes joked, "I ate so many I often wonder if I won't have web feet yet."[44]

Grimes was not alone in his affinity for the brisk Wisconsin winters.

Over the years numerous other ballplayers joined Grimes at Yellow Lake to unwind after the season, including Pie Traynor, Paul Waner, Dutch Henry, Leo Dickerman, Dave Bancroft, Andy High, Bubbles Hargrave and Heine Mueller. Many of them stayed at the Ike Walton Resort or in nearby cabins. A destination during the summer months, the retreat was deserted during the winter. The ballplayers had the run of the place, congregating on the porch during the fall and eating their meals in the large dining room. They were catered to by Jens Vorm, the resort proprietor, who became close friends with many players.

Back in the baseball world a change was made to help balance the growing disparity between pitchers and batters. In late January of 1926, it was announced that pitchers would be allowed access to a rosin bag while on the mound. The decision didn't seem to impress Grimes, who told Thomas Holmes of the *Brooklyn Daily Eagle*, "Batters have been using rosin and pitchers have been using it too. They rub it into the leg of their trousers between innings, then go out there and rub their hand on their trouser leg whenever they feel like doing so." But he added, "I've never used rosin myself. I don't need it."[45]

Grimes spent most of February in Arkansas. He went hunting with former teammate Leo Dickerman and then spent a few weeks soaking in Hot Springs before heading to Florida. The first spring training after the death of Charles Ebbets featured a laid-back environment. Robinson let players come and go in camp at their leisure, with some showing more interest in golf or their real estate holdings than in getting into baseball shape.

Robinson worked on rebuilding his roster, focusing on the depleted infield. He also spent a great amount of time tinkering with the team's portable batting cage. Measuring 75 feet long, 15 feet high and 20 feet wide and draped with cord netting, it was said to be "the first batting cage in history to be used by a big league club on a training trip."[46]

The off-season hadn't softened Robinson's view of either Wheat or Grimes. Instead of giving Wheat back his title of team captain, Robinson let Fournier keep it. Just when it seemed that the communication lines between Grimes and management couldn't get any worse, Robinson added Otto Miller to his coaching staff. With the return of the former Brooklyn catcher with whom Grimes had a combative relationship, Grimes's allies on the Robins' bench were few.

When it came time to pitch in live spring games, Grimes was given minimal opportunities. Although in the past he had welcomed a slow build-up, for the first time in three years Grimes was throwing to someone besides Zack Taylor. Grimes described the departure of Taylor as "a blow."[47]

Hank DeBerry was still on the roster, but his problems with receiving Grimes's spitter opened up an opportunity for either Charlie Hargreaves or Mickey O'Neil. Hargreaves had been a Dodger since 1923, but had played sparingly as a third-stringer behind Taylor and DeBerry. Hargreaves had the upper hand because of having caught Grimes during the 1924 barnstorming tour. He won the job in Clearwater and proved a good fit, starting all of Grimes's 1926 outings.

Grimes dropped his first two starts of the season, both to the New York Giants. After the second loss on April 23, Grimes and outfielder Dick Cox found themselves under the bleachers brawling with New York catcher Fred Snyder and manager John McGraw. The Giants were already upset about the number of times Grimes had backed team captain Frank Frisch off the plate with inside fastballs over the past couple of years. Finally, after Frisch was picking himself up off the dirt in the ninth, McGraw and Snyder (who was not playing) began jockeying Grimes from the bench. Grimes took exception to Snyder's words in particular, as did Brooklyn outfielder Dick Cox, who had had an incident with the Giants catcher during the previous season. Snyder finally told Grimes to meet him outside the clubhouses under the right field bleachers after the game.

Following the 6–3 Giants victory, Grimes, flanked by Cox, met Snyder as planned. Grimes and Snyder started to scrap as Cox looked on. Wilbert Robinson and John McGraw soon arrived on the scene. Robinson tried to play the peacemaker, but McGraw started jawing at Grimes, Cox and Robinson. Cox took umbrage and landed a wicked blow to McGraw's nose that sent the Giants manager to the ground. Snyder then went after Cox, who punched the catcher in the jaw. Before the scuffle escalated any further, police arrived on the scene and made sure everyone retreated to their respective clubhouses. The scuffle gave Cox a head start on his after-hours activities as a member of the 4 for 0 Club.

The brawl ignited the Robins. They went on a season-high six-game win streak and won 14 of their next 17 contests. Brooklyn moved from sixth place into first place, staying atop the National League standings for two weeks. All of this was accomplished without the services of Jack Fournier, who had suffered a severely sprained ankle injury in a collision with Braves second baseman Doc Gautreau in early May. Robinson inserted Babe Herman into Fournier's spot in the lineup and in the field. In his first game as Fournier's replacement, Herman suffered an injury of his own (later diagnosed as a cracked rib), but played through the pain. Although Fournier returned a week later, Herman never fully relinquished a spot in the lineup.

The May successes were the Robins' last time in first place for the season, and by the first week of June they had dipped into the second division. June turned out to be Brooklyn's only winning month of the year, posting a 14–12 record. Unfamiliar names were leading the pitching staff, most notably Jesse Petty. He was suddenly the staff ace after reeling off five wins to start the season, including two shutouts of the Giants, one of which was an Opening Day one-hitter. Petty added another defeat of the Giants in late May.

The actions of the 4 for 0 Club finally proved a public distraction for the ballclub. Jesse Petty was kicked out of the club for breaking its cardinal rule: "Raise all the hell you want but don't get caught." He got caught breaking curfew. Petty pleaded to get back into the club, even enlisting Joe Gordon of the *New York American* to ghost write a letter for him, explaining why he should be let back into the club.

Vance called Petty to his hotel room, where the other members of the 4 for 0 Club were "draped in sheets with bath towels wound, turban fashion, about their heads."[48] They spent a good amount of time grilling Petty on whether he actually wrote the letter. Petty was insistent that he had.

Vance finally said, "You were not only a big dope to be caught by Robbie, but you are deceitful. There are words in this letter that you can't even spell and don't know the meaning of. For that you are...."

Vance hesitated for the right word.

Rabbit Maranville piped up "Ignominiously!"

Vance continued, "Ignominiously thrown out again, and in case you don't know what that means, it means you can't come back."[49]

Word of Petty's shaming reached other teams, who mercilessly jockeyed the pitcher whenever possible. Joe Vila, sports editor and columnist for the *New York Sun*, was angered by the treatment of the man who had been the Robins' best pitcher to that point. Vila enlisted the *Sun's* sports cartoonist to take a shot at the high-priced and underperforming Vance, as well as Grimes, who in the *Sun's* estimation wasn't living up to his contract either. The caption under the cartoon of Petty read, "Jess Petty is winning while the higher-priced Dazzy Vance and Burleigh Grimes are losing. How much is Petty being paid?"[50]

After seeing the paper, an infuriated Wilbert Robinson made a call to the *Sun* demanding an explanation for the cartoon. When he was told it was to motivate Vance and Grimes, Robinson refused to accept the answer, instead insisting that it was a personal attack. He continued his tirade before being hung up on. From then on, the *Sun* made no contact with players, never mentioned Robinson's name and returned to referring to the team as the "Dodgers" rather than the "Robins."[51]

Absent from the win column for the first month and a half was Dazzy

Vance, who didn't record a victory until June 4. He had been more concerned with fishing and real estate during spring training and as the regular season began his abdomen was covered in boils. The painful skin abscesses made pitching unbearable. When the boils subsided, other problems arose, including family troubles (his sister passed away and his daughter had a lengthy illness), a sore arm and a severe case of the flu. Vance never fully got on track and had his worst season since joining the Robins in 1922, compiling a 9–10 record in limited duty (22 starts). Despite that, Vance still led the league in strikeouts for the fifth straight year with 140.

It was no longer a priority of Robinson for Grimes to pitch every fourth or fifth day — he frequently allowed a week to pass between the spitballer's starts. Grimes threw well when he got the opportunity, going 3–0 during Brooklyn's two-week reign in first and continuing to pitch well into June. He finished the month with a 4–1 record, including his only shutout of the year, a 3–0 defeat of the Pirates at Ebbets Field in front of 30,000.

Trying to improve the team, Robinson offered Grimes and Hank DeBerry to the Pirates in exchange for George Grantham, but Pittsburgh manager Bill McKechnie turned down the offer. Some thought McKechnie's refusal stemmed from bad blood from the Carey incident the previous August. Grimes was in fact booed lustily when he pitched at Forbes Field in May, but he and Carey had made up before the game, sharing a lengthy conversation during batting practice. "What's a punch more or less between friends on the ball field?" said Grimes.[52]

Robinson was growing increasingly aware of his bumbling image and he didn't help his public persona by openly arguing about game strategy with fans during the game. He also fed into the image when he devised a fine system for mental errors during the game. Robinson implemented the "Bonehead Club" before a game against Pittsburgh. "By God we ought to get some good out of the boners we make," said Robinson. "From now on, let's do this: Every time a player pulls a boner, he's got to put ten dollars into a fund, and at the end of the season we'll cut it up among all the players." He then quipped, "The way we're going, you'll each get as much money as the fellows who get in the World Series."[53] The players agreed to the system. That very afternoon Robinson flubbed the batting order by giving one to the umpire that differed from the one he had written for the team. The error ended in a loss for Brooklyn and put an end to the short-lived "Bonehead Club."

Trailing the Reds by six games, the Robins entered July in fourth place. However, they were scheduled to play 26 of their next 33 games on the road. When the month ended, the injury-plagued Robins were still in fourth place, trailing the Pirates by six and half games.

Offense as a whole was down over both leagues, but nowhere was that more apparent than on the Robins. Their .263 team batting average finished last in the National League. Babe Herman was the only regular to bat over .300 (.319). Despite a late-season slump that saw him benched, Herman also led the team in hits (158), doubles (35), triples (11), home runs (11) and RBIs (81). His fielding was putrid, however, as he finished the season with the lowest fielding percentage of any first baseman. Jack Fournier, who was hampered by leg problems the whole season, provided one of the more thrilling moments during the road trip when he pounded out three home runs in one game on July 13 in St. Louis.

On July 11, Grimes, scattered four hits in a 2–1 defeat of the Cubs in front of 29,000 at Cubs Park (Grimes dominated the Cubs in 1926 with a 5–1 record). Despite Robinson's reluctance to use him more than once a week, the *Brooklyn Daily Eagle* reported that "Grimes hasn't pitched a bad game of ball since the season started."[54]

In the woolen Brooklyn uniform, Grimes tired in the sweltering July heat. He was unable to finish his next three starts in St. Louis, Cincinnati and Pittsburgh. He finally reached double digits in wins at Ebbets Field on July 30, holding the Cubs to six singles in a 4–1 victory. Grimes's record stood

Grimes began to spend more time (both excused and unexcused) at his farm in Minerva, Ohio, as his relationship with teammates deteriorated (Charles Clark Photo Collection).

at a team-best 10–7, but he won only two more games over the remaining two months.

The Robins suffered a major blow to their lineup on August 5, when Zack Wheat was lost for nearly a month, except for pinch-hitting duties. Trailing 11–7 in the 10th inning, Wheat smacked his fourth home run of the season off the Cardinals' Jesse Haines. In the process he lost his balance and fell backward, stumbling over a loose board covering a hole that umpires kept extra balls in. Limping out of the batter's box, he barely made it to second base before collapsing to the ground. The umpires and managers convened to figure out what to do. They decided to bend the rule that states a runner must complete the circuit of the bases for the home run to count. Rabbit Maranville was announced as a pinch runner, but before Maranville made it to second Wheat arose and traveled the final 180 feet at a slow pace.

The injury, initially reported as a "Charlie horse" by the press, was in fact another devastating injury for Wheat. He had broken a bone in his right heel and ripped several ligaments. Wheat had been in a season-long slump, his numbers drastically down from the 1925 season, but now his presence in the lineup was sorely missed. The Robins lost 11 of their next 12 games, putting to rest their pennant hopes once and for all.

Grimes had his worst month of the season in August, going 1–4 with his only victory a 3–1 rain-shortened game versus the Cubs. As the end of the season neared his starts again became sporadic, even more so after Brooklyn picked up Max Carey. Carey had been exiled from Pittsburgh with Babe Adams and Carson Bigbee after an incident that became known as the "great Pirate mutiny." As team captain, Carey was standing up for his teammates, who were tired of former manager and now part-owner Fred Clarke sitting on the bench and frequently second-guessing manager Bill McKechnie's decisions. Before Carey could plead his case in front of Commissioner Landis, Pirates owner Barney Dreyfuss suspended and then released him along with Adams and Bigbee.

With Carey now in Brooklyn, Robinson began to tout him as the next Robins manager, taking over as soon as next year. That dismissed Wheat's chances to manage and led to intermittent playing time for veterans down the stretch, including Wheat, Fournier and Grimes. All three were mentioned as part of Robinson's impending off-season fire sale.

Grimes tried everything to break out of his losing ways, including growing a full beard rather than his customary stubble, but nothing seemed to work. His last win of the season came on September 4 against the Phillies and his final decision was a loss on September 19 to the Pirates. He finished the season at 12–13, his win total second on the team to Jesse Petty (17–17).

Brooklyn spent the final two months of the season in sixth place. It was the fourth time in five years that Brooklyn had finished in sixth place and the seventh time in Grimes's nine seasons that the team ended in the second division.

Before the final homestand, Grimes and his wife left Brooklyn and headed for their Yellow Lake retreat where he and Pie Traynor planned to spend the winter. The two men had bonded over their love of outdoor sports, particularly fishing and hunting. Since taking over as the Pirates' full-time third baseman in 1922, Traynor had become one of the game's best all-around players. At 6 feet he was large for a third baseman, but he was very mobile and had a quick accurate release on throws. Offensively, Traynor lacked power, but his speed was an asset, utilizing the large gaps at Forbes Field.

One important change had occurred during the 1926 season. Grimes's parents had recently moved to Owen, Wisconsin, some 150 miles from the cabin, to be close to their other son Shurleigh, who had moved back to Wisconsin to work as a fireman on the Soo Line Railroad. Shurleigh had spent the last half decade out east working for the Pennsylvania Railroad out of Delmar, Delaware. He also had played a few years of baseball in Cape Charles, Virginia.

While Grimes was renowned for staying in shape during the off-season, in the winter of 1926 he rededicated himself to the game. He instituted a lumberjack routine that would benefit him in the second half of his career. He explained his regimen to F.C. Lane: "I tramp miles ever day in the snow with my gun. I breathe crisp, frosty air many hours out of the twenty-four. I eat a lot of wholesome, well cooked food. I go to bed early and sleep like a badger in a burrow. And next season I'm fit for whatever deviltry the batters can invent."[55]

As the National League owners meeting rolled around in mid–December, Grimes and Wheat were still openly being shopped. The Giants, Cardinals and Reds showed the most interest in adding the four-time 20-game winner, while Wheat was said to be at best a pinch hitter if dealt to the American League. The meeting came and went, and Grimes remained a Robin. The Giants, however, had a huge move brewing.

Less than a week after the owners congregated in New York, the Giants made a blockbuster deal with the St. Louis Cardinals. The Giants sent fan favorite Frank Frisch and pitcher Jimmy Ring to the St. Louis Cardinals for player-manager Rogers Hornsby. Hornsby, who despite leading the Cardinals to their first World Series title a few months before, had had one too many disagreements with owner Sam Breadon, ranging from contract squabbles to Hornsby's penchant for betting on horses. Frisch had his own problems with

John McGraw, who publicly had called out his captain for not providing leadership down the stretch.

McGraw wasn't done beefing up his roster. On January 9, 1927, nine years to the day since Grimes had been acquired by Brooklyn, he was involved in a three-way trade with the Philadelphia Phillies and the cross-town rival New York Giants. The Giants sent Jack Scott and Fresco Thompson to the Phillies. Philadelphia sent George Harper to the Giants and Butch Henline to the Robins, who in turn dealt Grimes to the Giants. Grimes left Brooklyn near the top of every career pitching category in team history.

A few weeks after he was traded, Grimes seemed ecstatic with his situation. He took the opportunity to let the Brooklyn organization know that he was going to be just fine. After signing a $15,000 contract, he said, "I'm certainly tickled to become a Giant. I have just signed the contract tendered me by McGraw, and it is the first time in all my career that I ever signed such a document on the day it reached me. You can figure from that how well I have been treated by my new employers."[56]

6

Rejuvenation, 1927–1929

The winter of 1926 and 1927 was a monumental one for wheeling and dealing. The Hornsby-Frisch deal was arguably the biggest one-for-one trade in the game's history to that point and the Philadelphia Athletics' Connie Mack was opening his wallet to get his team back to prominence. After spending much of the past decade in the lower division, he doled out big money obtaining Ty Cobb, Eddie Collins, and Zack Wheat. It was estimated that Mack and the New York Giants' owner Charles Stoneham spent a combined $500,000 in salaries.

In addition to Hornsby and Grimes, McGraw also traded High Pockets Kelly to the Reds for outfielder Edd Roush. McGraw had dealt Roush to Cincinnati a decade earlier and had spent the intervening years trying to reacquire him. Roush didn't care for spring training or McGraw's dictatorial style of management, but eventually agreed to a contract. Although Roush's legs had begun to weaken, he was still one of the game's most-feared hitters. Grimes would finally be given a rest from having to face Roush, who remained one of the league's toughest outs for Grimes. In 1923, Grimes had figured out a temporary solution — breaking Roush's ribs with a pitch, causing the then-Reds star to miss two and a half weeks.

Within a month of his trade, Grimes made his annual pilgrimage to Arkansas to prepare for the Giants' preseason training in Sarasota, Florida. Once again the training in Hot Springs was nothing compared to his winter regimen back in Wisconsin, but he went along, taking in the spas, hiking about the mountains, and taking to the links. His golfing partners were Reds pitcher Carl Mays, Senators outfielders Goose Goslin and Sam Rice and former Brooklyn teammate Jesse Petty. Grimes even entered a few golf tournaments, but didn't place. He soon got the itch to be in Giants camp, leaving Arkansas after 15 of the scheduled 21 soaks.

When Grimes arrived in Sarasota, the scene wasn't what he had expected. Hornsby had replaced Frisch as captain and wasn't taking the label lightly. Furthermore, McGraw was absent from camp, making his annual trip to

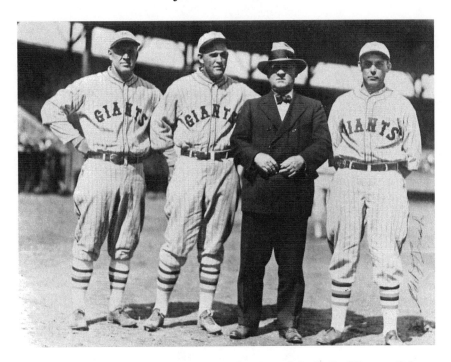

One of Grimes's favorite pictures, circa 1927. From left: Hall of Famers Grimes, Rogers Hornsby, John McGraw and Edd Roush (Charles Clark Photo Collection).

Havana to patronize the racetracks and casinos. Hornsby found himself running much of training camp and soon found ways to irritate his new teammates.

Many took exception to the way Hornsby ran camp, but third baseman Fred Lindstrom was one of the few who directed his displeasure directly at Hornsby. Lindstrom was entering his third full season, having finished ninth on the 1926 MVP ballot and at the age of 21 was already gaining a reputation as one of the elite third basemen in the league. The previous year, Grimes had paid him a very high compliment: "I think that in time Lindstrom will be a greater third baseman than Traynor. Fred's a great ballplayer now. With the experience of one or two seasons more he figures to be a much better one."[1]

After being lambasted by Hornsby for the cautious way he turned a double play, Lindstrom shot back that it was the way that McGraw himself taught him.

Hornsby barked at Lindstrom, "If that's the way the Old Man wants it, do it that way when he's in charge. When I'm in charge, do it my way."

Lindstrom didn't back down, telling Hornsby that "once he laid his bat down he was no bargain and not to get all puffed up with his own importance."

"I'm not arguing with you. I'm telling you," shouted Hornsby. "You do as I say and keep your mouth shut." He turned to the rest of the team red-faced, "And that goes for the rest of you."[2]

While some players may have disliked Hornsby's curt approach, Grimes — equally as terse while in uniform — had no problem with it. "Blunt as hell, but he never gave you any bullshit," Grimes said of Hornsby. "You might not have liked what he had on his mind, but you always knew what it was."[3]

Once McGraw arrived in Florida, it was his team. He encouraged Grimes to concentrate on pitching rather than the on-field coaching he was accustomed to doing. McGraw felt that the extra duties were affecting Grimes's concentration on the mound. Burleigh was somewhat taken aback that he only had to worry about the batter: "I always hustled and would fight to make my teammates hustle behind me. When I came to the Giants, McGraw said, 'You just pitch and I'll make the guys hustle behind you.' And he did. He didn't take any back talk from anybody."[4]

John Joseph McGraw was entering his 25th season as manager of the New York Giants. He had made his major league debut with the rough-and-tumble Baltimore Orioles of the American Association and never lost the competitive edge that he displayed as a slight teenager. McGraw was the game's premier tactician and years ahead of other managers around the league in his approach to running a ballclub. He often groomed prospects (sometimes for years) before their entrance into the lineup and freely used substitutions when the situation called for it. McGraw rarely sought out the big-name player, rather choosing those who fit into his system.

McGraw's system had taken a hit in recent years as the explosion of offense made his small-ball approach look obsolete. The Giants were coming off a fifth-place finish, ending with a disappointing 74–77. It was their first losing campaign in 11 seasons and McGraw and management had taken steps to make sure that they were back in the pennant hunt in '27. The Giants had seven future Hall of Famers going into the start of the season. Besides Grimes, the entire infield was made up of Cooperstown inductees: Bill Terry (first base), Hornsby (second base), Fred Lindstrom (third base), and Travis Jackson (shortstop). In the outfield were the newly acquired Edd Roush and teenager Mel Ott.

There would have been an eighth on the roster if not for the illness of Ross Youngs. One of McGraw's favorite players, Youngs had been accompanied by a specialist during the 1924 season. That year he was diagnosed with

Bright's disease, a disorder of the kidney. With a full-time nurse now traveling with the club, Youngs's condition worsened and by 1926 he was only able to play in 95 games. He was bedridden during the '27 season and passed away on October 22, 1927, at the age of 30.

After an impressive spring, Grimes went winless in April (0–1 in three starts) and never made it into the eighth inning. During the third start, his first at the Polo Grounds in a Giants uniform, Grimes allowed five runs on 12 hits to the lowly Braves in a no-decision. During the game McGraw noticed that right-handed Boston hitters were sitting on Grimes's 0–2 pitches (all spitballs), slapping them into right field. A decade into his career, the scouting report was out on Grimes. Of course, it didn't hurt that his former battery mate Zack Taylor was now catching for the Braves.

The next day McGraw approached Grimes. "Burleigh, how's your curveball?"

"Mediocre," replied Grimes, not missing a beat. He had tinkered with it in Brooklyn before settling on the nickel curve. When Grimes did throw the curveball, he threw it with a sidearm delivery, working the corners of the plate.[5]

McGraw convinced Grimes to throw the curveball straight over the top, aiming for the middle of the plate and low. Now, instead of throwing the spitter to right-handers, which they would inevitably bloop into right field, they had to either pull the ball or hit it to center. This addition to Grimes's repertoire proved crucial to his success during the '27 season, especially at the Polo Grounds.

Located in the shadows of Coogan's Bluff in upper Manhattan, the Polo Grounds had been hosting National League baseball since 1891. Following a fire on April 14, 1911, that decimated that mostly wooden ballpark, a steel, concrete and marble stadium had been built. The double-decker grandstands provided a horseshoe shape that resulted in the most obtuse dimensions of any baseball stadium before or since — down to the inch. The left-field line measured 279 feet, eight inches; right field was 257 feet, eight inches; and centerfield measured upward of 450 feet from home plate.

Grimes utilized his new approach in his next start against the Brooklyn Robins at the Polo Grounds. In his first start opposing his former team, Grimes went the distance, scattering six singles in the 4–1 victory, picking up his first win of the season.

The Giants were in first-place going into the last week of May. Before a May 22 game against the Pittsburgh Pirates, Grimes and his teammates were going over the scouting report. When it came time to talk about how to approach right fielder Kiki Cuyler, Grimes wouldn't even let the scouting report be read.

"I don't want to talk about him," muttered Grimes.

"Well, what are you going to throw the guy?" inquired a befuddled Dick Bartell. "I'm gonna stick it right between the shoulder blades," sneered Grimes, which he then went out and did.[6] The Giants lost 9–4 and Grimes didn't make it out of the fourth inning, but he earned the respect of his teammates. Grimes had no particular gripe with Cuyler beyond the fact that the speedy left-handed-hitting outfielder dominated the Giants. Grimes had also found difficulty retiring Cuyler while in a Brooklyn uniform, so he brought that disdain with him to Manhattan.

Despite his reputation as someone who threw at anyone, Grimes was actually selective of his targets. Two of the other three batters he hit during the 1927 season were close personal acquaintances. The first was his former catcher, Charlie Hargreaves. The second was his hunting companion, Pie Traynor. Grimes wanted to make it clear that their friendship ceased between the baselines.

Grimes lost his next two starts, but evened his record at 3–3 with 10⅔ innings of relief against the Reds at Crosley Field. He lost his next three starts and with a record of 3–6 his struggles began to be chronicled in New York City's plethora of news outlets.

Although Grimes was happy to be playing for McGraw, he had a hard time adjusting to the Giants manager's method of handling his pitchers. "It is true he has his pitching system and that system is hard on a pitcher," explained Grimes. "McGraw is likely to work a man out of turn, any old time. Pitchers don't like that, for their arms get sore and they burn out quickly."[7]

The Giants were in fourth place on June 7 (they stayed there for the next 77 games), and despite the prodigious offense, the pitching staff needed a spark. McGraw noticed that Grimes wasn't gelling with his new catchers. The two conferred and decided that a change needed to be made. On June 12 the Giants sent pitchers Hugh McQuillan and Kent Greenfield along with short-stop Doc Farrell to the Boston Braves in exchange for pitcher Larry Benton, utilityman Herb Thomas and catcher Zach Taylor. Benton pitched superbly (13–5) and Taylor caught all but two of Grimes's remaining 24 starts. The acquisition of Taylor didn't immediately turn around the spitballer's season, but it eventually proved to be a shrewd move on the part of McGraw.

As the Giants struggled to stay in the first division, McGraw — suffering from an upper respiratory ailment — was growing more concerned that he no longer could fulfill his managerial duties. Before a homecoming celebration in St. Louis for the return of Rogers Hornsby, McGraw announced that Hornsby would succeed him as the Giants manager starting in 1928. McGraw's admiration for Hornsby blinded him to the clubhouse turmoil likely to arise from this announcement. Believing that he was speaking on behalf of the team, he stated, "The members of the club all swear by Hornsby. He has proven the greatest inspiration a team could desire and he has more than fulfilled all expectations we had in signing him."[8]

The announcement caused a firestorm. McGraw, Hornsby and Giants owner Charles Stoneham all scrambled to explain that McGraw wasn't giving up on the team and that he would manage the Giants for as long as he was physically able. Even so, McGraw increasingly handed the managerial reigns over to Hornsby. He never admitted it, but all the distraction of whether or not he was going to be the next manager affected the play of Hornsby, who "struggled" during the month of July, putting up his lowest offensive totals of the season. He even struck out 13 times, nearly a third of his season total (39).

On July 1 and July 4 Grimes defeated Boston (4–1) and then Brooklyn (9–4). It was the first time since the previous July that he won back-to-back starts. Grimes had begun to adapt to McGraw's approach to dealing with pitchers and enjoyed working with Zack Taylor once again.

While with Brooklyn, Grimes had grown accustomed to the idea that if he started a game he was more than likely going to finish it. At times this led to lapses in concentration, but he liked to say that Robinson would need to bring help if he wanted to remove him from the game. With the Giants, Grimes had to be aware of every pitch he made due to McGraw's willingness to pull a pitcher from the game (evidenced by Grimes's complete game total of 15, the lowest since his injury-shortened season of 1919). He lost his next start, but on July 15 Grimes pitched a masterful 4–1, four-hit victory over the Reds at the Polo Grounds. The victory began a winning streak that spanned two months. When it ended his consecutive win total reached 13, a career high.

On July 19, New York City celebrated John McGraw Day at the Polo Grounds in honor of his quarter-century as manager of the Giants. A slew of activities were planned, but rained dampened the pre-game festivities. In front of Mayor Jimmy Walker, Commissioner Landis, assorted celebrities and former players, the Cubs spoiled the day with an 8–5 win. With the Giants clinging desperately to the bottom rung of the first division, it was becoming more apparent that Hornsby was calling more of the shots.

Abandoning McGraw's system, the Giants' offense was flourishing with a power game. All of the big-name players were living up to their reputations. Rogers Hornsby returned to form after his mid-season "slump" (.361, 32 doubles, 26 home runs, 125 RBIs) and Bill Terry was having a breakout season (.326, 32 doubles, 20 home runs, 121 RBIs). Newcomers George Harper (.331,

16 home runs, 87 RBIs) and Edd Roush (.304, 27 doubles, 18 stolen bases) provided a veteran presence, while youngsters Travis Jackson (.318, 29 doubles, 14 home runs, 98 RBIs) and Fred Lindstrom (.306, 36 doubles) were the up-and-comers.

Grimes evened his record at 9–9 in the second game of a doubleheader against the Pirates on July 24 in front of a season-high crowd of 50,000. Wins continued to mount for him and a month later on August 19 his string of victories was at six after a 5–2 defeat of the second-place Pirates. The win started a 10-game win streak for the Giants that moved them from fourth to second place behind the Pirates, who had regained first place. Grimes was instrumental, tallying four victories during that stretch.

In only one of those starts did Grimes fail to go the distance, pitching eight innings in a 7–3 victory over the Cubs on August 30. Grimes was cruising along, allowing one run heading into the ninth inning, but a single followed by a walk and another single produced a run. Expecting that the Cubs would use a left-handed pinch-hitter, Hornsby was set to take Grimes out of the game. More than a decade later Grimes explained what happened next. "The Cubs didn't use a pinch-hitter and Rog called for me to go back to the box, as I was walking off the diamond," Grimes said. "I kept right on walking to the clubhouse and as I passed him I let him have a few pointed remarks."[9]

What transpired after the game is up for debate. The talk among players was that Hornsby had been bungling McGraw's directives or flat-out ignoring them. Grimes took the opportunity to let Hornsby know that he and his teammates didn't approve of the way he was running the club. When the game ended Hornsby confronted Grimes in the clubhouse about his remarks. The next day Hornsby took the field with a black eye. Grimes downplayed the incident, blaming the shiner on a bad-hop groundball that Hornsby had taken off his cheek the day before.

On September 9, Grimes won his tenth straight game with a 7–2 defeat of the Cubs. It was the Giants 13th win in 14 games and brought them to within a half-game of Pittsburgh. A 9–6 record over the next two weeks dropped the Giants to three-and-a-half games behind the Pirates, but a sweep of a crucial four-game series in Pittsburgh on September 22–24 could leapfrog New York into first.

The Giants arrived in Pittsburgh early because of two off days before their showdown with Pirates. The rare "extended" hiatus gave the team an opportunity to see its upcoming opponents take on Brooklyn. The Robins defeated the Pirates 3–0 in front of the Giants, with spitballer Bill Doak tossing the shutout. Doak's gem gave an idea to Grimes and some of his teammates. Over the next 24 hours, Grimes drummed up enough interest to present McGraw with a signed petition to instruct Hornsby to start Grimes rather than Larry Benton in the first game of the series.

The petition infuriated McGraw. Benton started the game and didn't make it past the fourth inning of the 5–2 Pirates victory. The Giants won the final three games of the series to come within a game-and-a-half of Pittsburgh (who had already started taking applications for World Series tickets), but that was as close as they got.

Grimes notched his 19th victory with a 6–1 defeat of Brooklyn on the next-to-last day of the season. He led the Giants in nearly every pitching category and cracked the top 10 in the league in several of those. He also reached 100 strikeouts for the final time in his career.

In his third winter at Yellow Lake, Grimes entertained a cavalcade of major leaguers. Pie Traynor, Dutch Henry, Dave Bancroft, Andy High, Bubbles Hargrave and Heine Mueller all spent time at Grimes's cabin during the 1927 off-season. In late October, Grimes, Traynor, High, Henry and Jens Vorm motored to South Dakota for three weeks of duck and pheasant hunting. The hunting party returned in time for Grimes and Henry to spend Thanksgiving in Owen with Grimes's parents and his siblings, Shurleigh and Hazel.[10]

Grimes spent the next month in Owen helping his father with his growing ice business. Although Wisconsin's ice harvesting industry had peaked a few decades earlier, Nick Grimes seemed to have no problem finding business. In just a few years in Owen, the elder Grimes had earned a reputation as one of the more colorful characters in town. Seemingly well liked by all, Nick was always up before sunrise chatting with patrons at local restaurants before beginning his early-morning deliveries. Along his ice route Mr. Grimes continued his jovial greeting of townsfolk. It was said that one could tell how Burleigh performed in his most recent game by the way Nick delivered his ice. If his son had won, Nick would be his usual cheerful self. If Burleigh lost, his father bypassed a greeting and merely grunted as he slammed the ice into the box.[11]

Ice harvesting was just the type of strenuous off-season activity that Grimes craved. Using a horse-drawn ice plow he helped his father mark their patch of ice and then keep it clear of snow (which slowed down the freezing process). They then cut nearly through the ice with the plow before completing the task by hand with a cross-cut saw that only had a handle on one end. From there the large blocks were broken apart and sent to an area where it was safe to remove them from the water, which could be back-breaking work in its own right. The ice was then taken to the Grimes's ice house, where it was stored, insulated by sawdust. Nick harvested enough ice for a year-round business.

Shortly into the new year, Grimes made his way back to Minerva, Ohio. He planned to do more hunting and tie up loose ends before heading to Hot Springs, Arkansas, for some training. From there he was set to head to the Giants' new spring training site in Augusta, Georgia. His plans changed on February 11 when he was traded to the Pittsburgh Pirates for pitcher Vic Aldridge.

Over the years Grimes often commented upon the exceptional influence that McGraw had on him during the 1927 campaign. In a 1981 *Sports Illustrated* article about McGraw, Grimes explained his experience. "I worked for McGraw for only one year, but I learned more that season than in all the years before — or since. The science of pitching took on a new meaning," Grimes said. "I ended up winning 270 games in my career, but if I'd known earlier what McGraw taught me, I could've won 300. He was the smartest man I ever played for."[12]

Driving the roughly 80 miles from Minerva, Grimes arrived in Pittsburgh, where he signed a contract a few days after the trade at Pirates headquarters, located in the Flannery Building. Dreyfuss seemed to have no problem reacquiring a player he had once viewed as talented but detrimental. In the near decade since he left Pittsburgh Grimes had become a very successful pitcher, winning 177 ballgames along the way.

The Giants were initially thought to have come out ahead in the Grimes-Aldridge swap. A year younger than Grimes, Aldridge had won 15 games in 1927. John McGraw was in Hot Springs a few days after the trade giving a strange explanation for the exchange: "The main reason for that deal was because of Grimes's late start last season. He is older than Aldridge and I didn't think he would get started any sooner this spring.... I had to have a pitcher who could start winning games in April and May so I made the trade."[13]

A few weeks after the trade, Grimes and his wife boarded a train in Chicago with several members of the Pirates, heading west for the team's training camp in California. It had been a dizzying couple of weeks for Grimes, who had been preparing for another season as a Giant. Sitting at a layover in Kingman, Arizona, he spoke highly of his former manager. "McGraw by all means is the best manager for whom I ever worked," said Grimes. He was optimistic about his relationship with his new manager Donie Bush. "Of course, Bush does not figure in the comparison because I have not yet done any pitching under his leadership, but from all that the boys tell me I'm certain he is a fine fellow to work for and it is quite probable I will like him as much as I do McGraw."[14]

Owen "Donie" Bush was a former shortstop for the Detroit Tigers. Playing in the shadow of Ty Cobb, the diminutive Bush (5-foot-6 and 130 pounds) had a keen batting eye, was an excellent contact hitter and was regarded as one of the best shortstops of the Dead Ball Era. He had taken over managerial duties the year before from Bill McKechnie, who had led the Pirates to a World Series championship in 1925. In his first season, Bush piloted the Pirates back to the Series, where they were swept by the New York Yankees "Murderer's Row," considered by many to be the greatest team of all time.

Despite his success, Bush wasn't popular with Pittsburgh fans and media due to his benching of star outfielder Kiki Cuyler. The two had been at loggerheads all year after Bush moved Cuyler from right field to center field and bumped him up to second in the order, instead of his preferred spot in the three-hole. Their disagreement came to a head in early August against the Giants when Cuyler didn't slide to break up a double play. He played in just 10 more games the rest of the season (starting one) and was benched for the last 27 contests and all of the World Series.

Grimes was in the first wave of players arriving in Pablo Robles, California, where the Pirates had been training since 1924. Staying at the Hotel El Paso de Robles, the club utilized the area's hot springs and seasonable weather. No longer an unpolished youngster stubbornly getting by on his talents, Grimes relished the chance to go back to where it all began:

> Home again. I've been beating around the bush hither and thither, but now I am back to the old plantation, or steel plant, if it is better that way. I'm a little more experienced, perhaps a little more older, and probably just as good. I know that I am almost the last Mohican of the spitball pitchers, but I also know that as long as I can keep my arm moving freely in the shoulder socket I can throw winning ball games.[15]

No players remained from Grimes's first tour of duty with the Pirates. The franchise was also in a completely different place than the doldrums of a decade earlier, having won two of the last three pennants ('25 and '27) and the 1925 World Series. In his first stint in a Pittsburgh uniform, the team had been plagued by poor offense. With the Dead Ball Era over, the Pirates had some of the most potent hitters in the game. In 1927 the Pirates led the league in hits, average, and runs. Even without Kiki Cuyler, who had been traded in late November 1927 to the Chicago Cubs for slight infielder Sparky Adams (5-foot-5) and forgettable outfielder Pete Scott, the Pirates still had plenty of offensive clout. They were led by Grimes's hunting partner Pie Traynor and the left-handed-hitting Waner brothers, Paul and Lloyd.

Hailing from Harrah, Oklahoma, the Waners had taken the baseball world by storm over the past two seasons. Paul burst on the scene in 1926, batting .336 and leading the league with 22 triples. He followed that up with a monstrous '27 season, leading the league in average (.380), hits (237), triples (18) and RBIs (131). Paul was joined by his younger brother Lloyd that year and he had a breakout campaign of his own (which led to the shift of Cuyler), batting .355.

During the 1927 season Paul and Lloyd Waner gained their nicknames of "Big Poison" and "Little Poison." In Donald Honig's book *The October Heroes*, Lloyd recalled a doubleheader at the Polo Grounds that year:

> There used to be this Italian fellow who always sat in the center-field bleachers. He had a voice on him you could hear all over the park. When he hollered out you heard him no matter where you were ... one day we came out of he clubhouse between games of a doubleheader and this fellow started hollering at us. What it sounded like was "Big and Little Poison," but what he was really saying was "Big and Little Person."[16]

Grimes greatly respected the Waner brothers for their hitting skill, particularly Paul. "I saw a lot of good hitters but I never saw a better one than Paul Waner," recalled Grimes. "I mean I once threw a side-arm spitter right into his belly and he hit it into the upper deck. I may have got Waner out but I never fooled him."[17]

After a few years of being a solitary figure, Grimes was enjoying the camaraderie of the Pittsburgh camp. Back in the fraternity of the Pirates he received a letter from Honus Wagner, accompanied by a picture of a bearded Grimes, Traynor and Dutch Henry at their hunting cabin in Wisconsin. Wagner jokingly wrote, "I'm thinking of doing some scouting for the House of David and would like to know how you'd like to sign a contract," referring to the religious sect out of Benton Harbor, Michigan, whose men shaved neither their hair nor beard and had a competitive traveling baseball team that sometimes had major leaguers in their lineup while touring the country.[18]

Showing up in peak physical form and enjoying himself more than he had in years couldn't keep Grimes from enduring a few mishaps during training. While shagging fly balls he broke the nail on the middle finger on his right hand and the ring finger on his left. He then took a wicked bouncer off the throat that left him momentarily stunned. Neither of those compared to the flu bug that left Grimes incapacitated for the second half of camp and lingered for the first few months of the season.

The optimism of spring training met the reality of the Pirates' shortcomings over the first few months of the season. Pittsburgh's offense was never in question, but the holes in the pitching staff were evident. Only five of the 14 hurlers who pitched for the 1927 World Series team were on the '28 roster: Carmen Hill, Lee Meadows, Ray Kremer, Joe Dawson, and Grimes's former

Dodgers teammate Johnny Miljus, who had gone six seasons between big-league starts before being signed by the Pirates the previous July.

The flu that Grimes was suffering from spread to his teammates, leaving Pie Traynor, Sparky Adams and Fred Brickell weak and unable to play. Despite still feeling the effects of the flu and a recurrence of appendicitis (team doctors treated the organ with "plaster and heavy bandages"[19]), Grimes took on an enormous workload and by the end of May had already logged over 90 innings. His record stood at 5–5 for the sixth-place Pirates, who were 18–24. At least Grimes was making an impact. Vic Aldridge hadn't signed with the Giants until early May because of a contract dispute and had a record of 1–1 in three starts.

On June 8, Grimes's personal catcher Johnny Gooch was traded to Brooklyn along with first baseman Joe Harris for his former catcher with the Robins, Charlie Hargreaves. Before the end of June he had once again shown himself to be one of the game's most durable pitchers. From a purely statistical standpoint, the month turned out to be one of the best of his career. He started seven games, winning six and adding another in relief, for a total of seven wins in the month. Grimes threw 71⅓ innings, moving his total to 161, accounting for 50 innings more than his nearest teammate.

Grimes's June efforts seemed to go for naught, however, as Pittsburgh remained in sixth place, falling to 12 games out of first place. Not helping the Pirates effort was low team morale, due in part to stringent rules put in place by Bush. The manager forbade players from engaging in "any form of public entertainment — no movies, no shows, no concerts."[20]

The team that had abounded with camaraderie in California was now nowhere to be found. Bush kept loose reigns on Grimes, however, allowing the veteran pitcher to return to his home in Ohio whenever possible to tend to his stable of more than 20 horses.

The team's problems couldn't keep the Pirates from hitting the ball. Pie Traynor was returning to full strength and the Waner brothers (specifically Paul, who batted .370 for the season, finishing second to Rogers Hornsby) were tearing up league pitching. Several other Pirates enjoyed strong offensive campaigns, including George Grantham (.323, team-best 10 home runs), Glenn Wright (.310) and Fred Brickell (.322). Grimes also got in on the hit parade, contributing a career-best .321. In fact, the Pirates were the only team in either league to bat over .300 (.309). They also led the National League in hits and runs scored.

The weak link was the club's pitching. Grimes's masterful pitching carried over into July, but he was the only Pirates pitcher with double-digit wins until the second week of August. Ray Kremer had led the National League in

ERA (2.47) in 1927 but he stumbled to a 4.64 ERA in 1928 and won 15 games, three less than in '27. Lee Meadows had won 58 games over the previous three seasons, but he was plagued by a serious sinus infection for much of 1928, only appearing in four games and compiling a 1–1 record. Carmen Hill's win total dropped from 22 to 16. Johnny Miljus was put on waivers in July and picked up by the Cleveland Indians.

On August 7, Grimes became the first pitcher in either league to reach 20 wins with a 4–3 complete-game victory in Brooklyn. Dating back to July 9, Grimes had won eight of nine decisions. On August 9 he preserved another victory in the first game of a lengthy home stand (27 of the next 30 games were in Pittsburgh). All facets of the Pirates' game began to improve as they started to make a drive for the pennant.

Grimes won his 22nd victory of the season in a 16–5 laugher against the Giants in Pittsburgh on August 24. The Giants went through five pitchers, the last being Vic Aldridge. He gave up five runs in what turned out to be the next-to-last appearance of his major league career. A week later he was sent to the International League's Newark Bears. Grimes was further vindicated by his immaculate 5–0 record against the Giants in 1928.

On the final day of August, the Pirates were in St. Louis for a double-header against the first-place Cardinals, a slot they had held for the last two-and-a-half months. Pitching on a bruised leg and sore foot, Grimes threw the last inning-and-a-third to preserve a 6–5 Pirates victory. Having gone 23–9 in August, the Pirates moved to within six-and-a-half games of the Cardinals and catapulted from fifth to third place, their best standing since May 9. It was the closest Pittsburgh got to the top of the division. A few days later it fell into fourth-place where it finished the year, 21 games behind the Cardinals.

For the first time all season Grimes lost back-to-back starts, dropping one-run games to the Cubs (3–2) on September 2 and Cardinals (4–3) on September 6. He was 4–5 in one-run games for the year. Grimes then won three in a row. The last victory on September 29 was a 9–7 complete game at the Baker Bowl in Philadelphia, his 25th and final win of the season.

The season was the strongest statistical campaign of Grimes's career. He led or was tied for the major league lead in wins (25), games (48), complete games (28), innings-pitched (330⅔), and batters faced (1,377). The wins, games and innings pitched all were career highs. Grimes also received 53 points in the NL MVP votes, finishing third behind the Cardinals' Jim Bottomley and the Giants' Fred Lindstrom. It was the highest Grimes placed in voting for the award.

The off-season was a quiet one for Grimes. He signed a 1929 contract with little fanfare and spent most of the late fall and winter months in Wisconsin at his cabin on Yellow Lake. While there he showed his abilities as a hunter in a tale told by Pie Traynor:

> Grimes was easily the best shot in our camp. One day during the deer season a buck ran out in front of me. After taking a random shot and missing him I cut across through the snow and he turned in the direction of where Grimes was hunting. Burleigh saw him at a distance, which must have been almost a mile. The spitball king took quick aim and brought him down. Grimes had a high-powered rifle and the bullet nearly tore the head from the deer. It was the best shot I ever saw.[21]

Keeping up his busy outdoorsman routine, Grimes and Paul Waner traveled to South Dakota for a two-week hunting trip. The pair returned with their limit of pheasant in time to head to Grimes's parents in Owen for Thanksgiving. From there he traveled back to his stock farm in Ohio to tend to his horses and indulge in the local fox hunting club.

In New York City, the city's baseball writers didn't let John McGraw forget about the lopsided trade. At the writers' minstrel show during the winter they mocked the move:

From left: Grimes, Paul Waner and Dutch Henry posing with their cache of pheasants during their fall 1928 South Dakota hunting trip (Charles Clark Photo Collection).

They sent Burleigh Grimes away
Because he was too noisy, or so somebody said
Burleigh beat the Giants five straight,
Vic Aldridge went to "Joisey"[22]

In early February Grimes arrived in Paso Robles, California, where the
mood was nowhere near as jovial as the previous spring. Players were told to
leave their wives at home and Bush put out the decree that recreational activities would be kept to a minimum. Pie Traynor was still nursing a hip injury
from the 1928 season, but Bush seemed to be dead set on moving him to
shortstop. Absent from camp were the Waner brothers, which team treasurer
Sam Dreyfuss blamed on their love of the saxophone: "It is all the fault of
that devilish saxophone. Ever since Paul learned to play the instrument and
Lloyd also learned to make it moan, the boys have been trying to combine
two arts, music and baseball."[23]

Grimes was laid up with a cold that caused him to miss nearly all of
training in Paso Robles. On the evening of his return, Grimes was injured in
a bedtime mishap in his hotel room: "After turning off the light he was about
to hop into bed when he stepped on one of his baseball shoes in the darkness.
The shoe was lying upside down on the floor and Burleigh trod squarely upon
a spike, the blade of which penetrated the flesh beneath the big toe. He
stopped the flow of blood and bandaged his own spike wound."[24] The self-
imposed spiking kept Grimes out of workouts for a few days, but he quickly
distinguish himself from the gaggle of pitchers after returning to the mound.
Before the Pirates broke camp, manager Donie Bush announced that Grimes
was the Opening Day starter.

On April 16, Grimes took the mound in Chicago for the first and only
Opening Day start of his career. In front of the largest Opening Day crowd
in city history (a reported 50,000), Grimes went the distance, scattering 10
hits in the 4–3 victory over the Cubs. He followed that up with a complete-
game 5–4 win in Cincinnati and then tossed 11 innings of a 13-inning, 5–4
defeat of Chicago in the home opener at Forbes Field.

Grimes's next start at Sportsman's Park in St. Louis didn't go as well. In
the bottom of the third inning, Cardinals right fielder Ernie Orsatti lined a
ball back through the box. Grimes instinctively stuck his hand out and
knocked down the ball, with his thumb catching the brunt of the impact. It
broke the thumbnail, cut the flesh and left the thumb bruised and badly
swollen.

The Pirates and their fans breathed a sigh of relief when it was reported
that there was no fracture in Grimes's thumb. There was speculation that he
would miss a week to 10 days, but Grimes was back on the mound six days

later on May 5 when he threw all nine innings of a 7–2 victory over the Braves in Boston. The win bounced the Pirates from sixth place into fourth. Admiration for Grimes was growing. The *Pittsburgh Post Gazette* gushed, "Grimes is on his way to becoming a civic institution, a hero of almost mythical proportions."[25]

The Pirate climbed their way up the standings and by the end of May were tied for first place with the St. Louis Cardinals. Grimes was perfect during the month, winning all six of his decisions. He was again taking on a tremendous workload, with more than double the wins of any Pittsburgh starter and nearly twice as many innings pitched as the next closest teammate. He won his first two starts in June to make him a perfect 10–0 for the season and was just two short of the club record (for consecutive wins at any point) of 12, set by Frank Killen in 1893. Grimes's streak made it no further, as he lost an 8–1 decision to the Reds on June 16, with his teammates making six errors behind him. He won his next five starts, however, including a shutout of Cincinnati on June 29 to put his record at 15–1.

The Pirates' longest stay in first place lasted from July 4 to July 23, including a season-high eight-game win streak. Once again Pittsburgh boasted a stout offense. As a team the Pirates again hit over .300, led by Pie Traynor (.356, 108 RBIs), Lloyd Waner (.353, 20 triples), Paul Waner (.336, 43 doubles, 15 home runs), outfielder Adam Comorosky (.321), George Grantham (.307), and Dick Bartell (.302). The pitching staff also began to flourish. Ray Kremer returned to form (18–10), second-year player Erv Brame (16–11) had a breakout year and Grimes's former Brooklyn teammate Jesse Petty was a serviceable fourth starter (11–10).

Injuries started to take their toll on the club during the Pirates' stay in first place. Lloyd Waner suffered a mysterious thumb injury, George Grantham hurt his throwing shoulder on a slide and Pie Traynor was told to remain in bed to rest his ailing hip. The biggest blow of all came on July 20 when Grimes suffered another devastating thumb injury in the first game of a doubleheader at the Polo Grounds against the Giants.

After giving up a pair of runs in the first inning, Grimes was cruising along until the sixth. With one out, New York first baseman Bill Terry sent a shot back through the box. Grimes instinctively stuck up his bare hand to knock it down. The ball hit his hand with such force that the impact bent his thumb back against his wrist. Grimes recovered and threw to first for the out with his remaining four digits, but it was immediately apparent that he hadn't escaped injury this time. There was no shaking this one off as Grimes looked down at his dislocated thumb, the nail partially shattered. With teammates surrounding him on the mound, the grimacing Grimes "pulled the joint back into place and walked back to the clubhouse."[26] The Pirates held on to beat the Giants for Grimes's 16th victory, but it was certain that he would miss substantial time.

Grimes's injury had been foreshadowed by his manager. A few weeks earlier Bush expressed concerns about the "rabbit ball." "It's not a ball, it's a bullet," said the Pittsburgh manager. "Somebody's going to get killed if they don't watch out. A pitcher who has to put the ball over hasn't a chance. All he can do is to pitch and duck."[27] To add insult to injury, Bush thought about withholding Grimes from his start against the Braves, saving him for the opener against the Giants, but after a loss Bush sent him to the mound as a stopgap measure in Boston, thus pushing back his start against New York. Five days after the Grimes injury the Pirates relinquished their three-week reign in first place, never to regain it.

The Pirates trailed the Cubs by just six-and-a-half games when they started a 17-game east coast road trip. When they returned 19 days later, they were still in second place, but now 14½ games behind after dropping 12 of the road contests. Grimes returned to the mound during the fateful road trip, but was a shell of his former self. After his initial relief appearance against the Phillies (one-and-one-third innings, two earned runs on two hits and two walks), Grimes complained of soreness in his thumb and an inability to properly grip the ball firmly.

When the team arrived back in Pittsburgh, Donie Bush was summoned to the Flannery Building for a closed-door meeting with Barney Dreyfuss. On August 28, the two emerged with Dreyfuss accepting a resignation from Bush. The now former manager put forth the following statement: "I was thoroughly disgusted with the ways things were breaking for the team on the last trip and had made up my mind upon arrival here that I would hand in my resignation."[28]

There were doubts that it was an amicable split, but the two parties remained mum. Coach Jewel Ens was named interim manager. A former Pirates infielder, Ens had played sparingly (67 games) over four years in a Pittsburgh uniform. The Pirates and Grimes won Ens's first game as manager, a 10–3 thumping of the Cubs, but Grimes's relationship with Ens wouldn't be as close as it was with Bush due in part to reports that Grimes might "succeed to the managerial role next season, if not before."[29]

Although Grimes had some solid performances in September, the victory over Chicago was his last of the season. A September 28 start in St. Louis proved to be his final mound appearance of 1929. The premature end to his season came as a result of his actions during that game. Ens pulled Grimes in the fourth inning after allowing four runs, the last one coming when he threw the ball into center field trying to start a double play. Unhappy with the decision, Grimes vehemently argued with Ens on the bench, claiming that the base had not been covered in a timely manner. The dugout confrontation exacerbated the strained relationship between the two men.

The season had taken a toll on Grimes and toward the end of the season he began thinking about how much longer he wanted to play. "Please tell the fans for me that I have no idea of continuing in baseball after the season of 1930," he declared. "I have no ambition to run a marathon with Old Man Time. I want to have a good year in 1930 and then kiss baseball goodbye forever. This will be my last season regardless. I have saved my money, am fixed for the future and in 1931 I will buy a farm in Indiana or Kentucky and raise horses or cattle."[30]

Spalding's Official Base Ball Guide summarized Grimes's importance to the Pirates and what his injury meant to their pennant hopes: "The year's history in Pittsburgh is to be divided into two parts. The first is W.G.—'with Grimes'—and the second is also W.G.—'without Grimes.'"[31]

Despite the injury-abbreviated campaign Grimes placed fourth in the National League MVP voting and was named pitcher on *The Sporting News's* fifth annual Major League All-Star Team. The 187 members of the Base Ball Writers' Association of America also found his performance good enough to name him one of the two best pitchers in the Major Leagues alongside the Philadelphia Athletics' Lefty Grove.

The 1929 season marked the end of the first decade since the grandfathering of the spitball. Grimes had been one of the most successful pitchers of the 1920s. For the decade, he compiled the most wins (190), complete games (234) and innings pitched (2,797⅔). He was second in strikeouts (1,018) to Dazzy Vance and fifth in games pitched (373).

In late fall, Grimes's name was mentioned in trades to the Cubs, Cardinals and Reds. Also taking shape were discussions of Grimes taking over for Wilbert Robinson as manager of the Dodgers. A contentious situation was arising in Brooklyn, where Robinson's contract as manager had expired, but he was still team president. All of these rumors were swirling when Grimes made his way to New York for the league meetings at the Biltmore Hotel. It was here that Grimes made public his desire for a salary of nearly $25,000 before he signed a contract. Shortly thereafter, it was reported that he was asking for a two-year contract that would pay him $20,000 a year (up from roughly $18,000 in '29), which was at odds with his statement of just a month earlier that he wouldn't play beyond 1930.

As the negotiations spilled over into the new year, Barney Dreyfuss tried to squelch the rumors that Grimes wouldn't be accompanying the team to

Paso Robles for spring training. "Grimes is not a holdout and will sign," he reassured Pittsburgh fans before leaving with his wife for Hollywood, Florida, where he spent the duration of the winter due to health reasons.[32]

The contract negotiations didn't embitter Grimes enough to renege on his promise to speak at the Pittsburgh Sports Writers' Dinner at the William Penn Hotel. Never one to shy away from saying a few words, Grimes was one of the headline speakers for a large group that included Commissioner Landis and National League President John Heydler. Numerous players would also attend, including Hack Wilson, Lloyd Waner and the great Honus Wagner.

A few days before the dinner, Grimes received some leverage in his contract battle when well-respected umpire-turned-general manager Billy Evans penned an article naming the top pitchers from the last 25 years. Evans broke them into four tiers, the first consisting of Walter Johnson, Christy Mathewson, Grover Alexander, Rube Waddell and Cy Young. The second included Mordecai Brown, Chief Bender, fellow spitballer Ed Walsh, Eddie Plank and former teammate "Dazzy" Vance. Grimes was placed in the third tier alongside fellow Wisconsin native Addie Joss, Babe Ruth, Herb Pennock and Waite Hoyt. The fourth tier had Lefty Grove, George Earnshaw, Tommy Thomas, Charley Root, Pat Malone and Ted Lyons.

By all accounts the Sports Writers' Dinner was a gallant affair. Around 700 people attended the banquet and Grimes was given a "tremendous ovation" by the Pirates faithful. The show of love seemed to have little effect on the Pirates brass. On the following day, Grimes met with club vice president Sam Dreyfuss for more than two hours before leaving for his home in Ohio without a contract. Following the proceedings, Dreyfuss stated that the two parties were "miles apart" in their negotiation, finally conceding that Grimes was in fact now a holdout.[33]

A week later Grimes returned to Pittsburgh, this time with his brother Shurleigh in tow. The two drove from Minerva so that Burleigh could meet with Vice President Dreyfuss and Manager Ens at the Flannery Building. The two sides continued to be at odds, and about the only thing that came of the meeting was a photo opportunity for the newspaper. With the team leaving for Paso Robles in less than two weeks, Grimes became more aggressive in his pursuit of a contract, dropping in unannounced at Pirates headquarters as if hoping to catch Pittsburgh management in a giving mood. It was to no avail, as the team headed west without him.

Contract negotiations, the Ens conflict and trade rumors weren't Grimes's only concerns. After 17 years of marriage, Ruth Grimes filed for a two-year separation, hoping he "would settle down by that time, and all this foolish

Few details of the divorce of Ruth and Burleigh Grimes were left untold. This full tell-all was printed in papers from coast to coast.

wrangling would be forgotten."[34] Grimes wanted no part of a separation, instead filing for a divorce.

When the couple had their day in court on April 3 in Canton, Ohio, neither side held back in their accusations. Burleigh accused Ruth of gross neglect, extreme cruelty and extravagant and frivolous spending. He asserted that it was Ruth's malicious behavior toward the wives of his Brooklyn teammates that had caused the friction between him and his fellow Robins. Burleigh's parents, brother, housekeeper and numerous members of the Minerva community took the stand in his defense. These witnesses cited numerous incidents over the years in which Ruth had been verbally or physically abusive toward her husband and his family.

Ruth counteracted Burleigh's allegations, accusing him of infidelity. She brought forth a number of letters from women in Boston and Philadelphia that seemed to be more than the fan mail that Burleigh claimed them to be. He said he received more than 200 letters a year and even more last year due to his success. However, the letters in question, each of which was read aloud

Former teammates Grimes (left) and Clarence Mitchell during Grimes's short-lived stint with the Boston Braves (Charles Clark Photo Collection).

in court, were damning evidence. The words went beyond fandom, peppered with endearing terms that elicited snickers from those in the courtroom.

Just days later on April 9, less than a week before the start of the regular season, Grimes was dealt from the Pirates to the Boston Braves in exchange for left-handed pitcher Percy Jones and cash. Grimes agreed to an undisclosed salary and appeared to look forward to the challenge ahead. "Rebuilding the Braves is a three-year job," he declared, "and I want to be at my best to help the most."[35]

7

Meet Me in St. Louis, 1930–1931

The Boston Braves franchise was one of the most abysmal in the league. The team's owner, Judge Emil Fuchs, a former attorney for the New York Giants, was trying mightily to pull the club out of the doldrums it had been in for a decade and a half, but nothing seemed to work. After a failed experiment with Rogers Hornsby as manager in 1928, Fuchs took over managerial duties, leading the club to a last-place finish in 1929. For the 1930 season, he went out and hired "Deacon" Bill McKechnie, who specialized in pitching and defense.

McKechnie had managed the St. Louis Cardinals during the second half of 1929 and most observers assumed he would be back there in 1930. However, when Fuchs offered him a five-year deal to rebuild the Braves, McKechnie accepted. He inherited an aging roster with very few players who would have started on other major league teams. In a season that came to be known as the "Year of the Hitter," rookie centerfielder Wally Berg and veteran George Sisler (in the final year of his Hall of Fame career) were the team's lone offensive threats. The pitching staff was even thinner — Grimes was by far the best pitcher on the roster.

Shortly after Grimes was acquired, it was announced that he would serve as an assistant to McKechnie. However, it quickly became apparent that Fuchs didn't have Grimes in his rebuilding plans. He was already working on dealing Grimes to either St Louis or Cincinnati, a club that had spent the past several years trying to obtain the pitcher.

Although Grimes continued his usual off-season conditioning (he spent two weeks in Hot Springs working out with the Minneapolis Millers, a AA team), the contract negotiations and divorce proceedings kept him from the spring training and exhibition games that he found increasingly valuable as he grew older. His progress was further hindered when, after joining the Braves, he was hit in the ankle by a line drive while throwing batting practice.

On April 27, Grimes, started his first game of the season, a 13–4 defeat

Cardinals team picture on the day Grimes arrived in St. Louis. Grimes in street clothes (center, back row) had yet to receive a uniform. July, 1930 (Charles Clark Photo Collection).

of the Phillies at Braves Field. He looked spry on the mound and contributed a double and two RBIs at the plate. In his next start against the Pirates on May 3, Grimes had the shortest outing of his career, recording no outs and giving up six runs on four hits and two walks.

The victory over the Phillies proved to be Grimes's high point in a Braves uniform. For the next month-and-a-half he suffered from a debilitating flu that left him weakened. Rumors of Grimes's departure from Boston began to increase in late May and early June, but with a high salary and an unimpressive record (2–3 on June 1), it was unclear who would be willing to take him on.

Finally, at the midsummer league meeting in New York City, Fuchs and St. Louis Cardinals owner Sam Breadon worked out a deal. On June 16, Grimes was sent to the Cardinals for pitchers Fred Frankhouse and Bill Sherdel. While Grimes was thrilled to be heading to St. Louis, Sherdel and Frankhouse were devastated. Both had hoped that Grimes would be acquired, but neither thought they would be sent to Boston in the deal. Sherdel, who had spent his first 12 years in St. Louis, said that he would "be pulling for the Cardinals, except when I pitch against them."[1]

Breadon actually wasn't going to go through with the trade until being coerced to do so by Sam Muchnik of the *St. Louis Times* and Roy Stockton of the *St. Louis Post-Dispatch* on the previous evening. The three men had been sitting in Breadon's room at the Alamac Hotel, drinking Scotch and waters and discussing how to improve the struggling Cardinals. The sportswriters kept insisting that obtaining Grimes from Boston was crucial to turning things around.

"Oh, I can't get Grimes. I've been trying to get him!" lamented Breadon.[2]

The increasingly inebriated sportswriters convinced the Cardinals owner to call Boston owner Judge Fuchs just to make sure. Breadon retired to the other room and when he returned he announced that he had gotten Grimes in exchange for Frankhouse and Sherdel. The trade took place just before the midnight trading deadline.

Although the Cardinals had been trying to obtain Grimes for a few years, he had had mixed results when pitching in St. Louis. Since the Cardinals had moved into Sportsman's Park (sharing the facility with the Browns) in July 1920, Grimes's record was 14–13. Some changes to the dimensions of Sportsman's Park had been made in 1930 that were advantageous to pitchers during the heavy-hitting season. The left-field wall was moved back to 360 feet and center-field to 450. The right-field wall was just 320 feet from home plate, but a 37-foot high screen in front of the right-field bleachers knocked down balls headed for the stands.

St. Louis was an outstanding offensive team (all eight starters ended the season batting over .300), but they were in dire need of another pitcher to anchor the staff. Jesse Haines, who became a close friend to Grimes had been the team's best pitcher over the last half-decade (he won 20 games in '27 and '28, but dropped to 13 in 1929) and the talented yet inconsistent lefty Bill Hallahan was just starting to show his skills. Without the services of several top hitters and a rash of suspect pitching during the early part of the season, the Cardinals had suffered a freefall on a recent road trip to the east. They had been in first place on May 24, but had then lost 15 of 20 and fallen into fourth place, prompting the trade.

When the team returned to St. Louis, Breadon summoned Grimes to his office at Sportsman's Park. Grimes assured the Cardinals' owner that his arm wasn't the reason for his poor start to the season, but rather the flu bug, from which he had now fully recovered. Breadon responded, "Burleigh, if you win a dozen games, I think maybe we might make it."[3] According to Grimes, before their meeting was over, Breadon had offered him a bonus of $2,000 if he helped lead them to the pennant.

Being a veteran of nearly 15 years and having played for four different franchises, it was inevitable that there were familiar faces in the St. Louis clubhouse. There was Andy High, whom Grimes had forged a close friendship with during their three-and-a-half years together in Brooklyn, as well as Sparky Adams and Carmen Hill from Pittsburgh, and Doc Farrell from the Giants. The trade also teamed Grimes with his long-time nemesis, Frankie Frisch. After a decade of run-ins, the pair became roommates and forged a close friendship that lasted the rest of their lives.

The move from one end of the baseball universe to the other also reunited Grimes with his old battery mate from his minor league days in Chattanooga, Gabby Street. Street, known as "Old Sarge" from his World War I service, had managed the Cardinals for the final game of the '29 season while Bill McKechnie campaigned for town assessor in his boyhood home of Wilkinsburg, Pennsylvania. When McKechnie went to the Boston Braves for the 1930 season, Street was hired as manager, the fifth Cardinals manager to start the season in as many years.

Initially, Grimes didn't provide the spark that Breadon and the Cardinals had hoped. He won his first start, a 9–3 victory over the Phillies, but by the end of July Grimes's record with St. Louis was 4–3. He wasn't alone in his inconsistency. The Cardinals couldn't seem to budge from their spot at the bottom of the first division. They'd win three or four games in a row and then lose as many. Finally, St. Louis dropped to a season-low 12 games behind the first-place Brooklyn Robins on August 8. The complexion of the season began to change for Grimes and his teammates shortly thereafter, starting one of the greatest drives toward the pennant that baseball has ever seen.

On August 10, Grimes won his third straight decision (and fifth of his last six dating back to July 6). He lost his next start, 3–2, to the Boston Braves, but it was evident that Grimes was returning to the form that had made him one of the top pitchers over the past two years. One of the main reasons was his rapport with catcher Jimmie Wilson. For a brief time, Wilson, nicknamed "Ace," had been a two-sport athlete, playing soccer and baseball. The footwork he learned on the soccer pitch was essential to handling Grimes's spitball. Of all the catchers Grimes threw to during his career, Wilson was his favorite.

As the season was reaching its home stretch and pitchers were beginning to tire in the summer sun, the inevitable happened — the Cardinals began to hit the ball. In the "Year of the Hitter," St. Louis had one of the most dangerous lineups in the game. The team batted .314, including the eight starters who batted over .300: George Watkins (.373, 17 home runs), Frankie Frisch (.346, 46 doubles, 114 RBIs), Chick Hafey (.336, 39 doubles, 12 triples, 26 home runs, 107 RBIs), Jimmie Wilson (.318), Sparky Adams (.314), Jim Bottomley (.304), Charlie Gelbert (.304, 39 doubles, 11 triples) and Taylor Douthit (.303, 41 doubles, 10 triples). The bench also had some outstanding role players, including Ray Blades (.396), George Fisher (.374), Gus Mancuso (.366), and Ernie Orsatti (.321).

On August 19, St. Louis was 10 games out of first place. With the New York Giants in town for the last time, Sam Breadon entertained the New York sportswriters at his farm. A good-natured game of ball between the New York and St. Louis press took place, umpired by Gabby Street. As the day wore on, Breadon proclaimed, "It's too bad our club didn't start a little earlier; I would have all you guys back here for a World Series." Speaking of his team, Breadon said, "We're playing the best ball in the league right now, but we're too far behind to make up ground we lost earlier in the season."[4]

The next day, the Cardinals started a nine-game winning streak. The final victory on August 28 against the Cubs lasted 20 innings. Grimes won two games during the streak, but was tabbed with the loss when he pitched the final two innings of a 13-inning tilt on August 29. The Cardinals lost again the following day, but won their next seven to pull within two-and-a-half games of Chicago before heading east for a 14-game road trip.

The addition of Grimes was beginning to pay major dividends. He went 5–2 in August and won his first decision of September. Overall, he had won nine of his last 12, and was particularly effective at Sportsman's Park, where he won six of seven.

With only three weeks remaining and just four games separating the top four teams, New York City was hosting all four in a crucial series of games. The third-place Dodgers were entertaining the first-place Cubs, and the fourth-place Giants were hosting the second-place Cardinals. Grimes opposed former teammate Clarence Mitchell (who had begun the year with the Cardinals) on September 9 at the Polo Grounds. For six innings the two spitballers pitched scoreless ball, but in the top of the seventh the Cardinals pushed across a run. In the bottom half of the frame, the Giants responded with two runs of their own to win, 2–1. The Cardinals won their next three over the Giants and by the time they were on a train headed for Boston they were tied for second place with Brooklyn, just a half-game behind the Cubs.

In Boston, the Cardinals won the first two games (the second was a 9–2 victory behind Grimes) before dropping the third. The first win had moved them into a tie for first place with Brooklyn, but splitting the next two left them a half-game behind the Dodgers heading into a three-game series at Ebbets Field.

St. Louis won the first two games of the series in Brooklyn, the latter victory giving the Cardinals sole possession of first place for the first time since May 27. When Grimes took the mound for the final game on September 18, Brooklyn fans were in no mood to watch him keep them from a World Series. From the get-go, he was showered with jeers from the stands, and he goaded the crowd into a frenzy with his behavior. After getting out of a jam to end the sixth inning, he gave a mock tip of the cap to the crowd and brought his thumb down to his nose, playfully wiggling his other four digits at the Brooklyn faithful.

When the final out of the 4–3 St. Louis victory was recorded, Grimes found himself dodging the insults being hurled his way and a flurry of pop bottles. After the game, Grimes was asked if he was bothered by all of the yelling. "Naw I liked it!" he responded. "Hey, there's nothing I enjoy more than to have 'em hollering for my head and then to be able to strike a slugger out in a pinch. That's sweet music into my ears."[5]

The Cardinals were still just three games ahead of the Cubs with a four-game series against the Pirates ahead. Not wanting to appear overconfident, the St. Louis players tried to get off on a platform opposite the crowd. Reporters were able to corral them for a photo opportunity and a brief word from Gabby Street. "Now for Pittsburgh," was all the Cardinals manager would say at first.[6] Pressed for details of the team's amazing run to first place, Street emphasized that nothing had been won yet, but he did say, "We beat out those other clubs because every man on the team was hustling and giving his best. It was team play and the fighting spirit of one of the gamest clubs I ever saw."[7]

That the Cubs were the last team standing in the Cardinals' way was somewhat of a surprise. Chicago was coming off a World Series loss to the Philadelphia Athletics, but had battled through a tumultuous year. Reigning MVP Rogers Hornsby played in only 42 games and popular pitcher Hal Carlson, who won a game as recently as May 10, died of tuberculosis on May 28, a result of being exposed to mustard gas during World War I. Behind the hitting of Hack Wilson (.356, 56 home runs, 191 RBIs), Kiki Cuyler (.355, 50 doubles, 17 triples, 134 RBIs) and Gabby Hartnett (.339, 37 home runs, 122 RBIs) the Cubs persevered. A season-long feud between manager Joe McCarthy and Hornsby, along with hard feelings still lingering from managerial moves made in the 1929 World Series, led owner William Wrigley to ask for McCarthy's resignation with just four games left in the season. Hornsby was named as his successor.

After an off day, Grimes was scheduled to pitch the opening game against the Pirates. He arrived at the ball park early and went to Sam Breadon's office at Sportsman's Park to good-naturedly reminded him of the $2,000 agreement for a dozen wins, which Grimes had reached. Breadon pushed him for one more: "I said a dozen, Burleigh, If you could only make it 13...."[8] Grimes promised to do his best.

Pitching his first home game in nearly a month, Grimes was matched against Pittsburgh's Ray Kremer, already a 20-game winner. Kremer gave up a three-run homer to Jim Bottomley in the bottom of the first and was out of the game before the second inning ended. Grimes was masterful, compiling his only shutout of the season and contributing two hits in the 9–0 Cardinals victory. The win put Grimes's record at 13–6 in a Cardinals uniform and 16–11 overall. In a year of gaudy offensive numbers, Grimes compiled a stellar 3.01 ERA after the trade.

The Cardinals culminated their improbable pennant run the following day, clinching the pennant with a 10–5 victory. They split their last two games, the win coming on the last day of the season behind the hitting and pitching of upstart Dizzy Dean, who had to borrow a pair of spikes from Grimes.

The resurgence of the Cardinals was nothing short of miraculous. Dating back to August 8 when they sat in fourth place, 12 games behind the Brooklyn Robins, the Cardinals had won 39 of 49 games and 21 of their last 24. Their record in August had been 23–9 followed by a 21–4 mark in September.

The Cardinals' opponent in the World Series was the defending champion Philadelphia Athletics, a 102-win juggernaut. After years of non-contention and watching the Yankees dominate the American League, the venerable Connie Mack had rebuilt the A's into a powerhouse. They were led by the pitching tandem of Lefty Grove (winner of the pitching Triple Crown — 28 wins, 2.54 ERA, 209 strikeouts) and the effectively wild George Earnshaw (22–13). They also boasted the most prodigious middle of the lineup in the majors: Mickey Cochrane (.357, 42 doubles), Al Simmons (.381, 41 doubles, 16 triples, 36 home runs, 165 RBIs) and Jimmie Foxx (.335, 33 doubles, 13 triples, 37 home runs, 156 RBIs) drove American League pitchers to distraction.

Heading into the World Series, the Cardinals had some question marks on their roster. Catcher Jimmie Wilson was still on the mend from an ankle injury that he had suffered against the Giants in early September. That left Gus Mancuso as the main catcher for the series. Starting pitcher Sylvester Johnson had had an old rib injury flare up on him in his last start of the season. Frankie Frisch was also suffering from an attack of lumbago. The lower back pain was a residual effect of a cold he caught during the final series against the Pirates.

Much of the talk leading up to the first game dealt with the pitching match-ups. With five formidable starters, St. Louis was thought to have the upper hand over Philadelphia's two-man attack. Gabby Street named Grimes his starter for Game One, citing the struggles of the A's against spitballers, who now numbered just four (Grimes, Mitchell, Jack Quinn and Red Faber). "I pick him not because I think he is the best, but because the Athletics don't see much spitball pitching during the season, and Faber of the Chicago White Sox always gives them trouble," said the St. Louis manager.[9] On the other hand, Connie Mack remained tight-lipped about his choice of starter, a tactic he had used in the World Series the year before.

The night before Game One, Grimes was acting in a boastful mode in the Benjamin Franklin Hotel lobby. Surrounded by a gaggle of reporters, he spoke dismissively of the Athletics. "Bring on your Macks! Just three pretty good hitters and I've got the book on them," said Grimes as he pulled a small black book out of his breast pocket, its contents supposedly holding the batting deficiencies of Jimmie Foxx, Mickey Cochrane, and Al Simmons.[10] Gabby Street got in on the act: "Grove will never pitch against you! You are going to pitch the first game and Connie will be afraid to start Grove against you."[11] He was wrong.

On October 1, a capacity crowd of 32,295 jammed into Shibe Park, including President Herbert Hoover, who sat in a box above the Philadelphia dugout. Babe Ruth, who was writing a column about the series, was in attendance, standing out in his large tan overcoat and puffing on a cigar. Players from Mack's World Series teams of two decades earlier also looked on. The pregame entertainment included "baseball clowns" Al Schacht and Nick Altrock.

Grimes had suffered a gall bladder attack on the previous evening, but that didn't stop him from formulating his normal combative game plan. After a scoreless first, Philadelphia put a run on the board in the second inning. Jimmie Foxx rocketed a ball off the right-field wall that ricocheted by right fielder Ray Blades. By the time he corralled it, Foxx was on third base. The next batter, Mule Haas, hit a sacrifice fly to right field, scoring Foxx. In the top of the third, the Cardinals loaded the bases against Grove with no outs. The next two batters hit sacrifice flies to give Grimes a 2–1 lead. Philadelphia tied the game on a fourth-inning home run by Al Simmons and took the lead on a run-scoring double by Jimmy Dykes in the sixth.

After Dykes's double, Grimes turned to the jockeying portion of his repertoire. During Mickey Cochrane's at-bat, home plate umpire George Moriarty called a close pitch a ball. Grimes took a few steps toward the plate, barking his displeasure. Cochrane had some harsh words for Grimes, who didn't take kindly to Philadelphia's catcher interfering in the discussion. The two kept up their dialogue throughout the at bat, which ended in Cochrane striking out. Cochrane took a few steps toward the mound, barking expletives at Grimes, who responded by stepping toward home plate. "If I had a bird dog pup that looked like him and had no sense, I'd shoot him," he said, referring to Cochrane's protruding ears.[12] Cochrane said a few choice words before turning and heading to the Philadelphia dugout. Inspired by the pregame comedy routine, Grimes put his thumbs in his ears and wiggled his hands at Cochrane's back.

St. Louis had a chance to tie the score in the top of the seventh inning. With one out, Grimes rapped a single to right field. The next batter, Taylor Douthit, hit a hard grounder into the hole. Shortstop Joe Boley made a great backhanded stop. Grimes, thinking that the ball was going through, didn't run full speed right away, giving Boley time to pivot and make the force at second. The next batter, Sparky Adams, hit a single to left that might have scored Grimes, putting runners on first and second, before Frisch lined out to second. In the bottom of the seventh, Philadelphia added an insurance run which Haas tripled and scored on a perfectly executed squeeze by Boley.

The Cardinals squandered a double by Chick Hafey in the top of the eighth. In the bottom of the inning Cochrane came to the plate with two out. Grimes tried to sneak a fastball by the lefty, who yanked it over the right field wall, exacting revenge from their confrontation a few innings before. St. Louis went down 1-2-3 in the top of the ninth; the game ending 5–2 in favor of the A's.

Grimes allowed five hits, opposed to Grove's nine, but they all went for extra bases and resulted in runs. After the game, Grimes asked reporters disgustedly, "Whoever heard of a team getting five runs on five hits?"[13] He gave no credit to Philadelphia, instead attributing their success to getting all the breaks. Street concurred: "Say, those hits would have been singles in my ballpark out it St. Louis. They'd have hit that screen and bounded back onto the field."[14]

Street surprised many when he named Flint Rhem as his Game Two starter against George Earnshaw. Rhem had helped the Cardinals to the 1926 World Series, but since then he had struggled greatly with alcohol abuse (he was a drinking partner of Grover Alexander). He allowed six runs and was pulled from the game with one out in the fourth inning as Philadelphia won easily, 6–1. Grimes kept busy during the contest by mercilessly riding Cochrane with calls of "mule ears, mule ears."[15]

The series moved to St. Louis, where crazed fans cheered the Cardinals' every move, including batting practice. Game Three belonged to "Wild Bill" Hallahan. After working out of a bases-loaded jam in the first inning, he didn't let another baserunner past second for the rest of the game. A Taylor Douthit solo home run in the bottom of the fourth was all Hallahan needed in the 5–0 Cardinals victory.

Game Four matched Jesse Haines against Lefty Grove. The A's jumped out to a 1–0 lead in the first inning on an Al Simmons single. They threatened again in the second, prompting Street to warm up Grimes, but Haines was able to get out of the jam unscathed. He settled in and allowed just one more hit (a Simmons single in the third inning) the rest of the game. The Cardinals scored a run in the third and two in the fourth, giving them the 3–1 win and tying the series at two games apiece.

Game Five pitted the well-rested Grimes against Game Two winner George Earnshaw. As if he needed any more incentive, Grimes's father Nick was in attendance. The two teams exchanged singles in the first inning, but each went hitless over the next three innings. In the fourth inning Grimes dusted off Al Simmons, who entered the game batting .500 (7 for 14). Three times he ended up in the dirt to avoid being hit. One of the balls even bounced off his bat for a strike. The approach drew the ire of Philadelphia fans in attendance, but it worked. The game was Simmons's only hitless game of the series.

Grimes also kept up his verbal assaults. He spared no one, going after Connie Mack with particular vigor. As the always nattily dressed Philadelphia manager paced in front of the bench, his collar began to wilt from perspiration. Grimes called Mack's "attention to the fact that his collar was getting a rough deal and made a few suggestions of what an elderly gentleman should do under those circumstances"[16]

Pitching continued to dominate the game. Philadelphia managed another single in the fifth inning and St. Louis's Jimmie Wilson (playing on his sore ankle) legged out a two-out double in the seventh. Earnshaw intentionally walked the next batter, Charlie Gelbert, to get to Grimes, who ended the threat with an easy fly out to center.

The game's intensity rose to another level in the eighth inning. Philadelphia collected two infield hits, managing to put runners on first and third. Mack pulled Earnshaw from the game in favor of pinch hitter Jimmy Moore, who Grimes walked. With the bases loaded, Grimes coaxed two ground balls to get out of the inning unscathed. Mack put in Lefty Grove in the bottom of the eighth. Grove allowed a two-out single to Frankie Frisch (the Cardinals' third hit of the game), but retired the next batter on strikes.

In the top of the ninth Grimes walked Mickey Cochrane. Grimes continued his running dialogue with Mack while inducing Simmons to fly out to left field. The next batter, Jimmie Foxx, stepped to the plate with Grimes, who was still smirking from the exchange he had had with Simmons. Grimes tried to throw a first-pitch fastball by Foxx, a pitch that he had struck out on in his previous at-bat. Foxx didn't miss this one, sending a towering fly into the left-field bleachers. As he rounded the bases the only noise in the ball park was the Athletics' bench barking at Grimes. Between third and home Cochrane put his hands to his ears and mockingly flapped them toward the mound.

The Cardinals put one runner on in the bottom of the ninth, but that was all they could muster. The final score was 2–0. Grimes was once again the tough-luck loser, allowing just five base hits.

Grimes's effort was lauded by many, but not all. Following the game he was sitting in a taxi waiting to return to the team's hotel when two women approached him. He expected that they were going to pay their respects, but instead they chastised him for his behavior. "Two women stuck their heads into the door and bawled me out," recalled Grimes. "They said if I had my mind on my work instead of abusing Connie, I might have won the ball game."[17]

Two days later in Philadelphia, the Athletics won the Series behind Earnshaw, pitching on one day's rest. In a season dominated by hitting, the World Series was a showcase of pitching by both teams.

After the game, the players and their wives rode on a bus to the train station. From the back of the bus, rookie George Puccinelli sang "It's all over now.... It's all over now...." According to sportswriter Bob Broeg, Grimes, seated in the front of the bus, flew into a rage. He ran to the back and shouted at the reserve outfielder, "Listen, you big bastard, we all know it's over, but we don't have to have it rubbed in."[18]

A few days after the Series ended, Grimes received notice that Ruth Grimes had filed papers for divorce in Canton, Ohio. It was evident that she still had feelings for her husband and even seemed willing to reconcile. "If he can convince me that those fan letters I found were really fan letters I'll forgive him, but I'll never live with him again if he can't."[19] The relationship had been non-existent since the trial in April and Burleigh was dating Laura Virginia Phelan of St. Louis. The former wife of Leo M. Phelan, secretary of the Phelan-Faust Paint Company, she had been divorced since 1927 and was soon going to stop receiving alimony payments because she had deceived Phelan as to a previous marriage.

Instead of retreating to his cabin in Webster, Wisconsin, for solace, Grimes turned to the stage. Shortly after the World Series ended, Grimes had been approached by former major league pitcher George Crable to join a vaudeville quartet known as "Ball Four, Real Ballplayers in a Delightful Number." Grimes not only agreed to join the show, but he bought half of the production company. Along with Crable, Grimes joined professional comedians Gene McCoy and William Welch. The troupe planned a series of shows on the Orpheum vaudeville circuit, where Grimes could utilize his gift of gab.

The trip brought Grimes to Wisconsin, enabling him to visit his parents and brother in Owen and his sister in Stevens Point. When he traveled to the Orpheum Theater in Madison, Grimes was asked to compare baseball crowds to those in the theater. He replied, "No matter what you do on a baseball field, somebody is always squawking, but in the theaters, the audience is either silent or applauds."[20]

Newfound celebrity left Grimes with an abbreviated winter routine. It didn't seem to hinder his confidence any, as he talked about playing another five years and approaching the National League win record of 373 held by Grover Alexander and Christy Mathewson. At 37, Grimes had accumulated 240 wins. Another 134 seemed like a stretch, but with the way he had pitched over the last three seasons, it wasn't out of the realm of possibilities, either.

In February, Grimes and Jesse Haines traveled to Hot Springs before heading to Bradenton, Florida, for spring training. On March 7, Grimes married Laura Virginia Phelan, with Haines and his wife looking on.

Early in 1931 Grimes looked as though he could go on pitching for another decade (Charles Clark Photo Collection).

The Cardinals were a confident bunch during spring training, and rightfully so, since essentially the same team was in camp. "We're fixed fine," said a self-assured Gabby Street. "We've got practically the same team we had last year, and that was a pretty good team, wasn't it? Sure it was, and we're stronger this year."[21]

There were also some up-and-comers who were ready to take a spot on the roster if a veteran wasn't careful. Pepper Martin had had brief stints with the Cardinals in 1928 and 1930 and looked to finally earn a permanent place on the roster. The talented Dizzy Dean had wowed management with his skills on the last day of the 1930 season and seemed to be a lock to make the team, but constant bickering with Gabby Street and the emergence of Paul Derringer prompted team vice president and general manager Branch Rickey to send Dean back to the Texas League after the first few weeks of the season.

Grimes looked like he just might approach Alexander's record when he shut out the Reds in his first start of the season and ripped off five consecutive victories to start the '31 campaign. In New York to face the Giants in the middle of May, he discussed one of the secrets to his longevity. "As I grow older I become more careful. I found out that trying to strike out everyone that came up to the plate didn't pay," explained Grimes. "I realized that baseball is a business and the smart thing to do is to spread that salary they pay you over as many seasons as possible."[22]

Grimes's relaxed approach didn't mean that he had lost his edge. The same weekend that he discussed his pitching philosophy with reporters he started a year-long assault on the Giants' Bill Terry, who hit .401 in 1930 — the last National Leaguer to do so. Terry's first time up, Grimes walked within a few feet of home plate and asked him, "Bill, you must have gotten a pretty good raise for hitting .401 last year." Terry nodded his head in agreement. Grimes growled, "Well. You won't hit that much this year," before returning to the mound.[23]

Instead of the usual high-and-tight pitch, Grimes's first toss sent Terry jumping out of the way of a ball thrown at his feet. It wasn't until years later at Cooperstown that Terry got an explanation. "Because," said Grimes, pausing to take a puff from his pipe, "you hit with your feet so close together that you couldn't move them as fast as you could your head."[24]

The only thing that seemed to be able to slow Grimes down was a suspension. In the first inning of a game against Brooklyn during the same trip to New York City, Gabby Street was thrown out for arguing. In the second inning, coach Clyde Wares was also tossed. Grimes, who was not pitching that day, began ruthlessly heckling the umpires from the dugout. In the fourth inning, home plate umpire Charlie Moran called time and told Grimes to get off the bench. Grimes took Moran's order literally and simply stood up in the dugout before eventually moving to the bullpen. The game was again stopped and the umpiring crew threatened a forfeit if Grimes didn't go to the clubhouse, which he finally did. The result was a $50 fine and a three-day suspension, which caused him to miss a start.

Grimes lost his first start after the suspension, but won his next three decisions to put his record at 8–1 (including win number 250 for his major league career against the Reds on May 29). By the end of May the Cardinals were in first place, a spot they held for the duration of the season, but not without a struggle.

Although St. Louis had a very strong pitching staff, there were some complications during June. After winning his first two decisions of the month, Grimes lost four of his next five after knocking down a ball against the Giants and suffering another injury to his pitching hand. The most glaring defeats were against the Dodgers at Ebbets Field on June 26 and June 28. In both games he lasted just one-third of an inning, giving up six earned runs in each start.

In addition to Grimes's struggles, the Cardinals lost Jesse Haines to a back injury in early June. Street replaced him in the rotation with rookie Paul Derringer, whose skills had prompted the demotion of Dizzy Dean. A tall, imposing figure (6-foot-4, 205 pounds) with a wicked temper, Derringer mainly had been coming out of the bullpen, accumulating a 4–0 record to date. After being inserted into the starting rotation, he went 14–8 and matched Grimes's surly mound presence.

During June, Pepper Martin finally found his way into the Cardinals' everyday lineup. The quirky, energetic Martin, who hadn't started a game in nearly three weeks, brashly burst into Branch Rickey's office and declared, "Look Mr. Rickey, I'm a little tired chasin' up and down these minor leagues and if you can't use me here, why don't you trade me so I can play every day?"[25] Rickey, not one to be pushed into deals, especially by players, saw the potential in Martin and traded Taylor Douthit to the Reds on June 15 for outfielder Wally Roettger. Martin became the everyday center fielder and Roettger became a solid bench player for St. Louis.

With many of the same faces in the lineup, the Cardinals still had a high-powered offense. Batting numbers were down all over the league, a result of a change in the composition of the baseball. Before the season a newly crafted baseball had been introduced, giving pitchers some respite. According to a writer for *Baseball Digest*, the cushioned cork center of the new ball was a "small sphere of composition cork which is molded to a layer of rubber. The first layer of black rubber is made up of two hemispheric shells. The two openings where these shells meet are sealed with a cushion of red rubber and a layer of red rubber surrounds the entire center."[26] The seams were also raised, giving pitchers a further advantage.

At the beginning of July, St. Louis's lead dipped to just a game-and-a-half over the Giants. They were given a boost when Jesse Haines returned to the rotation. Grimes also turned around his fortunes when the stifling summer heat rolled in. He lost his first start of the month on July 1, but between then and August 7 he won five of six decisions. Three of the victories came against the Cubs, all at Sportsman's Park. The Cubs had the league's top offense, but Grimes dominated them during the 1931 season with a 5–0 record and 2.40 ERA. By the end of July the Cardinals' lead stretched to eight-and-a-half games over the second-place Cubs, aided by a 17–7 homestand and a record of 21–13 for the month.

The Cardinals stormed through the month of August with a 21–8 record, their first-place lead never dropping below seven games. On August 30, St. Louis had an 11-game lead on the Giants, but after a three-day layoff and five New York victories it shrunk to eight games. It dwindled to five-and-a-half after getting swept in Pittsburgh and things only got worse. In the last game of the series Jesse Haines suffered a major shoulder injury. Haines had gone 7–1 since returning from his back injury, but he was certain that he had torn something. "It kept me awake last night, and I am afraid I injured a muscle or leader [tendon] in the shoulder. It certainly feels like something is seriously wrong," he told reporters.[27]

The pitching staff suffered another blow when Grimes, who went 3–1 in August and split his first two decisions of September, started to suffer from a dead arm. More urgent was a flare-up of his appendicitis. Even with his high threshold for pain, Grimes started to waver. He had no appetite and when he did eat, he had digestive problems. It became so intensely painful that Grimes had trouble sleeping.

When the Cardinals returned to St. Louis, Breadon and Rickey instructed Street to give Grimes some rest before the World Series. Grimes didn't seem too concerned about his health and looked forward to an opportunity to pitch again during October:

> I'm ready to pitch the first, second, third or fourth game, or any two of them, if Manager Street wants me to.... I'm hoping that Jimmy Foxx, who was hurt the other day, gets well before the series. He's the guy that broke up that fifth game with a homer and I want to show him I haven't forgotten that pitchers aren't supposed to pitch high to him.[28]

Another reason that Grimes was looking forward to the World Series was that he had agreed to a $400 contract with the Universal Service for exclusive rights to a column he would write during the World Series.

Grimes's absence from the mound lasted 11 days. During that time the Cardinals clinched the pennant, setting up a rematch with the Philadelphia Athletics. Wanting to get some mound work, Grimes convinced Street that he was well enough to pitch against the Giants on September 18. Grimes struggled mightily with his control, walking seven and hitting two batters.

During an at-bat in the top of the fifth inning, Grimes quickly got two strikes on Mel Ott. For the past few years, Grimes had pitched the Giants slugger low and outside in this situation, but this time he decided to mix in an inside spitball. Anticipating an outside pitch, Ott stepped toward the plate as Grimes released the ball. Ott tried to adjust, but was only able to turn his back and duck. The ball broke down and hit him in the back of the head. Ott crumpled to the ground as Grimes came toward the plate to argue that it was a strike. Grimes quit his barking when he saw that Ott was unconscious (years later he still contended it was a strike, saying, "Course I was a bastard for saying it after hitting him in the head, but it was!"[29]). He retreated to the dugout and watched as Ott was carried off on a stretcher and taken to St. John's Hospital. It was the only time that Grimes hit a batter in the head and thoughts of Ray Chapman undoubtedly crossed his mind. Upon the urging of his manager, Grimes continued to pitch. After the game he rushed to the hospital, where he found that Ott had suffered a concussion.

For the second time that month, Cardinals management resolved to sit Grimes until the World Series, but he was called on again to pitch a week later in a charity game against the Browns. Grimes still wasn't right and was hit hard, but the game was a success, raising $30,250 for the unemployed of St. Louis.

The Cardinals concluded the regular season with a three-game sweep of the Reds in Cincinnati, pushing their win total to 101 games. They were the first National League team since the 1913 New York Giants to reach 100 wins. Even though Grimes missed a handful of starts he still finished with a record of 17–9, making him one of six Cardinals starters with at least 11 wins. The others were Hallahan (19–9), Derringer (18–8), Haines (12–3), Syl Johnson (11–9) and Rhem (11–10). Jim Lindsey (6–4) and Allyn Stout (6–0) provided stability out of the bullpen. They were backed by a rock-solid defense that tied the Giants for first in the league with a .974 fielding percentage.

Offensively, St. Louis was led by team captain Frankie Frisch (.311, 28 stolen bases) and Chick Hafey (.349, 16 home runs, 95 RBIs), who edged out Bill Terry by three percentage points for the batting title. He was the first batting champion to accomplish that feat while wearing glasses. Other contributors included Jim Bottomley (.348), Sparky Adams (46 doubles), George Watkins (13 triples, 13 home runs) and rookies Pepper Martin (.300, 32 doubles) and Ripper Collins (.301 in 89 games). Speed was an essential part of the Cardinals' offensive attack — they led the National League in stolen bases (114) and often utilized the sacrifice bunt and the hit and run.

Like the Cardinals, the Philadelphia Athletics clinched the pennant in mid–September and spent most of the season in first place. The 107 wins were the club's third consecutive 100-win season and the highest total of the three. Lefty Grove again won the pitching Triple Crown and was the leader in several other categories (31–4, 175 strikeouts, 2.06 ERA, 27 complete games, four shutouts). For good measure, he also won 16 consecutive decisions. George Earnshaw (21–7) and Rube Walberg (20–12) followed Grove in the rotation. Al Simmons won the batting title (.390, 22 home runs, 128 RBIs), while Mickey Cochrane (.349, 17 home runs) and Jimmie Foxx (.291, 30 home runs, 120 RBIs) again decimated opposing pitching. The only weak spot in their starting lineup was the platoon at shortstop (an aging Joe Boley and 21-year-old Dib Williams).

The Athletics were more or less healthy entering the World Series, but as had been the case in the 1930 series, the Cardinals were dealing with a few injuries heading into Game One, played on October 1 in St. Louis. Jesse Haines was out indefinitely with his shoulder injury. The rest over the past month had helped to heal Grimes's arm, but how he would deal with his increasingly problematic appendicitis was unknown. Pepper Martin was also ailing with a knee injury and his status was unclear.

There was no question in Grimes's mind that he would see plenty of action in the World Series. In the weeks leading up to it, he contacted his father to obtain some "original Wisconsin slippery elm bark."[30] He had run out of his off-season cache and had been making do, with the drug store variety in St. Louis, but it left him nauseous. Nick Grimes contacted the Clark County surveyor and the two men set out to find as much of the bark as they could. According to the *Wisconsin Rapids Daily-Times*, when they finished their expedition, "The men had enough slippery elm mark for Burleigh to win several world titles."[31]

Due to his newspaper obligations, there was no pre-series posturing by Grimes, but Pepper Martin was able to fill that void. Martin showed no signs of a sore knee as he strolled through the lobby of the Forest Park Hotel where the Athletics were staying, brandishing a shotgun. He was on his way to do some trapshooting with Grimes.

Gabby Street chose Paul Derringer to oppose Lefty Grove for Game One. The Cardinals scored two runs in the second, but the Athletics countered with four in the third, all with two outs. Although Grove was shaky, allowing 12 hits (three by Pepper Martin), he held St. Louis at bay. Derringer struck out nine, compared to Grove's seven, but an Al Simmons two-run home run in the seventh put the game out of reach.

Bill Hallahan and Pepper Martin were the stars of Game Two. In the bottom of the second, Martin hit a double to left field off Earnshaw. He then stole third and scored on a Wilson fly ball to deep center field. Hallahan didn't allow a hit until the fifth inning (a single to Bing Miller). He allowed two more singles. He also lived up to his nickname of "Wild Bill," walking seven and striking out eight. St. Louis scored one more run in the bottom of the seventh when Martin singled, stole second, advanced to third on a groundball and scored on a Charlie Gelbert sacrifice bunt. The game ended in a 2–0 Cardinals victory to tie the series at 1–1 as it shifted to Philadelphia.

On the train ride from St. Louis to Philadelphia, Street was undecided on his starter for Game Three, but alluded to Grimes as the most likely candidate, if he was feeling right. Connie Mack was in the same predicament, since Lefty Grove was suffering from an injury to a finger on his pitching hand. Al Simmons told a friend that Grove "will probably do relief work exclusively for the rest of the series and not start anymore games."[32] When the two managers wrote out their starting lineup, both Grimes and Grove were starting in a rematch of the 1930 Series opener.

On October 5, a sellout crowd of 32,295 filed into Shibe Park. Once again President Hoover, now a self-proclaimed Athletics fan, was in attendance along with several members of his staff. Other attendees included John McGraw (who was writing his own column), Commissioner Landis and league presidents John Heydler (National) and William Harridge (American). President Hoover's ceremonial first pitch sailed over catcher Mickey Cochrane's head and was caught by Dolly Stark, known as "the tallest and nimblest of the umpires."[33]

Both teams went down in order in the first inning, but in the top of the second the Cardinals scored two runs after Jim Bottomley walked and scored on singles by Pepper Martin and Jimmie Wilson. Gelbert followed with a single of his own, scoring Martin. Neither team had another base runner until the top of the fourth inning when Hafey hit a single to center and went to third after Martin boomed a double off the wall in right center. Grove got two outs and looked to be on the verge of getting out of the jam with Grimes coming to the plate. After fouling off several pitches, Grimes began frustrating the Athletics and their fans by repeatedly stepping out of the box to tug on his belt, or adjust his cap. When he stepped back in, Grimes ripped a single to right field, scoring Hafey and Martin to make the score 4–0 for St. Louis.

Relying heavily on his spitball, Grimes baffled the Athletics. He didn't allow a base runner until the fourth when Max Bishop led off with a walk. Grimes then faced the minimum in the next three frames, pitching masterfully. His arm felt better than it had in weeks, if not months, but Grimes was suffering from excruciating pain in his abdomen, a symptom of his enflamed appendix. During St. Louis at bats a doctor applied ice to numb the area. The tension of each throw and movement eventually caused a crick in his neck that also needed tending to by the team trainer. Just breathing, let alone talking, was a painful experience, which put an end to his jawing.

Grimes nearly added to the Cardinals' lead in the top of the eighth inning. With two outs, Wilson dropped a bunt down the third-base line for a hit and Gelbert lined a single to left. Grimes came up and lined the first pitch to deep left field. Simmons, positioned perfectly, barely had to move to make the final out.

When Grimes made his way to the mound for the bottom of the eighth inning, the park was abuzz because the Athletics had nary a hit. The crowd only got louder when he walked Foxx to begin the inning. Bing Miller then stepped to the plate and lined the first pitch to center field for a base hit, ending Grimes's shot at immortality. After the game Grimes said of the hit, "Well, it was a fastball right smack down the middle. All he had to do was stick out his bat and hit it. I could have hit it myself."[34] He bore down and retired the next three batters, the last of which was Doc Cramer's (pinch-hitting for Grove) screaming line drive that Frisch made a diving stab on.

In the top of the ninth inning, the Cardinals scored a fifth run on a Bottomley double off the scoreboard in right field that brought in Watkins. Grimes saw none of it as he received therapy in the dugout tunnel. According to the *Chicago Tribune*, "The husky trainer of the National League champions grasped him about the chest from behind and squeezed him until something cracked. Then he scrambled back out there, tears in his eyes and fighting mad, determined to pitch that last inning."[35] Grimes later claimed that the cracking noise had been his sternum.[36]

With a 5–0 lead, Grimes let the first batter of the bottom of the ninth, Max Bishop, work the count to 3–2 before grounding out to first base. Seeing that Grimes was tiring, Street had Sylvester Johnson hastily warm up. The next batter, Haas, hit a ball that looked destined for center field until Grimes deflected it with his bare hand. It bounced to Gelbert at shortstop, who made the relay to first base for the out. Grimes was in serious pain from the impact, shaking a finger in obvious discomfort. Street, the team trainer and his teammates rushed to his side, but after several minutes, Grimes convinced his manager to let him finish the game. Grimes walked Mickey Cochrane, bringing up Simmons. With the count 2–0, Grimes tried to get a fastball over for a strike. Simmons hit it into the right-field stands for a two-run home run. Grimes remained composed, striking out Foxx to end the game.

After the win, Grimes was showered with praise from both sides. Gabby Street called it, "One of the greatest games I ever saw."[37] Connie Mack said, "He surprised me both as a pitcher and a batter."[38] In a newspaper column of his own, Philadelphia's Eddie Collins said, "I think Burleigh Grimes deserves all the credit in the world for going in and pitching a whale of a game, and we are not going to try to alibi a thing." Looking ahead to a chance to see Grimes again, the Athletics captain added, "but [we] are ready and willing to hand it to him."[39]

Grimes, whose Universal Services contract said he was supposed to contain his commentary for his column, couldn't repress his happiness after finally getting some revenge for the 1930 World Series. "I knew I could take those guys," wrote Grimes. "They beat me twice last year when I had them all wrapped up, but they couldn't do it today."[40]

The badly swollen digit bothered Grimes so much during the night that he went to Jefferson Hospital in the morning for x-rays. Much to his relief

Commissioner Kenesaw Mountain Landis and Grimes exchange pleasantries before Game Three of the 1931 World Series in Philadelphia (Charles Clark Photo Collection).

they came back negative. In his column Grimes vowed that the finger would "not interfere with any more pitching I may be called on to do in the series."[41]

Later that day in Game Four, it was George Earnshaw's turn to allow only two hits to the Cardinals. Syl Johnson didn't pitch poorly for St. Louis, but a run-scoring double by Simmons in the first inning was all Earnshaw needed. He didn't allow a base runner until the fourth inning, nor a hit until the fifth (a Pepper Martin single). The Athletics tacked on two more in the sixth. The Cardinals' only other hit was a double to deep left by Martin in the eighth. The game belonged to Earnshaw, but everyone continued to talk about Martin, who was 8-for-14 with four doubles and as many stolen bases in the Series. Grimes didn't mince words in his assessment of Martin: "I consider him the greatest young player in the game today."[42]

Martin added to his growing legend in Game Five. Now batting cleanup, he went 3-for-4 with four runs batted in, including a two-run home run in the sixth inning. The Athletics went through three pitchers, while Bill Hallahan exhibited surprising control for the Cardinals, walking just one in the 5–1 victory to secure his second win of the series. The Cardinals were just a game away from the World Series crown as they headed back to St. Louis.

In a rematch of the first game, Game Six looked like it was going to be a pitchers' duel between Grove and Derringer. The two exchanged scoreless innings until the fifth when Philadelphia broke the game open. After Foxx reached on a throwing error by Gelbert, Derringer became rattled. By the time the inning ended, he had walked four and had allowed two hits and four unearned runs. St. Louis got one run back in the sixth inning on a Frisch single, but the Athletics responded with four more runs in the seventh, all with two out. Grove held Martin hitless for the first time in the series, as the 8–1 Philadelphia victory evened the series at three games apiece.

According to betting commissioner Jack Doyle, the odds for the deciding seventh game were "4 to 5 against the White Elephants [Athletics] and even money against the Red Birds [Cardinals]."[43] In the eyes of many, the Athletics had an upper hand with a healthy, rested Earnshaw going against the banged-up Grimes. It wasn't a good sign for the Cardinals when the smallest crowd of the series (20,805) showed up for the 1 P.M. start.

Before the game Grimes received the appendix "freezing" treatment. He then went out and retired the Athletics' first three batters before the Cardinals jumped all over Earnshaw in their half to take a 2–0 lead. The first two batters (Andy High and George Watkins) hit bloop singles and then scored on a wild pitch and a strikeout that bounced away from Cochrane. The Cardinals scored two more in the bottom of the third on a towering two-run home run by

George Watkins that sailed over the right-field pavilion, bouncing on the roof before dropping to the street below. St. Louis now led 4–0.

Over the next five innings neither team scored. Grimes continued his gritty performance and Earnshaw settled down and allowed just one hit, an Andy High single in the bottom of the eighth. Grimes's high point during those frames came in the seventh inning when he struck out the side, including Simmons and Foxx, the latter looking. His contributions at the plate were nonexistent, however. He struck out twice and barely made it out of the batter's box when he grounded out to third base. His focus was just on making it through the game on the mound; any nonessential energy exerted was a waste.

After each turn on the mound, Grimes returned to the dugout to have ice applied to his abdomen. In agony and sweating profusely, he shed several pounds during the contest. Exhausted and in extreme pain, Grimes walked to the mound in the ninth inning. The first batter, Simmons, worked the count full before walking. Grimes was laboring as he walked around the mound and took big, painful breaths in between each pitch, agitating his sternum. He then was helped by his catcher, Jimmie Wilson, who sprinted toward the box seats behind the plate to make an outstanding catch of a foul ball off the bat of Jimmie Foxx. The series momentarily looked to be over when Bing Miller hit an apparent double-play grounder to Gelbert at shortstop, but Miller beat Frisch's relay from second base, a call that was vehemently protested by the Cardinals.

Jimmy Dykes then walked, Grimes's fourth free pass over the last two innings. Dib Williams followed with a bouncer just over Andy High at third base, the ball tipping his glove as it bounded into left field. Doc Cramer was brought in to hit for the pitcher (Rube Walberg) and looped a single into center field to score Miller and Dykes, pushing the scored to 4–2 with runners on first and second. Grimes was completely fatigued and put up little fight when Street replaced him with Bill Hallahan. Grimes made his way to the Cardinals' dugout, where he collapsed. Max Bishop worked the count to full before lifting a fly ball to center. Pepper Martin made an easy catch to give the Cardinals their second World Series title.

Grimes finally had his elusive first ring. After the game he exchanged handshakes with Commissioner Landis at his box seat and made his way over to the Athletics clubhouse to congratulate them on a well-played series. After the game Grimes humbly said, "I had a hard time with those boys. They're great hitters. They had me bearing down all the way."[44]

Awards season brought more recognition to the Cardinals. 1931 was the first year that each league named an MVP. Frankie Frisch won the National

League's award, while Lefty Grove won the American Leagues. Three other Cardinals received votes: Chick Hafey, Sparky Adams, and Jim Bottomley. Grimes, Martin, Johnson and Hallahan all received no votes, but were given an honorable mention.

Grimes was enjoying his life in Missouri so much that he decided to take up residence full-time rather than spend another year living out of a hotel. He and his wife, Laura, purchased a sizable plot of land in New Haven, located in the Missouri River bluff land along the Lewis and Clark Trail. The couple then made the 230-acre manor their own, stocking it with horses and livestock from Grimes's Ohio farm. Though he was supposed to be convalescing, Grimes, with the help of his brother Shurleigh, cut timber and plotted land for crops for next year's harvest. They also put a modern heating system in the 70-year-old house and made plans for a number of updates for the following spring.

Grimes had declared his intent to remain in Missouri, but his contact with the Cardinals had been minimal. Unbeknownst to him, the team had begun taking offers on him shortly after the season ended. He had turned 38 in August, had a large contract ($18,000) and his health was a major question mark. Grimes also had expressed interest managing in the near future, something that seemed unlikely in St. Louis given the success that Street was having. St. Louis had a deep pitching staff and planned to add Dizzy Dean full-time after he had dominated the Texas League in 1931. All of those factors led to Grimes being traded on December 9 to the Chicago Cubs in exchange for outfielder Hack Wilson and left-handed pitcher Bud Teachout.

Wilson was just a few years removed from his remarkable 56-homer, 191-RBI season of 1930. He had had a down season in 1931, falling out of favor with player-manager Rogers Hornsby. Wilson's penchant for alcohol began to catch up with him, as he often showed up for games drunk or hung over and frequently got in scuffles on and off the field. He never suited up for the Cardinals and was traded a month later to Brooklyn. Teachout pitched just one inning with St. Louis before ending his professional career.

Grimes was disappointed, but took the trade in stride: "That's why baseball clubs usually make trades, to strengthen. I know of no other reason why the Cards should want to trade me." He had been playing professionally long enough to know that it wasn't anything personal: "I've done a lot of moving about in baseball, and must take it as part of the business."[45]

In late December, Grimes received an accolade for his time in a St. Louis uniform. He finished tied for sixth place with Yale football captain Albie Booth and heavyweight champion Max Schmeling for the Associated Press Male Athlete of the Year. The winner was Pepper Martin.

8

Grizzled Veteran, 1932–1934

In 1919, William Wrigley, then a shareholder of the Chicago Cubs, had bought Catalina Island off the coast of southern California. Two years later, he bought a controlling interest in the club and in 1922 he sent his team to the coast by train, making the last leg of the trip to the island by steamship. The players stayed at the swank Hotel St. Catherine and trained at a nearby ballfield in Avalon Canyon that Wrigley built with dimensions identical to Wrigley Field.

Grimes was one of the second wave of Cubs to head west for training in February 1932. He boarded the Los Angeles Limited in Omaha, Nebraska, and mingled with new teammates Kiki Cuyler, Riggs Stephenson, and captain Charlie Grimm. He talked pitching with Guy Bush and good friend Dutch Henry, who had been invited to camp but in the end wouldn't make the team. Due to his health issues, Grimes had skipped his annual trip to Hot Springs for the first time in more than a decade. He was overweight and looked forward to getting back into playing shape.

The mood on Catalina was different than in years past. The Cubs organization was in disarray. Less than a month earlier, on January 26, 1932, William Wrigley passed away at the age of 70 following a stroke. His successor as owner was his son, Phillip K. Wrigley, who professed to having no interest in the game of baseball. He soon passed over responsibilities to team president Bill Veeck. Veeck's new duties caused a large problem for the team — he despised manager Rogers Hornsby. In fact, Hornsby's only ally in the organization had been the late William Wrigley.

Hornsby, entering his second full season as manager of the Cubs, hadn't changed any in the five seasons since he and Grimes last shared a clubhouse. The disenchantment of his players was at an all-time high, since he had banned alcohol and tobacco from the clubhouse. Off the field he forbade them from frequenting the hotspots of the Chicago nightlife, while he continued to lose money at the racetrack. He even chided Catholic players who had the audacity to wear religious medals around their neck, particularly the devout Kiki Cuyler.[1]

When Grimes finally arrived on Catalina Island, he dove headlong into workouts. He wore a rubber shirt, nicknamed a "Goodyear kimono," whenever possible to drop the extra pounds. Grimes spent a lot of time working out with his new catcher Gabby Hartnett, who had never caught a spitball. Also in camp was his old catcher Zach Taylor, but he was buried in the depth chart behind Hartnett and Rollie Hemsley, whom Hornsby preferred over Hartnett for his receiving skills. Grimes overexerted himself and developed a sore arm, causing him to miss several days. Once he recovered, Grimes threw several innings with varying degrees of success.

As Chicago's elder statesman, Grimes looked to round out a veteran rotation of Charlie Root, Pat Malone and Guy Bush, but shortly before the Cubs headed east to start the season Grimes contracted influenza and an infected tooth that was eventually removed. The two ailments caused him to miss the first three weeks of the season, but led to the emergence of young right-hander Lon Warneke, who had added five miles an hour to his fastball since the previous season. He went 4–0 in place of Grimes. When Grimes did return in early May, the Cubs were in first place despite playing without offensive cog Kiki Cuyler, who had broken his foot while rounding first base against Pittsburgh on April 24.

Grimes's first appearance of the year came against Brooklyn on May 5, throwing the final two innings, giving up one hit and walking one. Three days later he made his first start opposing the Dodgers' Dazzy Vance. Grimes threw a complete-game victory, while Vance lasted all of 13 batters. Grimes won his next two starts, a 12-inning victory over the Reds on May 19, and a satisfying 3–0 shutout of the Cardinals in St. Louis on May 25 that moved his record to 3–0.

Besides veterans Charlie Grimm and Gabby Hartnett, the Cubs were succeeding with an unproven lineup. After playing sparingly in 1931, second-year players Billy Herman (second base) and Billy Jurges (shortstop) were starting frequently. Rookie Stan Hack had such a good spring training that he was given the third base job for the first month and a half. All three were spelled by veteran Woody English. In Cuyler's absence, Hornsby shuffled different players in and out, including Riggs Stephenson, Vince Barton, Johnny Moore, Danny Taylor and Lance Richbourg.

Hornsby wasn't sold on the lineup and his willingness to convey that sentiment to the press led to a blowup with Veeck. Hornsby inserted himself into the outfield and cleanup position during a two-week period in late May and early June, but was a shell of his former self. An ankle injury suffered during spring training only exacerbated his previous foot problems, making him slow in the field. He also provided little pop in the middle of the lineup

(.167, two doubles, 1 home run, 1 RBI). He finally took himself out of the lineup when Cuyler returned from his injury in mid–June.

Hornsby's lack of faith in the lineup and stifling rules couldn't dampen the spirits of the first-place Cubs. On a June afternoon in Brooklyn, *Chicago Tribune* reporter Ed Prell walked into a loose clubhouse. Charlie Grimm was picking his banjo, while Lon Warneke walked around with cotton taped to his chin, imitating an elderly man from his home state of Arkansas. Billy Herman discovered that his clothes were all tied in knots. Woody English, Stanley Hack and Bill Jurges hauled a ladder into the clubhouse to tie a pair of Grimes's moccasins to a ceiling pipe. When Grimes emerged,

Grimes wearing his "Goodyear Kimono" during Chicago Cubs spring training on Catalina Island, 1932 (Cleveland Public Library).

he was met by a round of applause before Pat Malone pointed to the ceiling where his moccasins hung.

The Cubs spent all but two games away from Wrigley Field during June, finishing with a 9–14 record for the month. Still, they returned to Chicago in second place, just a half-game behind the Pirates. Grimes accounted for over a third of the team's losses during June, going 1–5. His only win came on June 16, a 2–1 defeat of Carl Hubbell and the Giants at the Polo Grounds.

On July 4, in Pittsburgh, Grimes was knocked out in the second inning and charged with five runs. When the Cubs boarded the train for Chicago they were in third place, two-and-a-half games behind Pittsburgh and one-and-a-half games behind the surprising Boston Braves.

The new month got even worse when shortstop Billy Jurges was shot and nearly killed in the early morning hours of July 7 by a jilted lover. While Jurges slept in his room at the Hotel Carlos on Sheffield Avenue, Violet Popovich Heindel-Valli, a chorus girl whom he had dated on and off since arriving in Chicago in 1931, came to his door. The details have become muddled over time, but supposedly she was drunk and wanted to talk about their relationship. She requested a glass of water and when Jurges returned with it, Valli was holding a pistol. A struggle ensued and three shots were fired. One caused a minor wound to Jurges's left pinkie, but another bounced off his rib and exited through his right shoulder. Violet also was hit once in the arm. Jurges didn't press charges and was back in uniform 16 days later, but wasn't the same player.

Once again Hornsby, tried to spark the team by inserting himself into the lineup at third base for the struggling Stanley Hack, but his output was similar to a month earlier — slow of foot and a shaky bat. When Jurges returned, Hornsby took himself out of the lineup for good.

Grimes was dropped from the starting rotation in early July. He was given a spot start on July 20 at the Polo Grounds, but squandered the opportunity. He failed to make it out of the fourth inning and gave up seven runs, all earned. His record was now 4–9, after having started the season 3–0. Hornsby said that Grimes was again suffering from an attack of appendicitis. Grimes denied the assertion, saying it was "just old-fashioned misery in the stomach."[2] Reports also surfaced that he was suffering from arm problems, another claim that Grimes brushed off.

The Cubs held tight to their grasp on second place throughout July, going 17–15, but the five-and-a-half games between them and the Pirates seemed much larger. The club just couldn't seem to make a move on the wide-open pennant race. When the Cubs left on a three-week road trip in July 25, Bill Veeck accompanied the team to assess what could be done to improve their place in the standings. He soon decided what he needed to do — get rid of the manager.

Veeck and Hornsby had exchanged words one week earlier when Hornsby brushed off a scouting report meeting with his pitchers to discuss Pittsburgh's hitters. Hornsby told Veeck to "pay me off" if he didn't like the way he was managing.[3] What Veeck saw during the start of the road trip prompted him to do just that.

Questionable managerial decisions on Hornsby's part led to a conference with Veeck as the team traveled from Brooklyn to Philadelphia. Upon arrival, they went immediately to the Ben Franklin Hotel to discuss the matter further. A few hours later, they emerged from Veeck's room to announce that Hornsby had passed waivers and was now a free agent.

The two men appeared cordial during the impromptu press conference. When asked if there was a rift between them, Veeck replied, "There has been no quarrel, has there Rog?" Hornsby laughed embarrassedly and said, "I guess we won't call it a quarrel. Only big differences of opinion about the ball club and the way it should be handled."[4]

Similar to his exit from St. Louis following the 1926 World Series, an underlying reason for Hornsby's dismissal was his insistence on betting on horses. Veeck was particularly concerned with Hornsby's habit of borrowing money from his players. The team president denied these allegations to the press, however. "There is positively nothing to it," said Veeck. "The only reason Hornsby was discharged as manager is because we disagreed over his handling of the team."[5]

The managerial vacancy was a perfect opportunity for Grimes to step in, but immediately after talking to reporters Veeck summoned Charlie Grimm to his room. Grimm thought he was going to being punished for something, so he was shocked to find that Veeck wanted him to be the team's new manager. After making sure that Hornsby was already out, Grimm agreed. He expressed excitement about the opportunity: "I know that I have the friendship of all the other 22 active players on the team and I am confident that they will give me their support in my ideas about how the team should be handled."[6]

Grimm's first order of business was to name Woody English team captain. Grimm also indicated that he would rely heavily on the input of English, Gabby Hartnett and Billy Herman. Despite his disappointing record and being passed over as manager, Grimes became a valuable resource as well, taking on the role of informal pitching coach. According to the *Chicago Tribune*, "Grimes has assisted the Cubs in a way that is just as important as if he had won in the box with the same consistency of former years."[7]

A week after Grimm took over as manager, the Cubs returned to Chicago in first place, a half-game in front of the Pirates. A much better team at home than on the road, a 20-game homestand lay ahead. The long stretch at Wrigley gave them an opportunity to pad their lead.

Over the next three weeks, the Cubs played nearly flawless ball. They won the first three games against the Braves, including back-to-back extra-inning games that went 19 and 15 innings, respectively. They lost the series finale, 6–5, but then went on a 14-game winning streak, sweeping the Phillies, Dodgers and Giants and taking the first two games from the Cardinals. Dizzy Dean snapped the streak with a 3–0 shutout, but the Cubs came back the next day with a 3–0 shutout by Warneke. In all, Chicago won 18 of 20 games during the homestand and pushed its lead on the Pirates to seven games.

Grimes contributed to the impressive run, starting two games and pitching in five. He only came away as the pitcher of record in one game, a 6–1 complete-game victory in the first game of a doubleheader against the Giants on August 27. In that game, he also picked up two hits, stole a base, scored a run and drove in one.

During their winning streak, Chicago's spark came from an unlikely source. Mark Koenig, a former Yankee and now property of the Detroit Tigers, had been acquired from the Mission Reds of the Pacific Coast League on August 5. The utility infielder took over at shortstop for the struggling Jurges on August 19 and batted .353 in 33 games.

The Cubs didn't falter in September and when it became apparent that they were going to clinch the pennant, questions about Grimm's rotation for the World Series surfaced. His pitching staff had led the league in ERA and he had four solid starters, including MVP runner-up Lon Warneke, who led the league in wins (22–6), ERA (2.37) and shutouts (4). Warneke was backed by veterans Guy Bush (19–11), Charlie Root (15–10) and Pat Malone (15–17). Grimes (6–11) wouldn't be used as a starter, but the Cubs hoped that he would be able to replicate his performance from the previous October. Offensively, the Cubs were led by Riggs Stephenson (.324, 49 doubles), Billy Herman (.314, 42 doubles, 102 runs), Johnny Moore (.305, 13 home runs), Charlie Grimm (.307), Kiki Cuyler (.291, 10 home runs) and Gabby Hartnett (12 home runs).

Chicago's offense paled in comparison to the one fielded by its World Series adversary, the 107-win New York Yankees. The Cubs' priority was stopping Lou Gehrig (.349, 42 doubles, 34 home runs, 151 RBIs) and Babe Ruth (.341, 41 home runs, 137 RBIs), but Earle Combs (.321), Bill Dickey (.310), Tony Lazzeri (.300, 113 RBIs) and Ben Chapman (.299, 108 RBIs, 38 stolen bases) could also do some damage. The Yankees also had a formidable four-man rotation to match the Cubs. They were led by 23-year-old Lefty Gomez (24–7), followed by Red Ruffing (18–7), Johnny Allen (17–4) and George Pipgras (16–9).

Leading up to Game One at Yankee Stadium, a few subplots were taking shape. There was of course the obvious fact that Joe McCarthy, manager of the Yankees, was facing the team that had dismissed him in the middle of the 1930 pennant race. McCarthy saw the series as a "tossup," but Grimm spoke with the bravado that got the team there: "It's going to be a great series, and, naturally, I think we'll win."[8]

A much more inflammatory issue took precedence when Cubs players voted Mark Koenig only half a World Series share. When the Yankees caught wind of this, they were incensed, particularly Babe Ruth, who had been close to Koenig during his days on the Yankees. A war of words erupted in the days prior to the series, which then led to one of the most famous moments in World Series history.

An estimated crowd of 69,000 was expected for Game One on September 28, but it rained the night before and into the early morning. Storms were forecast during game time, leading to a smaller crowd of 41,459 for the opening game. The Yankees had gone an astonishing 62–15 at home during the regular season, but the loose Cubs got out to an early lead. In the top of the first inning, they scored two runs off Red Ruffing, highlighted by a Babe Ruth error that brought Chicago's bench jockeys (including Grimes) to the top step of the dugout. After Herman led off with a single, English followed with a single of his own to right field. The ball got by Ruth and rolled all the way to the wall, allowing Herman to score and English to move to third. He scored two batters later on a Riggs Stephenson single, giving the Cubs an early 2–0 lead.

Chicago starter Guy Bush faced the minimum number of Yankees over the first three innings. He was pitching with a badly injured index finger on his right hand, the tip having been pulled away from the nail while trying to field a ball during the last few weeks of the season. He was a fierce competitor, however, and gave no thought to missing the World Series. Bush had picked up the Cubs' only win in the 1929 World Series against the Philadelphia Athletics, and since then had mastered a screwball. With rain falling, the Yankees got to him the second time around the order. He walked Combs, who advanced to second on a Joe Sewell groundout. Ruth then rapped a single to score Combs, making the score 2–1. Gehrig, the next batter, sent a ball deep into the right-field bleachers. Just like that, the score was 3–2, New York.

The score stayed that way until the bottom of the sixth inning. Bush walked Sewell, Ruth and Gehrig to load the bases, prompting Grimm to send Grimes out to the bullpen to warm up. After retiring Lazzeri, Bush gave up a two-run single to Dickey, followed by a fielder's choice by Chapman that scored Gehrig. Bush then walked Frank Crosetti to load the bases again. Grimm had seen enough, replacing Bush with Grimes.

From the start Grimes was wild, but with a drawn-in infield he was able to induce a fielder's choice by Red Ruffing. Combs followed with a single to center, driving in two more runs to make the score 8–2. The Cubs got two runs back in the top of the seventh, but New York replied with two runs of their own off Grimes on an infield single, a sacrifice fly and a wild pitch. Grimes was removed for a pinch hitter in the eighth after the Cubs hit a double and triple to start the inning. The parade of runs continued until the game ended in a 12–6 New York victory.

With much more favorable weather conditions, nearly 10,000 more fans showed up for Game Two. The game featured two 23-year-old starting pitchers who were considered rising stars, Lon Warneke and Lefty Gomez. Once again the Cubs scored in the top of the first inning. The 1–0 lead was quickly erased in the bottom of the first. Warneke was wild, walking the first two batters. He struck out Babe Ruth, which the Chicago bench gave Ruth an earful about, but Gehrig singled in a run and Bill Dickey singled in another run two batters later for a 2–1 lead. The Cubs tied the score in the top of the third, but a two-out, two-run single by Chapman in the bottom of the inning gave the Yankees the lead for good. New York added one more run on a Dickey single in the fifth inning and Gomez shut down the Cubs the rest of the way.

Following the game Ruth ripped the Cubs publicly. "Sure I'm on 'em," he said. At the forefront of his mind was the poor treatment of his former friend and teammate Mark Koenig. "I hope we beat 'em four straight. They gave Koenig and Hornsby a sour deal in their players' cut. They're chiselers and I tell 'em so."[9]

It was a quiet train ride back to Chicago, but the Cubs were happy to be heading home, where even during the throes of the Depression they had led the major leagues in attendance (974,688). A crowd of nearly 50,000 flocked to Wrigley Field on Saturday, October 1. Inadequate turnstiles led hundreds of fans to stand in line for up to 20 minutes after the first pitch. By the time many of them had taken their seats, the Yankees were leading 3–0.

Chicago's veteran pitcher Charlie Root got off to a rough start. Leadoff batter Earle Combs got on base on a throwing error by Billy Jurges. Root walked Sewell and Babe Ruth pulled a low outside fastball for a towering home run to right-center field, where a stiff wind was blowing out. The Cubs countered in the bottom of the first inning on a wind-aided double by Cuyler to score Herman, but the Yankees added another home run in the third inning, this one by Lou Gehrig, who hit a low outside curveball into the jet stream in right field to make the score 4–1. The Cubs scored two in the bottom half, highlighted by a Cuyler home run to right and a Charlie Grimm run-scoring double, pulling them within a run. The next inning they tied the game on an error by Lazerri.

In the top of the fifth inning, Charlie Root was set to face Sewell, Ruth and Gehrig. What followed was one of the most famous and hotly contested incidents in the history of the game. After Sewell had been retired on a ground-out, Babe Ruth stepped to the plate. He was met by a series of acid-tongued barbs from Grimes, Pat Malone, Guy Bush, Bob Smith and team trainer Andy Lotshaw, who were at the edge of the dugout. Before Ruth stepped into the batter's box, out of the corner of his eye he saw a lemon rolling his way. When he looked up, Malone and Grimes had their thumbs in their ears wiggling their fingers.

Distracted, Ruth stepped into bat and got two quick strikes on him without taking the bat off his shoulder. This only increased the volume of his tormentors. According to Irving Vaughan of the *Chicago Tribune*, Ruth stepped out of the batter's box and addressed his tormentors with a smile. "That's only two strikes, boys. I still have one coming," he said, holding up one finger toward the Cubs dugout.[10] Ruth stepped back in and sent a low outside curveball from Root to center field. His second home run of the game was a mammoth blast that sailed over the 436-foot sign, past the flag pole and off the box office at Waveland and Sheffield avenues, putting New York in front, 5–4.

Sportswriter Edward Burns said, "Ruth resumed his oratory the minute he threw 'down' his bat. He bellowed every foot of the way around the bases, accompanying derisive roarings with wild and eloquent gesticulations."[11]

Gehrig was next up and sent the first offering from Root into the right-field bleachers for his second homer of the game, extending the lead to 6–4. Pipgras shut down the Cubs until the ninth inning when Gabby Hartnett led off with a home run to make the score 7–5 (the Yankees having added to their lead with a crucial insurance run in the top of the ninth). Jurges followed with a single and the Cubs had some momentum. McCarthy brought in Herb Pennock, who got the final three outs without further incident.

It wasn't until after the game that the legend of the "Called Shot" took shape. A few writers claimed that Ruth had pointed to center field, a story that the slugger didn't deny. However, it's unlikely that he did so. Billy Herman shared the sentiment of many. "I can tell you just what would have happened if Ruth had tried that — he never would have got a pitch to hit. Root would have had him with his feet up in the air," said Herman.[12]

The lore of Ruth's called shot became a source of irritation to Grimes as the years passed. In one of his conversations with author Donald Honig, Grimes expressed his displeasure with the myth: "Just to show you how people can be led along. I had a good friend who was at the game, and he swore to me later that Ruth pointed to the bleachers. 'Forget it,' I'd tell him, 'I don't want to hear about it.'"[13]

Another first-inning scoring barrage took place the next day. The Yankees started Game Four by jumping all over Guy Bush, whose raw right index finger greatly affected his grip on the ball. He lasted just five batters and was pulled with the bases loaded, one out and the score 1–0. Grimm put in Lon Warneke, who retired the next two batters without further damage. Yankees starter Johnny Allen didn't make it out of the first inning either. The Cubs batted around, highlighted by a Frank Demaree two-run home run. Chicago led 4–1 after one inning.

The Yankees got two runs back on a two-out Tony Lazzeri home run during a long third inning. Warneke retired the first two batters, but while pitching to Gehrig something suddenly snapped in his pitching arm. Without his fastball, the pitcher was in trouble. Lazzeri followed Gehrig with a home run and two successive singles came next, before Warneke coaxed a groundout from Crosetti. Warneke said nothing to Grimm about the injury and went back out for the fourth. After giving up a single and walk, Grimm came out and had to practically wrestle the ball away from Warneke, replacing him with 36-year-old long reliever Jackie May, pitching in the first World Series in the final season of his 14-year career.

The left-handed May held the Yankees scoreless in the fifth inning, but in the sixth New York took a 5–4 lead on a Gehrig single. The Cubs tied the game on a throwing error by shortstop Frank Crosetti in the bottom half of the inning, but in the top of the seventh the Yankees scored four runs for a 9–5 lead.

In the top of the ninth, with the game all but out of reach, Grimm gave a tip of the cap to Grimes by putting him in the game. Many thought this was the spitballer's farewell. Grimes was met by a cordial round of applause when he took the mound, but it was all downhill from there. Earle Combs swatted the first offering into the right-field bleachers. Sewell and Ruth hit sharp ground balls to Grimm at first base for outs. Grimes walked Gehrig, who then scored on Lazzeri's second home run of the game. Dickey singled and scored on a Chapman double to make the score 13–5.

The Cubs scored one run in the bottom of the ninth, but Grimes was already in the Chicago clubhouse, embarrassed by his performance. According to Irving Vaughan of the *Chicago Tribune*, when the rest of the team entered the room the mood was surprisingly upbeat. "The boys knew they had been beaten by a superior foe and that was sufficient consolation," Vaughn wrote. Grimes was the only one who was outwardly bothered by the loss. Stung by the thrashing he had taken in the ninth inning, Grimes "berated newspapermen who had dared to point out the team's weaknesses in the first two games."[14] Vaughan predicted Grimes would be playing elsewhere in 1933, if he played at all.

Shortly after the series Grimes convinced his teammates to join him in a scheme to cash in on their celebrity from the World Series. Woody English remembered Grimes saying, "Let me be the agent and we'll get all kinds of money from different companies. We'll let them use our names on this and that." The results were meager. "You know what we wound up with?" said English. "A hundred dollars from Wheaties and a hundred dollars from Camel cigarettes. There were so darn many boxes of Wheaties up in the clubhouse, you could never believe it!"[15]

There were more pressing issues for Grimes. A month after the World Series ended, he was scheduled for surgery. After a decade of dealing with problems with his appendix he traveled to St. Louis to have Cardinals physician Robert Hyland, a pioneer of sports medicine, remove the troubled organ.

Following the procedure, Grimes spent a month-and-a-half recovering at his farm near New Haven. He was told to rest and drink pitchers of milk to aid in the recovery process. The inactivity led his weight to balloon to nearly 200 pounds, but by early January he was already feeling much better. He regretted delaying the procedure, saying, "Haven't felt so good for years. Guess I put off the operation longer than I should."[16] He looked forward to returning to his old training regimen: "I'm a new man now. Jump out of bed every morning at 6 and turn in every evening at 7:30. Don't feel any weakness at all."[17]

Chicago's World Series team, though aging, was intact and had added another power bat to the lineup in Babe Herman. Herman, who had spent the 1932 season with the Reds after six seasons in Brooklyn, was acquired in November for catcher Rollie Hemsley, outfielders Johnny Moore and Lance Richbourg and pitcher Bob Smith. The addition of Herman (unrelated to new teammate Billy Herman) had many picking the Cubs to repeat.

When the 39-year-old Grimes arrived on Catalina Island he was noticeably more fit than the previous spring, when he had arrived out-of-shape and overweight. He took part in all the drills and even played right field in an intrasquad scrimmage. A few weeks into camp, however, he started to have digestive issues after eating a tainted abalone steak. He then came down with the flu, which kept him in bed for a number of days.

On March 10, Grimes was still on bed rest. Shortly after the team returned to the hotel after a workout, a severe earthquake hit California. As Grimes's eighth-floor room shook, he bolted out of bed and headed for the elevator, which wasn't running. He took the stairs and congregated in the street with his shaken teammates. Though no one was injured, several players, including Grimes, felt traumatized by the earthquake.

Grimes recovered from his illnesses and pitched on a regular basis during the last few weeks of spring training. The Cubs suffered a major blow when Kiki Cuyler fractured his ankle on March 29 while stealing a base against the Giants.

In a relief role, Grimes got into his first game of the season on April 15. He threw two innings, gave up three runs and picked up the loss in a 6–4 defeat at the hands of the Pirates on a bone-chilling day in Chicago. He didn't see the mound for another two weeks, when the Cubs, losers of five of their last six, needed a spark. Grimes provided it, shutting out the Reds 7–0 on just three hits. He won again a week later on May 7, going the distance against the Braves. He contributed two hits and three RBIs in the 11–2 win.

Grimes was beginning to turn some heads with the integral role he was playing in Chicago's struggling rotation. On May 13 he threw 4⅓ innings of one-hit ball to preserve a victory against the Phillies. His success forced Grimm to move him to the starting rotation. Grimes suffered a few hard-luck losses in his return to the rotation (a 3–0 loss to the Giants on May 18 and a 2–1 loss to the Pirates on May 30) and was hit hard in others, losing all five starts. Thereafter he was relegated to the bullpen.

From May 28 to July 8, the Cubs spent all but one day in fourth place. After years of support by their loyal fan base, the Great Depression and a perceived lackadaisical performance by veterans led to a decline in attendance at Wrigley Field. A sparse crowd saw Grimes pick up the victory on July 23 against the Phillies to move the club within two games of first place. However, the Cubs never got closer to the top of the standings.

A week later, on July 30, Grimes was released by the Cubs. The next day he was signed by St. Louis. Grimes looked forward to the challenge. "I still believe that if I can get enough work I'll be able to pitch winning baseball," said Grimes confidently. "I'm in good condition and will be ready for work when I report to Frisch."[18]

The Cardinals were in a state of change and looking for a spark. In the past week, Gabby Street had been relieved of his managerial duties after a 46–45 start. Frankie Frisch was named manager and Rogers Hornsby was released so that no friction would arise between the two. The Cardinals were ripe for the spark that Grimes had provided for them his first time around in St. Louis, but he was of little help.

Grimes started his first game for the Cardinals on August 4 in Pittsburgh and was as combative as ever. In the second inning, he exchanged words with his old friend Pie Traynor after the Pirates third baseman slid hard into St. Louis catcher Jimmie Wilson. The benches cleared, but the players were separated before any blows could be exchanged. Grimes pitched well, but three St. Louis errors in the bottom of the seventh allowed the Pirates to tie the game at four. He received a no decision in the 5–4 Pittsburgh win.

Less than a week later, on August 9, Grimes was on the mound at Wrigley Field against his former teammates. A few days before, Edward Burns of the *Chicago Tribune* had written a scathing article about the veterans on the Cubs. According to Burns, "William Veeck had soured on the idea of being kind to men possessed of loud voices, glowing reminiscences and little remaining talent." Burns singled out Grimes, referring to him as a "clubhouse lawyer" who "thought that through enthusiastic speeches and pep talks he would be able to hang around long enough to share in a fourth successive World Series pot in case the Cubs repeated."[19] Grimes recorded just one out in the first inning before being taken out. He gave up five runs (four earned), highlighted by a three-run home run by Babe Herman and was saddled with the loss in the 10–7 Cubs win.

Grimes finished up a 3–2 Cardinals victory on August 12 against the Reds, but his season ended just four days later in Philadelphia. Pain in his arm forced him to leave in the middle of the fifth inning. He consulted team physician Robert Hyland, who found "several strained ligaments in Grimes's throwing shoulder."[20] Grimes stayed on for a few weeks acting as a coach, but not being able to pitch was too much for him to bear. Frisch finally sent him home in late August and gave him permission to rejoin the team when he felt like it.

The move by Frisch sparked rumors that Grimes was going to manage the Brooklyn Dodgers in 1934. Frisch did nothing to squelch them, saying that he would not stand in Grimes's way if he had a chance to become a manager. Those rumblings were put to rest when the Dodgers re-signed Max Carey to mange again in '34.

Grimes retreated to his New Haven farm determined to play again in 1934. It was discovered that in addition to his lame shoulder, Grimes also had a rib injury and was suffering from a painful bout of colitis (an inflammation of the large intestine). He worked out daily with a personal trainer to regain his strength. When the Cardinals offered him a job as the team's pitching coach, he declined the offer. "No coaching job for me," said Grimes. "That would indicate I believe my days on the mound are over and I don't believe they are. For the first time in two seasons I feel good and strong again."[21]

Grimes got a break that winter when Dazzy Vance was claimed off waivers by the Reds. Vance had had modest success for the Cardinals in 1933 (6–2), but now St. Louis needed someone to fill that veteran role. On February 20, 1934, Grimes and the Cardinals agreed to a contract. He was told to report to Florida as soon as possible. He was now the last of the legal spitball pitchers with Red Faber and Jack Quinn having thrown their last spitter the year before.

In Bradenton, Grimes looked healthy and vowed to win 10 games, but he was informed that he would be working out of the bullpen with only the occasional start. The decision didn't sit well with Grimes, but he continued to work as diligently as he always had. He also worked closely with the pitchers in camp, but the headline-grabbing tutorial went to top female athlete Babe Didrikson.

Didrikson was making the rounds of different camps that spring, throwing an inning for the Cardinals, Brooklyn Dodgers, Philadelphia Athletics and Cleveland Indians. In her game for the Cardinals, she went up against the Athletics. After allowing two runners to get on base, Al Simmons lined into a double play. She then retired Jimmie Foxx on a deep fly ball that Paul Dean went into an orange grove to snag. After the game, Grimes said, "Babe Didrikson would be one of the best prospects in baseball if she were a boy."[22]

Grimes got into his first game in the Cardinals' second game of the season. He was the tough-luck loser, throwing three innings of one-hit ball in a 7–6 Pirates victory. He picked up wins in back-to-back games against the Reds on April 30 and May 1 and pitched a few innings of solid relief against the Braves on May 6. In between appearances, Grimes acted as de facto pitching coach, but his frustration mounted when he wasn't given a start after pitching well in relief. In a surprising move, St. Louis released Grimes on May 15 in order to get down to the 23-player limit.

It looked like it might be the end of Grimes's career, but on May 28 he was back in uniform when the first-place New York Yankees signed him to help bolster their pitching staff. Manager Joe McCarthy made no promises, saying he would use Grimes where he saw fit. It marked the first time in his long career that Grimes had suited up for an American League team.

Grimes showed that his spitball could still be nasty when thrown properly. In his first appearance in pinstripes on May 30 at Yankee Stadium, he entered the game in the eighth inning, with the score tied, 4–4. The first time Yankees catcher Bill Dickey, considered one of the game's better defensive catchers, called for Grimes's famous spitter, he completely missed it and had to go the backstop to retrieve it. Inspired by a crowd of 70,000, Grimes threw four innings of scoreless ball to pick up the win.

Over the next two months the Yankees bounced between first and second place. Grimes remained in the bullpen. The success of his first appearance had convinced McCarthy that he could best serve the Yankees as a reliever. Grimes respected McCarthy and accepted the assignment, but he still wasn't particularly happy with the role. Through the end of July, Grimes had appeared in 10 games, holding a record of 1–2.

Off the field, Grimes grew close to Lou Gehrig, Red Ruffing and Frankie Crosetti. As a result of McCarthy's pipe-smoking ban, the four often congregated in Gehrig's hotel room to puff on their pipes and talk ball.

A legendary tale that came from Grimes's time as a Yankee was his alleged bean ball of Tigers slugger Goose Goslin — while Goslin was on deck. Supposedly, Goslin was inching his way toward the plate to get a better view of Grimes's delivery. When he got too close for comfort, Grimes plunked him.

For the second time that season, Grimes was blindsided when he was given his release on July 31. He felt that McCarthy hadn't given him a fair opportunity to prove himself by only using him in relief. As Grimes packed his bags, he vented his frustrations to Jack Cuddy of the United Press: "When you get into a game as a reliever, with men on base and so forth, you can't have much on the ball if you've been warming up daily and constantly in the bullpen."[23]

Grimes added that he wasn't ready to retreat back to his farm: "If I can land with a club that needs a pitcher; a club that will give me a chance to work — which the Yankees didn't — I'll soon satisfy myself whether I'm washed up. I'm in excellent physical condition, and my arm never felt better."[24]

Less than ten days later, on August 8, Grimes signed on for his third tour of duty with the fifth-place Pittsburgh Pirates, almost 18 years to the day after he originally signed with the club (August 5, 1916). He was on the mound later that day, in the second game of a doubleheader against the Cubs. Grimes was walloped for eight runs (seven earned) over four-and-two-thirds innings, but provided some much-needed relief for a depleted pitching staff.

On August 14, in Pittsburgh, Grimes started a game for the first time in nearly a year and showed that he still had life in his arm. Grimes gave up a few early runs, but dueled New York Giants ace Carl Hubbell for eight innings before being removed for a pinch hitter in the bottom of the eighth with the score tied, 2–2. Waite Hoyt threw a scoreless ninth inning and the Pirates scored in the bottom of the inning for a 3–2 victory.

Grimes started again four days later on "Ladies Day," hurling against the Brooklyn Dodgers at Ebbets Field. Again he turned back the clock, stymying the Dodgers for the first seven innings and allowing just one hit. In the eighth inning he got two quick outs before walking the next two batters. A single followed to end the shutout, and another hit tied the game at two. Grimes was tagged with three more runs in the ninth and was taken out with one out. He received a standing ovation from the crowd of 7,000 as he walked back to the dugout with his head down. It was the last great pitching performance of his career.

Over the next 10 days Grimes started two more games and lasted just one-and-one-third innings in the first (August 23) and just one-third-of-an-inning in the other (August 28). He didn't pitch again until September 10, when he picked up the win in two innings of relief in a 9–7 victory over the Giants at the Polo Grounds. The victory was the final one of his career, number 270.

Grimes got into two more games in late September, both against the Dodgers at the Polo Grounds. In the final appearance of his major league career on September 20, Grimes retired the only three batters he faced.

On October 11, the Pirates gave Grimes his unconditional release.

9

Still in the Game, 1935–1964

During the late fall and early winter, Grimes weighed his options for the 1935 season. He still hadn't given up hope of pitching again in the major leagues, but there weren't any teams interested in a high-priced 41-year-old who struggled to stay healthy. However, a number of teams were interested in his services as a coach and possibly as a manager. The Cardinals, coming off a World Series victory over the Detroit Tigers, extended Grimes an intriguing offer as player-manager of one of their minor league affiliates. The problem now became finding a league that would allow him to throw a spitball.

Once again Grimes made the pilgrimage to Hot Springs, Arkansas, to round himself into shape. From there he worked with Branch Rickey to find a team, which proved to be a daunting task. Grimes was turned down by the Pacific Coast League, Western Association, Three-I League and the Piedmont League. In each case, at least one owner or manager voted against letting him use the spitter. Grimes grew so frustrated by the situation that he decided to go into umpiring instead, having a job lined up in the New York-Penn League. Finally, St. Louis Cardinals management stepped in and persuaded John Butler, manager of the Three-I League's Decatur Commodores to change his vote. The Three-I League (Illinois, Indiana and Iowa) was preparing for its first season since 1932, when the circuit had folded in mid–July. Having a name like Grimes in the league could only benefit the gate receipts.

On April 1, Grimes was announced as the manager of the Bloomington (Illinois) Bloomers, commonly referred to as the Cardinals because of their use of the St. Louis Cardinals' old uniforms. Grimes wasn't bashful about his prospects, stating that he not only expected to win the league championship, but that at least 25 of those victories would come from his arm. He would be doing so while making $2,500, or a tenth of what he had the year before.

The Bloomers got off to a rough start, losing four of their first five games. Grimes was so disgusted that he took over calling pitches, whether on the mound or in the dugout. It didn't matter what league Grimes was playing in, he was going to play and manage the only way he knew how.

Crowds were started to flock to the newly renovated Fans Field as the young and impressionable Bloomington players were playing Grimes's brand of ball. When the parent club St. Louis Cardinals came to Bloomington for an exhibition game, leadoff batter Pepper Martin was hit square in the back. Manager Frankie Frisch pulled his starters after the first inning to give them a rest and the Bloomers won easily, 11–1.

Managing a group of young players was not always easy for Grimes and he didn't mind setting them straight when the need arose. Before one game, pitcher Max Macon slightly hurt his foot and went to the clubhouse instead of the bullpen for the game. Macon's situation wasn't explained to Grimes, who called for the youngster to get ready to pitch late in the game. According to one retelling of the story, Grimes "gave the youngster an old-fashioned tanning and then phoned Macon's father to come and get his son." When Macon's father arrived, he told Grimes, "Do it again if you think it will help. Maybe it will make a ball player out of him."[1]

Bloomington finished in second place during the first half of the season and by the end of July they were leading in the race for the second-half title. On the mound Grimes was dominant, with a league-leading 9–1 record. He was also terrorizing umpires and frequently calling on his pitchers to utilize intimidation tactics. The practice drew the ire of nearly every fan base in the

Grimes (arm raised) leading the Louisville Colonels in spring training (Charles Clark Photo Collection).

league. According to the *Hammond* (Indiana) *Times*, it led to police "escorting Burleigh out of the ball park almost daily because of his bean ball tactics."[2]

Grimes was increasingly enjoying his new-found role. When he went to discuss the Bloomers' progress with Branch Rickey in St. Louis, Grimes was asked if he wished he were still playing in the majors. Grimes responded, "Do I get discouraged because I'm in the minors? The answer is 'no,' we don't get paid in baseball for playing, we get paid for winning. That is just as true in the minors as it is in the majors."[3] His managing wasn't going unnoticed by Sam Breadon either. The Cardinals owner was telling some people that he would make Grimes manager "when a change is made."[4]

As much as Grimes was disdained in opposing towns, the people of Bloomington adored him. On August 1, "Burleigh Grimes Day" was held at Fans Field and more than 1,200 fans saw Grimes have his worst outing of the season. After the Springfield Senators got to him for a run in the second inning and three more in the third, Grimes took himself out. Springfield won 5–2 and Grimes's record dropped to 9–2. He beat Springfield a week later, but that was Grimes's last mound victory of the year, finishing 10–5 (2.34 ERA).

The Bloomers won the second-half title, setting up a mid–September best-of-seven series against first-half champion Springfield. The Senators won the first three games in convincing fashion (9–0, 3–2 and 6–0) and with the championship on the line Grimes started Game Four. After allowing three runs in the first inning, Grimes kept Springfield in check until the seventh inning, when he allowed two runs and then two more in the ninth. He was credited with the win as Bloomington's bats came alive in a 10–7 win. The Bloomers won a wild Game Five, 6–5, in a contest that was marred when Springfield's Clyde Smoll "climbed into the stands and punched a loudmouth fan."[5]

It appeared that Springfield won Game Six and the postseason crown, 5–2, but controversy surrounded the win. In the third inning a Bloomington player hit a home run and while rounding third shook hands with a teammate, thus negating the home run. Grimes and the Bloomington players were irate at the call, but filed no formal complaint until after the game. Three-I League President L.J. Wylie ruled that the game be replayed, but Springfield declined, saying that Wylie, who was in attendance at the game, could have easily over-ruled the call at the time. The Senators' refusal to play made the Bloomers the champion by default.

Due to financial woes, shortly after the completion of the 1935 season the Three-I League folded again. Grimes wasn't out of a job for long, however, taking over as manager of the Louisville Colonels of the American Association. Doubling his income to $5,000, Grimes went head-to-head against a few managers whom he had played under in the big leagues. Former St. Louis Cardinals manager Gabby Street was heading the Saint Paul Saints and ex–Pittsburgh Pirates skipper Donie Bush was directing the Minneapolis Millers. Grimes abstained from any preseason prognosticating beyond saying, "We'll give 'em plenty of trouble."[6]

Immediately, the Colonels found themselves near the bottom of the eight-team standings. Grimes went on a rampage, getting kicked out of three games in the first two weeks of the season, including an incident in St. Paul in which he stepped on an umpire's foot with his cleats, resulting in a $25 fine and 48-hour suspension. His antics didn't keep Louisville fans away — instead they were coming out to Parkway Field in droves to see what Grimes was going to do next. Sportswriter John Lardner wrote, "The renaissance of baseball in the City of Juleps is an old gaffer named Burleigh Grimes, who is colorful from the bugle in his cheek to the hungry hooks on the bottom of his shoes."[7]

Grimes didn't let up on his pestering of umpires; before the season was half over he had been kicked out of 14 games, fined three times and suspended twice. Umpires weren't the only ones who took a beating during Grimes's blowups. Once he actually knocked himself out. After making his way back to the dugout after getting tossed, Grimes picked up a bucket of ice water and tossed it into the air. As he explained, "When I threw the pail, I hoped it would land on the umpire's head, but after I was revived, I learned that the pail had knocked me out."[8]

In early June, the Colonels were in seventh place, but it seemed they were coming up with win after win against the league's top teams. Around that time Grimes's name began to surface as a candidate to take over for Casey Stengel as manager of the Brooklyn Dodgers. (Also being considered were Babe Ruth and Jimmie Wilson, Grimes's former catcher with the Cardinals.) In the second year of his managerial career (and a three-year contract), Stengel was struggling to gain control of a team that was short on talent and long on characters. He had had two players quit the ballclub only to return, including the talented yet combative pitcher Van Mungo. The rumor of Grimes taking over for Stengel lingered for the rest of the season.

In late June, Grimes, was arrested by Stark County (Ohio) sheriffs while the Colonels were playing in Columbus. He was taken in on a contempt warrant stemming from an alimony suit filed by his first wife Ruth. He was released on bond, but the issue dragged out for nearly two months before being resolved in late August when Grimes settled the $6,000 claim by giving Ruth $4,000.

Louisville never climbed out of the second division, ending the season in seventh place with a 63–91 record. Even with the team's poor record, Grimes never took the mound for a game. He finally found his way into an exhibition game on August 31 when the Colonels defeated the Ohio State League All-Star team, 4–3, in 12 innings. Grimes picked up the win, allowing one run on three hits over the final five innings.

A week later Grimes was in Brooklyn taking in the Dodgers' 60th anniversary celebration. He stuck around the city for a few more weeks to watch the Giants-Yankees World Series. After Game Four, Grimes was walking across the Yankee Stadium field when he was approached by a Dodgers official and told that Casey Stengel was going to be removed as Brooklyn's manager that night and that Grimes was at the top of the list to replace him.

Stengel was in fact let go as manager that evening, and for the next month the names of possible successors were thrown around. The team's ownership was in limbo, so it was anybody's guess. Colonel T.L. Huston, a former part owner of the Yankees, wanted to purchase the team and insert Babe Ruth as manager. Former Dodgers including Grimes, Zach Wheat, Dutch Reuther and Max Carey were also said to be in the mix.

On November 5, 1936, Grimes was introduced as the new Dodgers manager. "I'm going to give Brooklyn a hustling ball club," he said in an interview from his farm in New Haven, Missouri. "I don't know how good we'll be, whether we'll win a lot of games or not, but I can tell you it will be the kind of scrappy ball club that Brooklyn fans and all other fans like."[9] He did vow to rid the Dodgers of their "Daffiness Boys" label, but he had no idea of the trials and tribulations that lay ahead over the next two years. Years later Grimes said, "Every man thinks that he can do something that somebody else can't do when he starts managing."[10]

One of Grimes's first actions was to name Andy High as his lone assistant coach. He tried to get Jesse Haines to come aboard as a pitching coach, but Grimes's former teammate and close friend wasn't ready to retire. Grimes and High spent the next month assessing the roster and what they felt were the greatest deficiencies in preparation for the minor league meetings in Montreal. Their focus was on the middle infield.

The annual minor league meetings usually featured much talk and little action. Grimes took the event by storm, making the weekend's only trades. On December 4, he traded pitcher Ed Brandt to the Pirates for young second baseman Cookie Lavagetto and pitcher Ralph Birkofer. The next day, he sent shortstop Lonny Frey to the Cubs for veteran infielder Woody English and pitcher Roy Henshaw. Grimes wasn't done. When he returned to Brooklyn, he signed free agent outfielder Heinie Manush.

In January 1937, Grimes was put in the precarious position of discussing

There was little for Grimes to smile about during his tenure with the Dodgers (Charles Clark Photo Collection).

the topic of integrating major league baseball. During an August 1936 interview with *The Daily Worker*, National League president Ford Frick had circumvented the issue by saying that the decision of signing black ballplayers was up to the owners of each ballclub. Armed with this answer, sportswriters were asking owners around the league to explain their stances. Brooklyn owner Steve McKeever avoided the question by saying that he was open to the possibility, but that ultimately it was up to the team's new manager, Burleigh Grimes. This led to an interview with Grimes by Lester Rodney, who had written the original piece for *The Daily Worker*. Rodney asked Grimes, "How would you feel about putting a Dodger uniform on Satchel Paige and Josh Gibson?"[11]

The question made Grimes uncomfortable. Since Rodney's article had been published, a reported 5,000 signatures had been collected in support of signing a high-profile player from the Negro Leagues. Grimes had grown up playing against black ballplayers in Clear Lake when the Minneapolis Keystone and St. Paul Colored Gophers had come to western Wisconsin during barnstorming tours. However, he gave Rodney a discouraging answer. "You're wasting your time," responded Grimes. "That'll never happen as long as there are segregated trains and restaurants." When Rodney asked him if he could at least assess the talent level of black ballplayers, Grimes declined to do so. "He didn't want to stick his head out," recalled Rodney.[12] The issue gained steam and 5,000 more signatures were gathered pressing Grimes to take steps to sign a black player.

Notorious for spring holdouts during his playing days, Grimes the manager was irked when some of his players did so. He told the holdouts: "I don't remember seeing a plaque of you in the Hall of Fame!"[13] At the top of Grimes's list was Brooklyn's best pitcher, Van Mungo. The Dodgers had received numerous offers for Mungo, but Grimes insisted that he wanted to build the team around the big right-hander.

The spring didn't go without incident. Grimes got into a heated exchange with Reds manager Charlie Dressen during another exhibition game. Grimes lost his temper and had to be physically restrained after Dressen quipped, "What the hell do you know about managing a major league ball club? You were a lousy manager in the bushes."[14] When asked whether the dispute stemmed from a duster Grimes had thrown at Dressen during their playing days, Grimes snidely dismissed the assertion: "I knocked down a lot of guys in my day, but I never wasted a pitch on a .250 hitter."[15]

Grimes did everything conceivable to try to make the most of his players from early-morning workouts after a poor game to bringing in Percy Beard, an Olympic silver medalist in the high hurdles in 1932, to teach them track methods on the bases.[16] When the Dodgers broke camp to start the season, they still were picked to finish near the bottom of the league.

Brooklyn management appeased Grimes's desire to give the team a fresh start by changing the color scheme. According to author Bob McGee, "The Dodgers had new green hats with a plain unadorned 'B' on the caps; the new flannels had 'Brooklyn' printed across the front in plain block letters in Kelly green on white flannel, instead of blue or blue-red trim on white, as they had in the past. On the road they wore Kelly green and tan, which looked awful."[17]

The regular season didn't get off to a good start for Grimes. In the first week of the season, he was kicked out of back-to-back games, leading to a summons to Ford Frick's office. After a heated exchange in which Grimes at first denied any wrongdoing and then questioned Frick's baseball credentials, a fine of $25 was assessed along with a stern warning from Frick. "The next time you get put out the punishment will be a good deal more severe than the $25 you have already been taxed," said the league president.[18]

The situation didn't get any easier. The Dodgers worked themselves back into the first division in the second week of May, but then the season began to unravel. On May 23, Grimes fined Van Mungo $1,000 and suspended him three days for fighting with a teammate. An intoxicated Mungo allegedly came back to the team's hotel in St. Louis and picked a fight with Jim Bucher and Woody English in their room. Mungo missed a start, but when he returned he won his next four decisions. Then he developed a sore arm, which plagued him the rest of the year.

The Dodgers were in the second division for good by the end of May. An already suspect pitching staff was thrown into flux by Mungo's injury and the offense wasn't responding to Grimes's small-ball approach. Grimes was also having problems with sportswriters, many of whom were Casey Stengel sympathizers. As hard as he worked to rid the organization of the "Daffiness Boys" label, the press replaced it with "Dem Bums." The new moniker came from Willard Mullin, the sports cartoonist for the *World-Telegram*, who hopped in a cab after a game and was met by the question, "Well, what'd dem bums do today?"

In mid–July, Grimes was again fined and suspended for arguing with umpires. He was kicked out of a total of nine games in 1937. In late August, the Dodgers sank into last place, but Grimes continued to manage as if they were in a pennant race and expected his players to act the same way. Since late June, Van Mungo had been nursing a sore arm. When he repeatedly failed to take part in a rehab program set up by a specialist, Grimes suspended Mungo indefinitely without pay. Of the incident, Grimes said, "There was only one thing to do — suspend him. Mungo has lazed about and disregarded instructions. A specialist prescribed diathermic treatments for him, but with three days off in which to undergo these treatments he always said he had no time."[19]

Later that evening, a drunken Mungo confronted Grimes in the lobby of the team's headquarters at the Hotel St. George. The pitcher was infuriated that Grimes had told him of the suspension in the clubhouse in front of the whole team. Grimes didn't back down on his stance, going nose-to-nose with Mungo and reiterating his thoughts from earlier in the day. Grimes gave Mungo the opportunity to win a spot back: "Van can work out with the club if he wants to. It's up to him. If I think he is in shape to pitch again I'll lift the suspension. Otherwise, it sticks."[20] Mungo never took Grimes up on the offer.

Mungo was one of the few players who had the courage to confront their manager. Earlier in the season a young pitcher had objected to the way Grimes was picking apart his game. He threatened Grimes, "Why if you weren't such an old man...."[21] Grimes didn't let the player finish the sentence, punching him in the mouth and knocking him to the ground. The two were separated before the fight could go any further.

The Dodgers won six of seven games after Mungo's suspension, moving into sixth place, but were still 22½ games out of first-place. On September 7, Grimes was given a day off, while the Brooklyn board of directors discussed his future with the team. Andy High stepped in to manage. The meeting recessed to watch some of the game, which the Dodgers won 6–1. Grimes watched from the stands. "I'm just taking a day off, that's all," said Grimes.[22] He sat out one more game before it was announced that Grimes was not only managing the Dodgers next year, but that he would be given a $5,000 raise.

There were whispers that Grimes was simply re-signed to ensure that the Dodgers wouldn't keep switching managers. It was thought that the club already had another person in mind to manage and that Grimes would simply run the club for another year. The Dodgers continued to play uninspired ball, culminating with a 14-game losing streak from September 16 to September 30. Brooklyn finished the season in sixth place (62–91).

On October 4, the Dodgers sent Johnny Cooney, Jim Bucher, Joe Stripp and Roy Henshaw to the St. Louis Cardinals for Leo Durocher. A mouthy shortstop nicknamed "The Lip," Durocher was named team captain and was ultimately the man who would succeed Grimes.

On January 18, 1938, the Dodgers announced Larry MacPhail as the club's executive vice president, replacing Joe Gorman, who had stepped down as general manager after one season. A former general manager for the Reds, MacPhail came on the recommendation of Ford Frick, who had lobbied for him to take the same position one year earlier. MacPhail vowed to improve the team in all areas. When asked if he was going to keep Mungo, who was voicing his displeasure with Grimes in the press, MacPhail responded, "I don't know yet, but I'll tell you this: I'll trade Mungo — or Grimes — or MacPhail if I think it will help the ball club."[23]

That his job might be on the line didn't bother Grimes in the least. "I'm tickled to death," said Grimes. "MacPhail always was a go-getter. He has a lot of fire and has got results. I'll be happy to be associated with him."[24]

Brooklyn pitching was a concern, but MacPhail also felt that the team's offense wasn't taking advantage of the short dimensions of Ebbets Field. Free-agent Kiki Cuyler was added in February. MacPhail then traded for Phillies first baseman Dolph Camilli, who was expected to be the answer to the team's power-hitting needs. Of average size (5-foot-10, 185 pounds), the left-handed-hitting Camilli was a dead pull hitter and had taken advantage of the 280-foot right-field line at the Baker Bowl. He had hit 55 home runs over the past two seasons, only 15 less than the Dodgers as a whole had hit over that span. MacPhail hoped he would do the same at Ebbets Field, which featured a 297-foot right-field line.

MacPhail became even more involved with the team after the death of Steve McKeever on March 7, 1938. A shrewd businessman whose wealth had continued to grow despite the Depression, MacPhail talked banks and loan agencies (that the Dodgers owed thousands of dollars) into lending the franchise more money. Before the season MacPhail spent $200,000 upgrading Ebbets Field by installing modern plumbing and giving the ushers a more prominent role. He even vowed to put in lights for night baseball at some point and he restored blue as the team's primary color.

The offseason moves by MacPhail didn't leave Grimes too optimistic about Brooklyn's chances. During spring training, Grimes was asked about the prospects for this year's team. Instead of giving a stock answer about how optimistic he was about the upcoming season, he gave a not-so-glowing review. "This club — I think it will finish last," he said matter-of-factly. When he was reminded that the Phillies were a competitor for the last spot, he laughed and responded, "Oh yes, the Phillies. I had forgotten about them. Just say we'll finish seventh."[25]

Grimes denied having said such a thing, but it was to no avail. When MacPhail heard about the statement he was irate. "If the Dodgers are in seventh place on May 15, there will be some changes made," he declared.

The proclamation put Grimes on the hot seat before the season even had begun. Unfortunately for him, the Dodgers were fulfilling his low expectations and were in the second division by the end of April. Rumors spread that Grimes was going to be replaced by former Cincinnati manager Charlie Dressen. MacPhail tried to defuse the situation, saying, "How long do I have to keep denying these reports? Grimes will manage the Dodgers throughout the season of 1938. As far as I'm concerned he'll be here as long as I am."[26]

Following that vote of confidence, Grimes went out the next day (May 1) and got kicked out of a game for the first time that season. That was followed a few days later by an argument on the mound between Grimes and pitcher Luke Hamlin. The Dodgers led the Pirates 5–3 in the fifth inning with one out and a runner on first base. After the count went to 2–0 on Lee Handley, Grimes popped out of the dugout to take out Hamlin, who refused to leave. Only after numerous choice words between the manager and player did Hamlin retreat to the bench. After the game, Hamlin blasted his manager in the papers: "There wasn't any reason in the world for yanking me and don't you think I didn't say something to the manager about it."[27] It didn't help that Hamlin's replacement, Bill Posedel, got hit hard and the Dodgers ended up losing, 9–5.

MacPhail flew to Cincinnati, where the Dodgers were scheduled to play next. Before their game against the Reds, MacPhail addressed the team to

The signing of Babe Ruth (center, greeting Tony Lazzeri) as a coach only added
to an already difficult situation for Grimes (left) (Cleveland Public Library).

reinforce his stance to the players. He said, "When I say Grimes is boss I
mean he is going to be boss and I'll find 23 ball players who want to play for
him. And I mean I'm not telling him who to pitch or who to play in the outfield."[28]

The endorsement by MacPhail did nothing to ignite the club. At the
end of play on May 15, Brooklyn sat in seventh place with a 10–15 record.
The newspapers clamored for a change, but one never came. MacPhail was
too immersed in trying to get lights added to Ebbets Field to get involved
with a managerial change.

Grimes was also distracted. In April he filed papers for divorce from his
wife Laura, accusing her of constantly pestering him with accusations of
infidelity with their maid, Rose Porter. He also claimed that Laura lied to
him about her prior relationships. Originally he was led to believe that she
had been married just once previously, when she was actually three times
divorced. Furthermore, the girls she had told him were her nieces were actually
her daughters.

In her own petition, Laura said that the first few years of marriage were happy, but then Burleigh became abusive, began an intimate relationship with Rose Porter and even tried to seduce her daughters. In court documents, Laura claimed, "Burleigh left her for long periods of time to have affairs with other women, that he struck her and threatened to kill her while she was sick, and that he was cruel to a 3-year-old child for whom the couple had once cared."[29]

On June 15, the Dodgers played their first night game against the Cincinnati Reds. With a start time of 8:37, some 38,000 seats were sold after 5 P.M. Pre-game activities included a long-jumping demonstration by Olympic hero Jesse Owens, who then raced several Dodgers players. Adding to the event was the fact that pitching for Cincinnati was Johnny Vander Meer, a former Dodger farmhand who had pitched a no-hitter in his last start against the Boston Braves on June 11. In the stands were hundreds of family members and friends who came from Midland Park, New Jersey, to cheer Vander Meer on.

Before the game even began there were fights in the stands and by the end of the third inning the Reds were leading, 4–0. The innings went by and the Dodgers continued to go hitless. According to Brooklyn fan Edie McCaslin, "Around the seventh inning, everyone wanted to see him do it."[30] In the ninth inning, everyone in the park was on their feet. When the final out was recorded on a soft fly to center field by Durocher, the stadium erupted with cheers and applause.

MacPhail outdid himself three days later when he announced that Babe Ruth would be joining the coaching staff. Ruth, who had been in attendance the evening of Vander Meer's no-hitter, had caused quite a stir with his presence. MacPhail saw an opportunity and went for it. "Babe Ruth belongs in baseball," said MacPhail. "To prove that I mean what I say, I have signed him as a coach, and he will be in uniform at Ebbets Field tomorrow."[31]

Ruth claimed to be serious about wanting to break in as manager, but he delayed joining the Dodgers until he was finished with a golf tournament. "The Babe doesn't belong out on any golf links," said an irritated Grimes. "He is an institution in baseball, and that's where he ought to spend every day of his life."[32]

The move was nothing more than an attendance ploy by MacPhail. Ruth did little to contribute to the team. He clashed mightily with former teammate Leo Durocher (whom Ruth had once nicknamed "The All-American Out"). Durocher got revenge by berating Ruth after he forgot the signs while coaching third base. About the only thing Ruth was good for was pregame entertainment, when he would launch a few balls over the fence.

Ruth was extremely out of shape, so his batting practice sessions led him to the trainer's room for a rubdown from trainer Ed Froelich. Froelich, who had worked for the Cubs since he was a boy and was around during 1932 World Series, questioned Ruth on the supposed "Called Shot." According to Froelich, one day while on the trainer's table Ruth confessed that it was all media hype. "You tell those people, that Baby says they're full of crap right up to their eyeballs. I may be dumb, but I'm not that dumb," said Ruth. He explained his reasoning. "I'm going to point to the center field bleachers with a barracuda like Root out there? On the next pitch they'd be picking it out of my ear with a pair of tweezers. No!"[33]

The Ruth situation was not an easy one for Grimes to maneuver. There was more trouble for Grimes when Woody English, a friend from his days on the Cubs, left the team after he became disenchanted about playing behind Durocher. Grimes also had to deal with the backlash of a story that he had punched a teenage autograph seeker in the stomach when approached after a loss.

On August 3, the Dodgers were involved in an experiment. In the first game of a doubleheader against the Cardinals, the teams used a yellow baseball. Brooklyn won, 6–2, but the reviews were mixed. Pitcher Fred Fitzsimmons found that the ball became harder and harder to grip as the dye came off on his perspiring fingers. "I could follow it well enough from the bench," Grimes said after the game. However, he didn't feel it suited the dynamics of Ebbets Field. "I really think it would be a good ball to use against a white-shirted background, such as the one in Chicago's Wrigley Field."[34]

On August 7, Grimes was kicked out of a game for the sixth and final time of the season. This time it wasn't for what he said, but rather what he did. After Leo Durocher hit what looked like a home run, umpire Larry Goetz ruled it a double because of fan interference. Instead of arguing, Grimes covered his face with a red bandanna, with just his eyes visible, emulating a bandit. Goetz ejected Grimes, who was fined $25 and given a three-day suspension.

In late August, the cheers that Ruth had been hearing during batting practice got him itching to return to the field. After a particularly good round of hitting in Pittsburgh, Ruth approached Grimes about playing again. Grimes was still throwing batting practice at the time and probably wouldn't have embarrassed himself if he had to play an inning or two, but he knew Ruth was a shell of his former self.

At Brooklyn's next stop in Cincinnati, Jerome Holtzman of *The Sporting News* told Grimes that Ruth was talking more and more about playing. Grimes put out a statement designed to put an end to any thought of Ruth playing. "Babe's a great coach, but he can't help either himself or our club in the lineup.

He quit in 1935 because of that fading right eye. He complains about pain wracked knees daily," said Grimes, adding, "He asks to play. In his enthusiasm he has forgotten the fragilities of the flesh."[35]

In late September, it was announced that Grimes would not be returning as the manager in 1939. According to MacPhail, it wasn't a move that caught Grimes off guard: "I told Burleigh the situation several weeks ago, and he agreed with me that his going was the sensible thing. He wasn't pleased over my decision — but he saw my side."

Publicly, MacPhail had nothing but praise for Grimes: "He is a swell manager, and a great fellow — but he is just not the right man for our particular set-up."[36] The blow of the news was lessened when it became known that Grimes was a leading candidate to manage the Cardinals in 1939. When nothing came of that, Brooklyn decided to keep him in the organization.

On December 5, Grimes, signed on to manage the Dodgers' new Double-A affiliate, the Montreal Royals of the International Association. He was given free reign to trade players as he saw fit and promptly did so. A few days after being introduced as manager, he traded away fan favorites Harry Smythe and Alex Hooks. Grimes completely dismantled the roster, focusing on youth and speed.

Grimes had had troubling off-seasons in the past, but the one leading up to the 1939 season had to be one of the most trying. In February he was granted a divorce from his second wife, Laura, but was ordered to pay $150 in per month in alimony and $500 in legal fees. A few months later, tragedy struck the Grimes family when 11-month-old Jerry Burleigh Grimes, the son of Burleigh's brother Shurleigh and wife Mildred, died unexpectedly in Owen, Wisconsin. While sitting in a bouncy chair hanging from a door, Jerry fell, striking his head and fracturing his neck. By the time a doctor arrived, he was dead.

Grimes did his best to turn his attention back to the upcoming season, but he wasn't too optimistic about the Royals' prospects. He was confident in his re-tooled infield and outfield, but the pitching staff was going to be a glaring problem. His gutted roster consisted of just three players from the year before. The Montreal fans took to neither Grimes nor the unfamiliar roster. By June, there were already rumors that he was going to be fired. His preseason worries had come to fruition, as the Royals were plagued by thin pitching and a weak lineup. True to form, Grimes mercilessly rode his players. According to William Brown, author of *Baseball's Fabulous Montreal Royals*, "One veteran complained that the hard-nosed manager was always on somebody's back and that made everyone nervous."[37]

In an attempt to beef up the roster, Grimes added a power bat in Gene

Hasson, but on Memorial Day, his first day in a Royals uniform, Hasson's skull was fractured by a pitch. Grimes fashioned a batting helmet for Hasson to get him back into the lineup. The helmet, which slightly resembled horse blinders, was made of hard fiber with sponge rubber knobs to protect the temple. It was kept in place by a spring steel band that fit around the back of the head. The device was so well received that International League president Frank Shaughnessy took the idea to the Spalding sporting goods company, which then mass-produced them. Grimes received no credit for his invention.

Even when the Royals fell into the sixth place, Grimes felt the team could make a move. When asked by a reporter for *La Presse* whether the season had been a disappointment thus far, Grimes responded tersely, "We have been in first section most of the time, and we are very close to the first division. We have lost a few exciting games, we have known a lot of bad luck."[38]

Grimes continued to try anything to better the team (sometimes making poor roster moves), but the Royals never made it out of the second division. The season didn't get any easier when Larry MacPhail began to talk about Rogers Hornsby taking over for Grimes in 1940. By August, the Royals were out of playoff contention and the tense situation finally got to Grimes, who took it out on an umpire in Buffalo. He took up the argument for a player who had been ejected, berating home-plate umpire Chet Swanson for 10 minutes, his anger growing with each passing minute. Finally, Swanson threatened a forfeit if Grimes didn't leave the field, which he finally did under the escort of Royals coach Red Rollings.

By September, Grimes, was on his last nerve. He had lost 10 pounds and was agitated by every question asked of him. When sportswriter John Whoric asked the reason for the Royals' struggles, Grimes gave a biting assessment: "Three reasons: Hasson's accident, no shortstop worth a damn and a lost quality in baseball pitchers today."[39] The season mercifully came to an end on September 10 when a doubleheader split with the Toronto Maple Leafs ensured a seventh-place finish for the Royals, just a game-and-a-half ahead of Toronto.

Rumors about Hornsby (whose Baltimore Orioles finished in sixth place in the International League) taking over for Grimes continued through the fall and into the winter. On December 6, just a day before he was set to attend the winter meetings in Cincinnati, Grimes resigned as manager of the Royals. He was guaranteed his 1940 salary of $10,000 unless he caught on with another club.

Grimes wasn't out of a job for long. Early in the new year, he was reassigned within the Brooklyn organization. He was tabbed to run the Dodgers' new affiliate in Grand Rapids, Michigan, part of the newly started Class C Michigan State League. Grimes was by far the biggest name in the league, coach or player, and the prospect of him coming to Michigan caused a stir. The team started out being known as the Dodgers, but they were soon dubbed "Grimes's Growlers" and "MacPhail's Folly's." Fans were given the chance to write in suggestions for the new name of the club and by the end of May the team was officially known as the Colts.

Personally, Grimes was in a good place. On May 16, he married Miss Inez Martin, a former nurse from Des Moines, Iowa. He also won an appeal, with the court finding his claims in his divorce from his ex-wife Laura to be true, thus making him the injured party and ending his alimony payments. On the field, he was minding his manners, making it through the first month of the season without getting tossed from a game. That came to an end when an on-field altercation led to his dismissal and year-long banishment from the game.

On July 7, in Saginaw, Grimes began arguing with umpire Robert Williams over a disputed call. During the squabble, Williams accused Grimes of spitting in his face, earning him an ejection. Immediately following the game Williams filed a complaint with National Association of Minor Leagues president W.G. Bramham and Michigan State League president T.J. Halligan describing Grimes's actions. Halligan levied Grimes with a $50 fine and five-day suspension, but Bramham wanted a stiffer penalty. "I didn't do it," said Grimes after he was fined and suspended.[40]

Grimes kept on managing the second-place Colts and his actions hadn't made him any less popular. By mid–July he was the top vote-getter to manage one of the teams in the league's All-Star game. The directors of the Michigan State League also showed support for Grimes, moving to restore him to "good standing as manager of the Grand Rapids Colts."[41] In a unanimous decision, they had league president Halligan contact National Association of Minor Leagues president W.G. Bramham on their behalf to "reopen the case for the taking of such further testimony as may be presented." They also asked if Grimes could be reinstated pending a hearing.

The directors took matters even further, dismissing the umpire in the incident, Robert Williams, "for the good of the league."[42] Williams's firing stemmed from going directly to Bramham rather than consulting the league first, causing negative publicity for the league. Defiantly, there was talk of holding a Burleigh Grimes Day and presenting him with a gold watch.

Bramham reviewed the league's claim and denied it. That didn't deter the directors. Halligan traveled to Chicago to present the league's case to Kenesaw Mountain Landis. Landis ordered a hearing by the executive committee of the National Professional Baseball Leagues on August 20. It didn't take long for the committee to make its decision, upholding Grimes's fine and suspension. The final verdict was fines in excess of $300 and a year-long ban from any on-field involvement in all levels of the professional game. Landis also stepped in and fined the Michigan State League $500 for firing Williams and made them pay his year's salary in full.

Grimes had a right to appeal the suspension, but it was of little use. He returned to his parents' home in Owen, Wisconsin, devastated and tried to figure out what he would do for the next year. It only got more painful when ex-teammate Jimmie Wilson took over as manager of the Cubs and said he wanted Grimes as his pitching coach. With a full year away from the game ahead of him, Grimes threw himself into farming full-time, buying a 354-acre farm in southern Missouri.

In January, 1941, Grimes put in a request for reinstatement to Commissioner Landis. His request was denied. For the most part Grimes stayed clear of baseball. The Cardinals did call on him to do some regional scouting in St. Louis. He was asked to go watch a young ballplayer from "the Hill," the heavily populated Italian section of the city. According to Grimes, he watched as the youngster emerged from the dugout, shuffling his feat and dragging his bat "so that it made a trail in the dirt on his way to the plate."[43] The player, Lawrence Berra, later known as "Yogi," put on a hitting display that day. Despite that, Grimes still doubted that Berra had a future in the majors and told the Cardinals to pass.

The strain of being away from baseball paled in comparison to the personal grief that Grimes encountered during 1941. On March 1, his sister Hazel passed away at her home in Stevens Point, Wisconsin, from the complications of a brain tumor. A few months later, his father Nick was admitted to a Madison, Wisconsin, hospital for treatment for cancer. On September 8, he passed away. In his obituary, Nick was described as "one of Owen's best known and most colorful characters." The obituary added that "no one in the community has as many friends and as many friendly words and gestures of greeting them as Nick did."[44]

In December 1941, Grimes was reinstated and accepted the job of manager of the International League's Toronto Maple Leafs, an affiliate of the Pittsburgh Pirates. The league kept a close eye on the managers and even had an "anti-squawking" rule. When asked whether he was going to be harder on the new manager, league president Frank Shaughnessy said he held the same expectations of Grimes as for the other managers in the league. "He deserves the same treatment as the others get, at least before the season starts," Shaughnessy said. "I am not going to judge him by things that have happened in the past."[45]

The prospect of missing any more time away from the game was something Grimes didn't want to entertain. With his father gone, he sought counsel from umpire Bill Klem. Klem's advice was simple: "It is impossible to do your job right if you fight with the umpire."[46]

Grimes took his new outlook into his daily interactions with players, umpires, fans and the press. "This is another season, a new one, with new hope for everyone and we shall see what it will bring," he said optimistically.[47]

The Toronto players raved about Grimes's demeanor, even referring to him as the "ideal boss."[48] In talking about the anti-squawking rule, Grimes said with a smile, "Honestly, it's just like a vacation for me."[49] The new Grimes didn't lead to much on-field success in 1942, as the Maple Leafs finished in sixth place with a record of 74–79. Despite their second-division showing, Grimes got good reviews for keeping the club in the first division for much of the season.

After a slow start in 1943, Grimes began to show some frustration. Following another loss, he gave an early assessment of his club: "I don't exactly think my club as now constituted can win the flag, although I haven't seen most of the other clubs. Therefore I can't tell how they stack up. My club just doesn't suit me yet." He hadn't completely given up on the season, however. "We may come around though and surprise, but only time can tell."[50]

Shortly afterward, the Maple Leafs turned things around. By the beginning of June they were in first place and never looked back. Toronto won the International League title with a record of 95–57, but ended up losing in the league playoffs to the Syracuse Chiefs. Over the winter, the "new" Grimes was a favorite for a few major league vacancies, including the Braves and Cubs, but again nothing materialized.

The 1944 season wasn't as successful: Toronto finished in third place with a record of 79–74. In September the Maple Leafs were acquired by a new group of owners led by Peter Campbell. One of their first moves was relieving Grimes of his managerial duties. Once again, praise was showered on Grimes as he made his exit. Campbell said, "It is not through lack of ability that Grimes will not be coming back. Rather it was just that we couldn't see eye to eye in all matters and it was finally decided the best way was to part. I still regard Grimes as one of the shrewdest and best managers in baseball."[51]

Grimes stayed in the International League, returning to the St. Louis Cardinals organization to manage the Rochester Red Wings. He was expected to turn around a once-proud minor league franchise, but had little to work with. In 1945 Grimes went through 51 players while trying to find the right combination, but nothing seemed to come together. The Red Wings led the league in errors and were given the nickname of the "Dead Wings." The club finished in last place with a record of 64–90 and as one sportswriter quipped, "Abner Doubleday would have committed hari-kari managing this club."[52]

The 1946 season looked like it was going to be a repeat of 1945. In addition to another poor start, Grimes wasn't getting along with new Red Wings general manager Joseph Ziegler. On June 14, Ziegler had seen enough and fired Grimes, giving a biting assessment of the job Grimes had been doing: "I have been of the opinion that this team has been poorly handled all season. I believe we have a much better ballclub than our present league standing indicates. I don't think Grimes has gotten the most out of the players we have. It is my belief that a managerial change will benefit this club."[53] The change did little to help the Red Wings, who ended up with a record of 65–87 for a seventh-place finish.

Grimes's dismissal from Rochester ended up being a blessing in disguise. A month after he was let go, Lee MacPhail (son of Larry), head of the Yankees farm system, contacted him about being an interim manager for one of their affiliates. The Kansas City Blues of the American Association were in a predicament after the team's manager, Bill Meyers, had been told to sit out a month because of a heart ailment. The Blues were not in the hunt for the pennant, but Grimes decided to take job. When the month was up, Meyers returned and Grimes began a five-year relationship as one of the Yankees' top scouts.

Grimes spent parts of 1955 and 1956 working in the Kansas City Athletics organization (Charles Clark Photo Collection).

In 1947, Burleigh and

Inez Grimes sold their southern Missouri farm because the land was too rocky. They bought a 545-acre spread in Hickory Creek near Trenton, Missouri. They rebuilt the old farm house into a large ranch-style layout, facing away from the road, so that they could enjoy a breathtaking view down across the fields to the confluence of the Thompson and Grand rivers. Grimes was rarely there, but the homestead was maintained by a number of farmhands, who also tended to the fields and helped raise horses, mules and prize-winning hogs.

When Grimes was on the farm, he showed the same determination that he brought to the baseball field. According to Rex Gray, a former sharecropper for Grimes, he didn't like to give up on a plan. After a well-drilling firm failed to reach any water at 240 feet, Grimes told them to drill on despite the fact that the water would be too salty for consumption. They never hit water. Exasperated, Grimes said, "I just pissed all my bean money on a hole in the ground."[54]

Over the next five years Grimes traveled all over the midwest holding tryout camps. His prize finds included Bill Skowron and Bobby Richardson. He was promoted to Yankees minor league supervisor and instructor in December 1947, and became a mainstay at spring training, working with pitchers. He also had brief stints as interim manager for the Independence (Kansas) Yankees of the Kansas-Oklahoma-Missouri League during the 1948 and 1949 season while the club was between permanent managers. While with New York he worked closely with many of the players who played key roles in the Yankees dynasty of the 1950s.

During Grimes's travels he saw thousands of ballplayers pass through his tryout camps. He became aware that the game of baseball was changing and that the players who were coming into the league were much different than the ones from his playing days. Grimes recognized that "the most important qualifications for a young ballplayer today are a good disposition and character. With these things he cannot get into trouble, he will listen to instruction and he will not be discouraged by criticism."[55]

Grimes got the urge to manage again in July 1952. He resigned from what he described as a "lifetime job with the Yankees" to return to Toronto to manage the Maple Leafs. "There is nothing like managing, especially in Toronto," said Grimes with a smile.[56] He was still the last manager to lead the Maple Leafs to an International League pennant, but Grimes had less success in his second tour of duty, recording identical 78–76 records in 1952 and 1953. That proved to be his last full-time stint as a manager.

In October 1953, Grimes returned to Clear Lake, Wisconsin, where the newly lighted athletic field was christened "Grimes Field" during halftime of the Clear Lake High School football game. It was the second field to be named after him. In the late '40s, Burleigh Grimes Field had been erected in Trenton, Missouri.

He was out of baseball in 1954, but in November Grimes was inducted into the Wisconsin Athletic Hall of Fame, joining former major leaguers Ginger Beaumont, Addie Joss, Charles "Kid" Nichols, Al Simmons, George McBride and Billy Sullivan. He was also named Wisconsin Man of the Year in 1954.

In January 1955, Grimes was drawn back into the game after serving as master of ceremonies at a Kansas City Athletics banquet at Chillicothe (Missouri) High School. He introduced the club's manager, Lou Boudreau, and head American League umpire Cal Hubbard. A month later Grimes was named the head of midwest scouting for the Athletics organization.

Even though the spitball had been banned three-and-a-half decades earlier, it was still a topic of conversation. There were so many pitchers that were illegally using it that Ford Frick, who was now the commissioner of baseball, was thinking about reinstating it. When asked his opinion, Grimes said, "All they've done is cause a lot of pitchers to cheat." He also felt that reinstituting the pitch would give pitchers an advantage that they hadn't had in decades: "If they would bring it back you would see a lot more pitchers going nine innings and pitching good ball up into their 40s."[57]

Grimes adamantly defended the spitball and what it did for his career: "Everything that has been good to me has come out of baseball. What I have in material possessions, the thrills I've gotten, the wonderful experiences — I owe to baseball. And I owe all this to the fact I learned to throw the spitter and was permitted to continue to throw it."[58]

In late March, Grimes was summoned to West Palm Beach, Florida, and hastily named Athletics pitching coach. He reassured his fellow coaches and team management about a rash of sore arms in camp: "The sore arm pitcher quite often develops into a good pitcher because he is forced to learn how to pitch."[59] Grimes didn't end up remaining with the club full-time. Over the next two seasons, he was occasionally called upon to dispense advice to the team's pitchers, but spent most of his time scouting and running tryout camps throughout the midwest.

During spring training 1956, Grimes was scouting a Dodgers game. After a rookie baserunner flubbed a perfectly executed hit-and-run he got up to leave. When asked if he was leaving, Grimes said over his shoulder, "Sure I'm leaving. I've seen this before. They're still using our old plays."[60] This was, of course, said in jest, as Grimes continued to scout until his mother's death.

Shortly after his mother Ruth died in September 1956, Grimes once

From left: Charles Clark, Burleigh Grimes and Shurleigh Grimes at Burleigh Grimes Field during the Burleigh Grimes Day Celebration, May 16, 1964 (Charles Clark Photo Collection).

again stepped back from the game. Now living full-time at their farm in Hickory Creek, Burleigh and his wife Inez were able to travel freely. They visited her family in Des Moines, Iowa, and often returned to Wisconsin to relax at the cabin on Yellow Lake or to stop by Clear Lake to see old friends and visit Burleigh's brother's family in Owen. About the only thing that slowed Grimes down was a hernia surgery in early 1959.

In February 1960, after a three-year hiatus, Grimes signed on as a part-time midwest scout for the Orioles. Baltimore's general manager was Lee MacPhail, whom Grimes had worked with when he was a scout with the Yankees. Over the next decade, Grimes was instrumental in putting together Baltimore's World Series clubs, scouting both Jim Palmer and Dave McNally, his two biggest contributions to the team.

10

The Hall Calls

For years, Grimes's Hall of Fame credentials had been debated. In 1937, his first year of eligibility, he received just one vote. Over the next 18 years, he was on the ballot nine times and never received more than seven votes, garnering that total in 1948. Then beginning in 1956 he had three straight ballots where his votes grew: in 1956 he received 25 votes, in 1958 he tallied 71 and in 1960 he had 92. His vote total dipped to 43 in 1962, but then his name returned to the news when some of his long-standing Dodgers pitching records began to be broken by Sandy Koufax.

Many former players spoke highly of Grimes and felt he belonged in Cooperstown. One of those was Ty Cobb. When asked to put together an all-time team, Cobb named Grimes as one of the pitchers. According to author Don Rhodes, in Cobb's later years while in a hospital bed suffering excruciating pain, his "pet project was to get Hall of Fame recognition for some of the older stars including Eppa Rixey, Sam Rice, Joey Sewell, Edd Roush, Red Faber and Burleigh Grimes."[1]

On February 2, 1964, the Veterans Committee met at the Commodore Hotel in New York City to review a list of 50 names to be considered for induction into the Hall of Fame. Many of the committee members were contemporaries of Grimes, either as players, sportswriters, executives or league officials. The group included Warren Brown, Frank Graham, Branch Rickey, Frank Shaughnessy, William Harridge, Paul Kerr, Warren Giles, Charlie Gehringer, Charles Segar, Roy Stockton, Dan Daniel, Joe Cronin, Ford Frick and Fred Lieb. When the committee concluded its deliberations, it had selected seven new inductees: Grimes, Luke Appling, fellow spitballer Red Faber, Miller Huggins, Tim Keefe, Heinie Manush and John Montgomery Ward.

He had come up short so many times that Grimes actually missed the official phone call. According to Dan Daniel, Grimes was "probably out hunting ducks."[2] When he finally received the news, it was a joyful moment for him and his wife Inez. Many newspapers ran a picture of Inez planting a kiss on the cheek of a grinning Burleigh. Grimes became the third Wisconsinite inducted, joining Charles "Kid" Nichols (1949) and Al Simmons (1953). In 1978 Addie Joss joined the trio.

Following his selection, Grimes was bombarded with requests for interviews and public appearances. In April he threw out the first pitch at County Stadium for the Milwaukee Braves' 1964 home opener against the San Francisco Giants. A week later, he was at the inaugural game at New York's Shea Stadium, where he was honored along with several other Hall of Famers.

In May, Grimes returned to Clear Lake to celebrate Wisconsin's "Burleigh Grimes Day." On May 16, the town honored its hometown hero with a day full of activities. He lectured about what he looked for in a ballplayer and signed autographs at the town hall, all the while visiting with faces from the past.

That evening more than 500 people filled the school auditorium for a banquet, including former major leaguer Cy Williams (now living in Three Lakes, Wisconsin) and pro football Hall of Famer Johnny "Blood" McNally of nearby New Richmond. Many letters and telegrams from well-wishers were read, including ones from St. Louis Cardinals great Stan Musial, Wisconsin

Following the morning Hall of Fame ceremonies. From left: Faber, Appling, Manush and Grimes show their plaques (Charles Clark Photo Collection).

State Senator and Clear Lake native Gaylord Nelson, Los Angeles Dodgers president Walter O'Malley, San Francisco Giants president H.C. Stoneham and New York Mets manager Casey Stengel. Humbled by the many tributes and honors bestowed upon him, Grimes said he had "received more this one evening than what he ever had before in his life."[3]

Around this time, several Clear Lake citizens were formulating plans for a Burleigh Grimes Museum at the Wiley Davis Post 108 American Legion post to hold numerous mementos and artifacts from Grimes's career. Spearheading the effort was Charles Clark. He had grown up hearing stories about Grimes and over the past decade the two had forged a close friendship. Clark would become Grimes's closest friend, as well as his unofficial business manager and historian. According to Eau Claire area author Jerry Poling, for Clark, whose father died when he was 13, Grimes became "a father figure who happened to know everything about baseball and everybody in baseball."[4]

On the evening of July 25, Grimes, Clark and their wives arrived in Cooperstown for the induction ceremonies to take place on July 27. Clark had been to the National Baseball Hall of Fame and museum before, but incredibly it was Grimes's first trip there. They took in the various exhibits

Grimes's last job was as a scout for the Baltimore Orioles. Here he is instructing pitchers in Miami, Florida, during spring training (Charles Clark Photo Collection).

and presented the museum with an oil painting done by western Wisconsin artist M. Checklund that depicted Grimes in a St. Louis Cardinals uniform.

Being the museum's 25th anniversary, an unusually plentiful group of legends from the past were in town. The following day was spent meeting and visiting baseball luminaries or their widows. In the evening Grimes shared a simple meal with Clark and childhood friend Elmer Swanson and their wives.

The next morning Grimes and the other five inductees were enshrined in the Hall, with Grimes giving a reverent speech. According to Clark, "The ceremonies were very impressive and in Burleigh's acceptance speech he thanked the baseball writers, sports casters, the players he played with and against, and he added a special thanks to all the good folks in Clear Lake, Wisconsin and Trenton, Missouri."[5]

In the afternoon the four living inductees — Grimes, Faber, Manush and Luke Appling (who had been selected in the runoff election) — were introduced

Grimes holding court with members of the Hall of Fame Veterans Committee at a meeting in Florida. From left: Grimes, Joe Cronin, Al Lopez, Charlie Gehringer, Birdie Tebbetts, Stan Musial and Roy Campanella (Charles Clark Photo Collection).

at a game between the Mets and Senators at Doubleday Field. Even after receiving baseball's highest honor, at a dinner that evening with some of top people in baseball, Grimes said that "the party given him in Clear Lake on May 16 was the high-water mark of his career and added that it was the finest organized banquet he had ever attended."[6]

On August 25, less than a month after the Hall of Fame induction ceremony, Inez Grimes died of a sudden heart attack at their home in Trenton. There had been no signs of illness. Devastated, Grimes buried her at the family plot in the Clear Lake Cemetery.[7] He returned to the Trenton farm and continued his scouting duties for the Orioles. He also increased the frequency of his visits to Clear Lake. Following the death of Inez, his friendship with Charles Clark, his wife and their young family became even more important to him.

11

Twilight Years

On September 30, 1966, a month past his 73rd birthday, Grimes married Zerita Brickell. The two had reconnected after knowing each other decades earlier when he had been a teammate of Brickell's late husband Fred, during Grimes's second tour with the Pirates (1928–1929). The couple split their time between Trenton, Wichita and Wisconsin, but over the next five years Grimes spent extended time on the road scouting all over the midwest.

Always maintaining an allegiance to Clear Lake, Grimes made appearances whenever the chance arose, even when higher-profile opportunities were available. In 1969 he was invited to the White House by newly elected president Richard Nixon to take part in a 100th anniversary celebration of professional baseball.[1] He turned it down, instead choosing to attend the Polk County Fair in Balsam Lake, where he spoke in front of about 40 people. According the Charles Clark, "Burleigh didn't once second-guess his decision."[2]

Finally on December 31, 1971, at the age of 78, Grimes officially retired from baseball. It ended more than five decades of being involved in the game. He and his wife sold their farm in Trenton and retired to a cabin on Lake Holcombe in Wisconsin's Chippewa County, where the fishing was prime. He split his time between there and Wichita, where Zerita remained due to illness until her death in June 1974. Deeply pained by losing another spouse, he found solace in Lillian Gosselin, a divorcée whose parents owned a cabin next door to Grimes. The 33-year age difference meant little to the two and on October 17, 1974, they were married.

In 1976, Grimes suffered a mild heart attack while chopping wood, but it did little to slow him down. Now into his 80s, he and his wife traveled around Wisconsin in a car adorned with the license plate "BAG 270" when making public appearances (BAG for his initials and 270 for his career win total). He threw out the first pitch at a baseball tournament in Eau Claire, helped the Withee Public Library celebrate "Super Sports Week" and traveled to Winter, Wisconsin, to ride in the rumble seat of a 1929 Model A Ford as part of the July 4th parade.

**From left: Gaylord Nelson, Grimes and Charles Clark during Clear Lake's 1976
United States Bicentennial celebration (Charles Clark Photo Collection).**

Grimes also became a regular at autograph sessions, often telling the
venue to make out a check to the Clear Lake Historical Museum in lieu of
an appearance fee. He enjoyed signing autographs and always made a point
of taking the time to write legibly, displaying great pride in his penmanship.
He applied his signature to any number of items and seldom turned down a
request.

The Grimeses and Clarks continued to make the annual trip to Cooperstown and in 1977 Burleigh was named to the Veterans Committee. He
never outgrew the camaraderie of baseball and loved his time in upstate New
York, swapping endless stories with Edd Roush, Lloyd Waner, Bill Terry and
many other players from his generation. It was common to see Grimes surrounded by a who's who of ballplayers hanging on his every word. He also
had the unique experience of sitting in Commissioner Kenesaw Mountain
Landis's chair to sign autographs. When he was done, Burleigh quipped to
Clark, "I sat in front of this chair a number of times, but that was the first
time I ever got to sit in it."[3]

On September 1, 1979, after nearly two years of preparation by countless
volunteers, the Clear Lake Historical Museum held a dedication ceremony.
In a renovated schoolhouse, various rooms displayed aspects of Clear Lake's
history, but the two "celebrity rooms" were the biggest draw.

The "Grimes Room" housed hundreds of artifacts from Grimes's playing
days. There were jerseys, jackets, photographs, contracts, newspaper clippings,

signed baseballs and correspondence between Grimes and everyone from Richard Nixon to actor Gilbert Roland, who waxed poetic about his childhood idolatry of Grimes. The other room belonged to Wisconsin State Senator Gaylord Nelson. Lining the walls of the "Nelson Room" were "pictures of past presidents, political leaders, newspaper clippings, service plaques and other memorabilia."[4] Only Nelson matched Grimes's affinity for Clear Lake.

As time passed, Grimes grew more nostalgic about his playing days. He confided to Clark that he often sat by the fireplace in the basement of his house smoking his pipe and wondering if it all really happened. He had few regrets, but the fact that he failed to make it to 300 wins irked him.

The length of Grimes's career and the fact that he played with 36 Hall of Famers often sparked the question of what his all-time team would be. Besides an off-the-record list that he made with Clark, Grimes said that he liked to "confine myself to those players with whom I am most familiar."[5] He chose the following from former teammates:

Pitchers — Rube Marquard, Al Mamaux, Sherry Smith, Leon Cadore, Ray Kremer, Lee Meadows, Waite Hoyt, Dizzy Dean, Dazzy Vance, Jess Haines, Red Ruffing and Lefty Gomez.

Catchers — Bill Dickey, Gabby Hartnett and Jimmy Wilson.

First base — Lou Gehrig, Jim Bottomley and Bill Terry.

Second base — Rogers Hornsby and Frankie Frisch.

Third base — Pie Traynor.

Shortstop — Travis Jackson, Glenn Wright and Leo Durocher.

Left field — Riggs Stephenson, Zach Wheat and Chick Hafey.

Center field — Edd Roush, Lloyd Waner, Earle Combs and Kiki Cuyler.

Right field — Babe Ruth.[6]

In July 1983, a month shy of his 90th birthday, Grimes traveled to Chicago to celebrate the 50th anniversary of the first All-Star Game at Comiskey Park. For the first time in years he donned a baseball uniform. Surrounded by some of the greats of the game, Grimes stood out with his spry behavior. He even jumped up and clicked his heels when he was announced. When asked whether it was exercise that kept him in such good shape, Grimes snipped back, "Exercise? Hell no. I spent most of my life exercising. I get out in my garden a lot and spend time there."[7]

When his birthday came around in August, Grimes was showered with attention, highlighted by an open house birthday party at the Clear Lake Historical Museum. Flattered by the attention, Grimes said, "This birthday's been a real big one for me. It's the 90th, and everybody wants to get into the act. I've gotten so many calls and cards."[8]

Grimes started his 90th year by permanently moving back to Clear Lake, where he lived across the street from his good friend Charles Clark. He was a regular at the museum, where he was happy to engage in baseball talk with anyone who happened to drop in. He also enjoyed sitting on his back porch with friends, smoking a pipe and drinking ice water. Across a pond in his backyard sat the town's grade school. It was the site of the pasture where Grimes got his start playing as a nine-year-old for the Clear Lake Red Jackets.

On one occasion Grimes was hosting Clark and former major leaguer Andy Pafko of nearby Boyceville. As the three men sat on the back porch musing about long ago days, Pafko pointed toward some children playing ball at the school across the pond and said, "You think we'll ever see another Burleigh Grimes come out of Clear Lake?" Grimes took a puff off his pipe and pondered the question. In his three-plus decades as a scout Grimes had seen a shift in the drive and desire of youth when it came not only to the game he loved, but also their approach to life in general. He finally answered with a nod, "Oh, I think so." Pafko thought differently. "Not too many!" he said. "I don't think there'll ever be another Burleigh Grimes."[9]

A year later, in the summer of 1984, *Life* magazine was in Clear Lake doing an article on Grimes. The crew traveled over to Grimes Field (which had been rededicated in 1982) where Grimes, in his old Dodgers cap, threw some pitches for the camera. Inevitably, the topic of the spitball came up. When asked if he still believed it should be made legal, Grimes didn't hes-

Grimes's simple grave at the Clear Lake Cemetery.

itate. "Hell yes!" he said. "Legalize it today, tomorrow, Monday, Tuesday and Wednesday."[10]

Grimes was energetic as ever for the camera, but shortly thereafter he was found to be suffering from cancer. In the succeeding months, his health deteriorated rapidly, but he didn't lose his feistiness. According to St. Louis sportswriter Bob Broeg, when a nurse attempted to take out Grimes's teeth prior to undergoing colon surgery, he snapped, "Hey, kid, those are mine and a lot of times I didn't keep my mouth closed either."[11]

In one of his last public appearances, Grimes entertained several members of the Minneapolis chapter of the Society for American Baseball Research at the Clear Lake Historical Museum. He was as sharp as ever, musing on the difference between the modern-day player and himself. "Why is it there are so many nice guys interested in baseball?" he said wryly, puffing his pipe. "Not me. I was a real bastard when I played."[12] He also got riled up when talking about Babe Ruth's called shot. "I've been listening to that bullshit so long," said Grimes, annoyed. "If he'd a done that our pitcher would have had him in the dirt."[13]

In the fall of 1985, Grimes fell out of bed. His wife Lillian called the Clarks to come over and help get Burleigh back into bed. Grimes confided to Clark, "I don't think I'm going to last much longer."[14] It was the first time that Clark had heard his close friend admit that he was losing his battle with cancer.

On December 6, 1985, Grimes succumbed to cancer. He passed away with his wife Lillian and the Clarks by his side. Five days later, a memorial service was held at St. Barnabas Episcopal Church. The organist softly played "Take Me Out to the Ball Game," as people filed into the church. His body was cremated and his ashes were interred in block 88, lot 3, space 2, at the Clear Lake Cemetery next to his third wife Inez. The headstone bears a modest Hall of Fame logo.

Tom Giordano, then executive director for minor league scouting for the Baltimore Orioles, eloquently eulogized Grimes's impact on the baseball world: "His contributions to our national pastime are a matter of fact of history. I remember him as an acquaintance, as a baseball professional, and as a colleague…. I've been in baseball 39 years, and the name Burleigh Grimes is synonymous with baseball."[15]

Appendix I

Major League Statistics

Burleigh Arland Grimes

Born: August 18, 1893 Emerald, WI
Died: December 6, 1985 Clear Lake, WI
Height: 5'10"
Weight: 175 lbs.
Throws: Right
Bats: Right
First Game: September 10, 1916
Final Game: September 20, 1934

Year-by-Year Regular Season
Major League Pitching Statistics

Year	Team	LG	G	GS	W	L	IP	H	R	ER	BB	SO	CG	SHO	ERA
1916	PIT	NL	6	5	2	3	45.2	40	19	12	10	20	4	0	2.36
1917	PIT	NL	37	17	3	16	194	186	101	76	70	72	8	1	3.53
1918	BRO	NL	40	30	19	9	270	210	94	64	76	113	19	7	2.13
1919	BRO	NL	25	21	10	11	181.1	179	97	70	60	82	13	1	3.47
1920	BRO	NL	40	33	23	11	303.2	271	101	75	67	131	25	5	2.22
1921	BRO	NL	37	35	22	13	302.1	313	120	95	76	136	30	2	2.83
1922	BRO	NL	36	34	17	14	259	324	159	137	84	99	18	1	4.76
1923	BRO	NL	39	38	21	18	327	356	165	130	100	119	33	2	3.58
1924	BRO	NL	38	36	22	13	310.2	351	161	132	91	135	30	1	3.82
1925	BRO	NL	33	31	12	19	246.2	305	164	138	102	73	19	0	5.04
1926	BRO	NL	30	29	12	13	225.1	238	114	93	88	64	18	1	3.71
1927	NY	NL	39	34	19	8	259.2	274	116	102	87	102	15	2	3.54
1928	PIT	NL	48	37	25	14	330.2	311	146	110	77	97	28	4	2.99
1929	PIT	NL	33	29	17	7	232.2	245	108	81	70	62	18	2	3.13
1930	TOT		33	28	16	11	201.1	246	119	91	65	73	11	1	4.07
1930	BOS	NL	11	9	3	5	49	72	53	40	22	15	1	0	7.35
1930	STL	NL	22	19	13	6	152.1	174	66	51	43	58	10	1	3.01
1931	STL	NL	29	28	17	9	212.1	240	97	86	59	67	17	3	3.65
1932	CHI	NL	30	18	6	11	141.1	174	89	75	50	36	5	1	4.78
1933	TOT		21	10	3	7	83.1	86	42	35	37	16	3	1	3.78
1933	CHI	NL	17	7	3	6	69.2	71	29	27	29	12	3	1	3.47
1933	STL	NL	4	3	0	1	13.2	15	13	8	8	4	0	0	5.27
1934	TOT	MLB	22	4	4	5	53	63	38	36	26	15	0	0	6.11

Year	Team	LG	G	GS	W	L	IP	H	R	ER	BB	SO	CG	SHO	ERA
1934	TOT	NL	12	4	3	3	35	41	27	25	12	10	0	0	6.43
1934	STL	NL	4	0	2	1	7.2	5	3	3	2	1	0	0	3.52
1934	NYY	AL	10	0	1	2	18	22	11	11	14	5	0	0	5.50
1934	PIT	NL	8	4	1	2	27.1	36	24	22	10	9	0	0	7.24
Total			616	497	270	212	418.0	4412	2050	1638	1295	1512	314	35	3.53

World Series Pitching Statistics

Year	Team	LG	OPP	G	GS	W	L	IP	H	R	ER	BB	SO	CG	SHO	ERA
1920	BRO	NL	CLE	3	3	1	2	19.1	23	10	9	9	4	1	1	4.19
1930	STL	NL	PHA	2	2	0	2	17	10	7	7	6	13	2	0	3.71
1931	STL	NL	PHA	2	2	2	0	17.2	9	4	4	9	11	1	0	2.04
1932	CHI	NL	NYY	2	0	0	0	2.2	7	7	7	2	0	0	0	23.63
Total				9	7	3	4	56.2	49	28	27	26	28	4	1	4.29

Year-by-Year Regular Season
Major League Batting Statistics

Year	Team	LG	G	AB	R	H	2B	3B	HR	RBI	AVG
1916	PIT	NL	6	17	1	3	0	0	0	0	.176
1917	PIT	NL	42	69	7	16	3	0	0	4	.232
1918	BRO	NL	41	90	5	18	2	1	0	4	.200
1919	BRO	NL	26	69	8	17	4	0	0	12	.246
1920	BRO	NL	43	111	9	34	8	3	0	16	.306
1921	BRO	NL	37	114	10	27	6	0	1	11	.237
1922	BRO	NL	36	93	15	22	3	1	0	11	.237
1923	BRO	NL	40	126	15	30	3	1	0	15	.238
1924	BRO	NL	40	124	11	37	3	0	0	7	.298
1925	BRO	NL	34	96	12	24	4	1	1	14	.250
1926	BRO	NL	31	81	4	18	4	0	0	9	.222
1927	NY	NL	39	96	10	18	4	0	0	6	.188
1928	PIT	NL	48	131	17	42	8	1	0	16	.321
1929	PIT	NL	33	91	11	26	3	3	0	12	.286
1930	TOT		34	73	12	18	5	0	0	13	.247
1930	BOS	NL	11	16	3	3	1	0	0	3	.188
1930	STL	NL	23	57	9	15	4	0	0	10	.263
1931	STL	NL	30	76	4	14	0	0	0	8	.184
1932	CHI	NL	30	44	4	11	1	0	0	5	.250
1933	TOT		21	25	1	4	1	0	0	5	.160
1933	CHI	NL	17	20	1	3	0	0	0	4	.150
1933	STL	NL	4	5	0	1	1	0	0	1	.200
1934	TOT	MLB	22	9	0	1	0	0	0	0	.111
1934	TOT	NL	12	7	0	1	0	0	0	0	.143
1934	STL	NL	4	0	0	1	0	0	0	0	.000
1934	NYY	AL	10	2	0	0	0	0	0	0	.000
1934	PIT	NL	8	7	0	1	0	0	0	0	.143
Total			632	1535	157	380	62	11	2	168	.248

World Series Batting Statistics

Year	Team	LG	OPP	G	AB	R	H	2B	3B	HR	RBI	AVG
1920	BRO	NL	CLE	3	6	1	2	0	0	0	0	.333
1930	STL	NL	PHA	2	5	0	2	0	0	0	0	.400
1931	STL	NL	PHA	2	7	0	2	0	0	0	2	.286
1932	CHI	NL	NYY	2	1	0	0	0	0	0	0	.000
Total				9	19	1	6	0	0	0	0	.316

Regular Season Major League Managerial Statistics

Year	Team	LG	G	W	L	W-L%	Finish
1937	BRO	NL	155	62	91	.405	6 of 8
1938	BRO	NL	151	69	80	.463	7 of 8
Total			306	131	171	.434	

Source: Baseball-Reference.com

Appendix II

36 Hall of Fame Teammates

Jim Bottomley

Max Carey

Kiki Cuyler

Earle Combs

Dizzy Dean

Bill Dickey

Leo Durocher*

Frankie Frisch

Lou Gehrig

Lefty Gomez

Chick Hafey

Jesse Haines

Gabby Hartnett

Billy Herman

Rogers Hornsby

Waite Hoyt

Travis Jackson

George Kelly

Tony Lazzeri

Freddie Lindstrom

Rabbit Maranville

Rube Marquard

Joe Medwick

Mel Ott

Edd Roush

Red Ruffing

Babe Ruth

George Sisler

Bill Terry

Pie Traynor

Dazzy Vance

Arky Vaughan

Honus Wagner

Lloyd Waner

Paul Waner

Zack Wheat

*Inducted as a manager

Chapter Notes

Introduction

1. National Baseball Hall of Fame and Museum, *Burleigh Arland Grimes — Induction Speech*, http://baseballhall.org/node/11156.

2. Veteran Committee Members included Warren Brown, Frank Graham, Branch Rickey, Frank Shaughnessy, William Harridge, Paul Kerr, Warren Giles, Charlie Gehringer, Charles Segar, Roy Stockton, Dan Daniel and Joe Cronin.

3. Interview with Charles Clark, Clear Lake, WI, June 11, 2011.

Chapter 1

1. George Forrester, *Historical and Biographical Album of the Chippewa Valley Wisconsin* (Chicago: A. Warner, Publisher, 1891–1892), p. 742.

2. Interview with Charles Clark, Clear Lake, WI, September 18, 2010.

3. Donald Honig, *The Man in the Dugout: Fifteen Big League Managers Speak Their Minds* (Chicago: Follett, 1977), p. 32.

4. Clippings File, Clear Lake Historical Museum, Clear Lake, WI.

5. William J. McNally, "Early Days of Burleigh Grimes," 1941, Clear Lake Historical Museum Burleigh Grimes file.

6. *New Richmond Centennial, 1857–1957* (New Richmond, WI: Dairyland Press, 1957), p. 39.

7. *St. Paul Daily Globe*, March 30, 1894, p. 5.

8. Interview with Charles Clark, Clear Lake, WI, September 18, 2010.

9. *Capital Times* (Madison, WI), June 15, 1961, 28.

10. *St. Paul Pioneer Press* (St. Paul, MN), September 26, 1965, p. 6.

11. Robert Kemp Adair, *The Physics of Baseball* (New York: Harper & Row, 1990), p. 38.

12. *Ibid.*

13. *Ladysmith News* (Ladysmith, WI), May 22, 1980, sec. B, p. 1, 3.

14. *Sporting News* (St. Louis, MO), March 7, 1964, p. 5.

15. *Montreal Gazette* (Quebec, Ontario), April 19, 1939, p. 14.

Chapter 2

1. *Sporting News* (St. Louis, MO), February 24, 1938, p. 4.

2. Jerry Poling, *A Summer Up North: Henry Aaron and the Legend of Eau Claire Baseball* (Madison: The University of Wisconsin Press, 2002), p. 72.

3. Burleigh Grimes Interview, Withee Public Library "Super Sport Hero" Week (Withee, WI), July 17, 1979.

4. Honig, *The Man in the Dugout*, p. 33.

5. *Capital Times* (Madison, WI), June 15, 1961, p. 28.

6. Honig, *The Man in the Dugout*, p. 34

7. *Austin Daily Herald* (Austin, MN), July 5, 1913, p. 2.

8. *The Sports Magazine* (St. Louis, MO), April 1931, p. 4.

9. *New York Times,* August 24, 1915, p. 8.

10. *Ottumwa Daily Courier* (Ottumwa, IA), February 3, 1913, p. 7.

11. *The Sports Magazine* (St. Louis, MO), April 1931, p. 4.

12. *Detroit Free Press* (Detroit, MI), June 4, 1913, p. 13.

13. *Atlanta Constitution* (Atlanta, GA), January 19, 1914, p. 6.

14. Terry Simpkins, "Kid Eberfeld," *The Baseball Biography Project*, http://bioproj.sabr.org/.

15. *New York Journal American*, date unknown, Hall of Fame Burleigh Grimes clippings file.

16. *Capital Times* (Madison, WI), June 15, 1961, p. 28.

17. Herman Weiskopf, "The Infamous Spitter," *Sports Illustrated*, July 31, 1967, p. 17.

18. *Ladysmith News* (Ladysmith, WI), May 22, 1980, sec. B, p. 1, 3.

19. *Miami Daily News-Record* (Miami, OK), May 18, 1930, p. 30.

20. *The Sports Magazine* (St. Louis, MO), April 1931, p. 4.

21. *Sporting Life* (Philadelphia, PA), January 31, 1914, p. 3.

22. Charles Alexander, *Ty Cobb* (New York: Oxford University Press, 1984), p. 116.

23. Ben Bernston, "Rickwood Field," *Encyclopedia of Alabama*, http://www.encyclopediaofalabama.org/face/Article.jsp?id=h-2392, August 11, 2009.

24. *Birmingham News* (Birmingham, AL), May 6, 1914, p. 10–11.

25. *The Times-Dispatch* (Richmond, VA), May 9, 1914, p. 8.

26. He was kicked out of a game on August 7 in Petersburg, Virginia, for arguing from the 3rd base coaching box.

27. *The Times-Dispatch* (Richmond, VA), June 17, 1914, p. 8.

28. Robert Peyton Wiggins, *The Federal League of Baseball Clubs: The History of an Outlaw Major League, 1914–1915* (Jefferson, NC: McFarland, 2009), p. 104.

29. Daniel and Mayer, *Baseball and Richmond*, 64.

30. He hit a home run in August that was said to be the "longest hit ever made in the local park" in Portsmouth, Virginia, only to have it be washed away by a rainout.

31. *Birmingham News* (Birmingham, AL), March 1, 1915, p. 5.

32. *Birmingham News* (Birmingham, AL), January 26, 1915, p. 8.

33. *Birmingham News* (Birmingham, AL), April 19, 1915, p. 5.

34. Frank McGowan and Zipp Newman, *The House of Barons: Record of the Barons Since 1900* (Birmingham: Cather Brothers, 1948), p. 41.

35. *Birmingham News* (Birmingham, AL), July 4, 1915, p. 9.

36. *Birmingham News* (Birmingham, AL), April 19, 1915, p. 5.

37. *Birmingham News* (Birmingham, AL), August 1, 1915, p. 7.

38. The first 8⅓ innings were no-hit ball.

39. *Birmingham News* (Birmingham, AL), August 31, 1916, p. 10.

40. *Birmingham News* (Birmingham, AL), September 1, 1915, p. 9.

41. *Birmingham News* (Birmingham, AL), January 31, 1916, p. 8.

42. *Birmingham News* (Birmingham, AL), August 5, 1916, p. 5.

43. *Birmingham News* (Birmingham, AL), September 11, 1916, p. 8.

44. *Birmingham News* (Birmingham, AL), August 25, 1916, p. 9.

45. *Birmingham News* (Birmingham, AL), August 7, 1916, p. 3.

Chapter 3

1. All of the franchises except for Louisville had become part of the newly formed American League in 1901.

2. David Jones, ed. *Deadball Stars of the National League* (Dulles, VA: Potomac Books, 2004), p. 149.

3. *Ibid.*

4. Daniel Okrent and Steve Wulf, *Baseball Anecdotes* (New York: Oxford University Press, 1989), p. 68.

5. They had won the twelve previous and would win the next fourteen.

6. *Pittsburgh Press*, September 21, 1916, p. 26.

7. *Sporting Life*, October 14, 1916, p. 8.

8. *Ibid.*

9. Jones, ed. *Deadball Stars of the National League*, p. 178.

10. Frederick G. Lieb, *The Pittsburgh Pirates* (Carbondale, IL: Southern Illinois University Press, 2003), p. 176.

11. *Philadelphia Inquirer* (Philadelphia, PA), March 1, 1917, p. 14.

12. Mamaux went on to have an exceptional minor league career both as a player and manager.

13. Arthur D. Hittner, *Honus Wagner: The Life of Baseball's Flying Dutchman* (Jefferson, NC: McFarland, 2003), p. 217.

14. Jennifer D. Keene, *World War I: The American Soldier Experience* (Lincoln: University of Nebraska Press, 2011), p. 10.

15. *Brooklyn Daily Eagle*, January 9, 1918, p. 2A.

16. *Pittsburgh Press*, May 16, 1917, p. 32.

17. *New York Times*, June 7, 1971, p. 12.

18. *Sports Illustrated*, July 31, 1967, p. 16.

19. *Spalding's Official Base Ball Guide* (New York, NY), 1919, p. 8.

20. *Pittsburgh Press*, August 27, 1917, p. 24.

21. Lieb, *The Pittsburgh Pirates*, p. 180.

22. *Baseball Magazine*, December 1917, p. 253.

23. *Milwaukee Journal*, October 25, 1979, p. 4.

24. *Brooklyn Daily*, February 13, 1918, p. 2A.

25. "Burleigh Grimes," http://www.baseball-reference.com/bullpen/Burleigh_Grimes.

Chapter 4

1. Jones, ed. *Deadball Stars of the National League*, p. 302.

2. *Ibid.*, p. 271.

3. J.K. Taubenberger and D.M. Morens, "1918 Influenza: The Mother of All Pandemics," Emerging Infectious Diseases, January 2006. http://www.cdc.gov/ncidod/EID/vol12no01/05-0979.htm, August 20, 2011.

4. *Pittsburgh Post-Gazette*, March 19, 1918, p. 30.

5. *Brooklyn Daily Eagle*, October 3, 1920, p. 2.

6. Honig, *The Man in the Dugout*, p. 36.

7. Interview with Charles Clark, Clear Lake, WI, June 4, 2011.

8. *New York Times*, June 22, 1918, p. 1.

9. *Ibid.*

10. *Brooklyn Daily Eagle*, July 3, 1918, p. 2A.
11. *Sports Illustrated*, July 31, 1967, p. 17.
12. Interview with Charles Clark, Clear Lake, WI, August 14, 2011.
13. *New York Times*, July 20, 1918, p. 7.
14. *Ibid.*
15. *Baseball Magazine*, December 1918, p. 83.
16. *Brooklyn Daily Eagle*, February 2, 1919, p. 14.
17. *Pittsburgh Post-Gazette*, March 21, 1919, p. 32.
18. *Ibid.*
19. Frank Frisch and J. Roy Stockton, *Frank Frisch: The Fordham Flash* (Garden City: NY: Doubleday), p. 107.
20. *New York Times*, February 9, 1920, p. 17.
21. *Wisconsin Rapids Daily Tribune*, April 16, 1948, p. 3.
22. *Brooklyn Daily Eagle*, March 12, 1920, p. 2A.
23. *Brooklyn Daily Eagle*, March 23, 1920, p. 2A.
24. *New York Times*, May 2, 1920, p. 20.
25. *Brooklyn Daily Eagle*, June 14, 1920, p. 2A
26. *Ibid.*
27. *Brooklyn Daily Eagle*, June 23, 1920, p. 2A.
28. *The Sporting News* (St. Louis, MO), September 25, 1976, p. 6.
29. Glenn Stout, *The Dodgers: 120 Years of Dodgers Baseball* (New York: Houghton Mifflin, 2004), p. 75.
30. *Brooklyn Daily Eagle*, July 7, 1920, p. 2A.
31. Jones, ed. *Deadball Stars of the National League*, p. 302.
32. *New York Times*, March 26, 1920, p. 14.
33. John Bennett, "Jeff Pfeffer," *The Baseball Biography Project*, http://bioproj.sabr.org/.
34. Harold Seymour, and Dorothy Seymour Mills, *Baseball: The Golden Age* (New York: Oxford University Press, 1971), p. 76.
35. Steve Gelman, *The Greatest Dodgers of Them All* (New York: Putnam, 1968), p. 137.
36. *Brooklyn Daily Eagle*, October 1, 1920, sec. 2, p. 2.
37. Stout, *The Dodgers*, p. 79.
38. *New York Times*, October 19, 1920, p. 21.
39. *Ibid.*
40. *Brooklyn Daily Eagle*, November 7, 1920, p. 4D.
41. Stout, *The Dodgers*, p. 82.
42. *Brooklyn Daily Eagle*, October 10, 1920, p. 1.
43. *Brooklyn Daily Eagle*, October 11, 1920, p. 2A.
44. *Brooklyn Daily Eagle*, October 11, 1920, p. 3A.
45. Stout, *The Dodgers*, p. 84.
46. *Brooklyn Daily Eagle*, October 13, 1920, p. 2A.
47. *Brooklyn Daily Eagle*, October 13, 1920, p. 5A.

48. Interview with Charles Clark, Clear Lake, WI, August 14, 2011.
49. *Brooklyn Daily Eagle*, October 21, 1920, p. 2A.
50. *Baseball Magazine* (New York, NY), October 1920, p. 529.
51. *Brooklyn Daily Eagle*, November 7, 1920, p. 4D.
52. *New York Times*, December 15, 1920, p. 20.
53. *Brooklyn Daily Eagle*, April 13, 1921, p. 2A.
54. Frank Graham, *The Brooklyn Dodgers: An Informal History* (New York: G.P. Putnam's Sons, 1947), p. 83.
55. *Cleveland Plain-Dealer* (Cleveland, OH), March 27, 1921, p. 20.
56. *Brooklyn Daily Eagle*, April 1, 1921, p. 2A.
57. *Ibid.*
58. *Brooklyn Daily Eagle*, April 9, 1921, p. 14.
59. Graham, *The Brooklyn Dodgers*, p. 84.
60. *Brooklyn Daily Eagle*, April 13, 1921, p. 2A.
61. *Brooklyn Daily Eagle*, June 17, 1921, p. 2A.
62. Honig, *The Man in the Dugout*, p. 35.
63. Bob Broeg, *Bob Broeg: Memories of a Hall of Fame Sportswriter* (Champaign, IL: Sagamore, 1995), p. 113.
64. *Janesville Gazette* (Janesville, WI), October 7, 1921, p. 14.
65. *Eau Claire Leader* (Eau Claire, WI), October 9, 1921, p. 2.
66. *Austin Daily-Herald* (Austin, MN), October 17, 1921, p. 2.
67. *Brooklyn Daily Eagle*, March 14, 1922, p. 3A.

Chapter 5

1. *New York Times*, March 13, 1922, p. 22.
2. John C. Skipper, *Dazzy Vance: A Biography of the Brooklyn Dodger Hall of Famer* (Jefferson, NC: McFarland, 2003), p. 32.
3. *New York Times*, March 16, 1922, p. 22.
4. *Brooklyn Daily Eagle*, March 23, 1922, p. 2A.
5. *Brooklyn Daily Eagle*, April 15, 1922, p. 14.
6. *Brooklyn Daily Eagle*, April 29, 1922, p. 11.
7. *Brooklyn Daily Eagle*, May 11, 1922, p. 2A.
8. *Brooklyn Daily Eagle*, April 29, 1922, p. 11.
9. Honig, *The Man in the Dugout*, p. 41.
10. *New York Journal-American* (New York, NY), February 3, 1964, p. 18.
11. *Baseball Digest* (Evanston, IL), January/February 1955, p. 50.
12. *Brooklyn Daily Eagle*, August 10, 1922, p. 2A.
13. *Ibid.*
14. *Brooklyn Daily Eagle*, August 14, 1922, p. 2A.
15. *Brooklyn Daily Eagle*, March 20, 1922, p. 2A.
16. Graham, *The Brooklyn Dodgers*, p. 89.

17. *New York Times,* February 16, 1923, p. 11.
18. *Sporting News* (St. Louis, MO), February 24, 1938, p. 4.
19. Graham, *The Brooklyn Dodgers,* p. 90.
20. *Baseball Magazine* (New York, NY), May 1924, p. 559.
21. Skipper, *Dazzy Vance,* p. 52.
22. Graham, *The Brooklyn Dodgers,* p. 89.
23. *Brooklyn Daily Eagle,* September 8, 1924, p. 2A.
24. Tom Meany. *Baseball's Greatest Pitchers* (New York: A.S. Barnes, 1951), p. 75.
25. *Ibid.,* p. 76.
26. *Ibid.*
27. *Ibid.*
28. *Baseball Digest* (Evanston, IL), May 1960, p. 85.
29. *New York Times,* September 25, 1924, p. 17.
30. *Brooklyn Daily Eagle,* September 26, 1924, p. 2A.
31. Graham, *The Brooklyn Dodgers,* p. 94–95.
32. *Washington Post* (Washington, D.C.), January 12, 1925, p. 13.
33. Charles Einstein, *The Third Fireside Book of Baseball* (New York: Simon & Schuster, 1968), p. 305.
34. *Brooklyn Daily Eagle,* March 19, 1925, p. 2A.
35. *Brooklyn Daily Eagle,* April 18, 1925, p. 1.
36. Meany, *Baseball's Greatest Pitchers,* p. 75.
37. Stout. *The Dodgers,* p. 90.
38. *Brooklyn Daily Eagle,* August 8, 1925, p. 8.
39. Graham, *The Brooklyn Dodgers,* p. 102.
40. *Sporting News* (St. Louis, MO), August 13, 1925, p. 4.
41. *New York Times,* February 25, 1926, p. 21.
42. *Sporting News* (St. Louis, MO), March 29, 1926, p. 3.
43. *Sporting News* (St. Louis, MO), March 4, 1926, p. 4.
44. *Baseball Magazine* (New York, NY), April 1926, p. 36.
45. *Brooklyn Daily Eagle,* March 1, 1926, p. 2A.
46. *Brooklyn Daily Eagle,* March 2, 1926, p. 2A.
47. *Baseball Magazine* (New York, NY), April 1926, p. 36.
48. Graham, *The Brooklyn Dodgers,* p. 103.
49. *Ibid.*
50. *Ibid.*
51. *Ibid.*
52. *Brooklyn Daily Eagle,* June 7, 1926, p. 2A.
53. Graham, *The Brooklyn Dodgers,* p. 104–105.
54. *Brooklyn Daily Eagle,* July 12, 1926, p. 2A.
55. *Baseball Magazine* (New York, NY), October, 1929, p. 484.
56. *Sporting News* (St. Louis, MO), January 27, 1927, p. 2.

Chapter 6

1. *Brooklyn Daily Eagle,* July 7, 1926, p. 2A.
2. *Baseball Digest* (Evanston, IL), August 1972, p. 79.
3. Honig, *The Man in the Dugout,* p. 48.
4. *Reading Eagle* (Reading, PA), November 17, 1980, p. 50.
5. Honig, *The Man in the Dugout,* p. 41.
6. *Lawrence Journal-World* (Lawrence, KS), April 17, 1987, p. 5B.
7. *Baseball Magazine,* November 1931, p. 543.
8. *Billings Gazette* (Billings, MT), June 16, 1927, p. 10.
9. *Sporting News* (St. Louis, MO), February 24, 1938, p. 4.
10. *Burnette County Enterprise* (Webster, WI), November 29, 1928, p. 1.
11. *Manitowoc Herald-News* (Manitowoc, WI), March 25, 1932, p. 9.
12. *Sports Illustrated* (New York, NY), April 13, 1981, p. 61.
13. *New York Times,* February 20, 1928, p. 17.
14. *Pittsburgh Post-Gazette,* February 21, 1928, p. 15.
15. *Pittsburgh Post-Gazette,* March 5, 1928, p. 15.
16. Donald Honig, *The October Heroes* (New York: Simon & Schuster, 1979), p. 120.
17. *Sporting News* (St. Louis, MO), April 20, 1955, p. 18.
18. *Pittsburgh Post-Gazette,* March 1, 1928, p. 15.
19. *Pittsburgh Post-Gazette,* June 1, 1928, p. 15.
20. James Forr and David Proctor, *Pie Traynor: A Baseball Biography* (Jefferson, N.C.: McFarland, 2010), p. 104.
21. *Pittsburgh Post-Gazette,* February 20, 1929, p. 19.
22. Meany, *Baseball's Greatest Pitchers,* p. 82.
23. *Pittsburgh Post-Gazette,* February 28, 1929, p. 19.
24. *Pittsburgh Post-Gazette,* March 15, 1929, p. 18.
25. *Pittsburgh Post-Gazette,* May 11, 1929, p. 12.
26. *Pittsburgh Post-Gazette,* July 22, 1929, p. 15.
27. *Pittsburgh Post-Gazette,* July 9, 1929, p. 16.
28. *Pittsburgh Post-Gazette,* August 29, 1929, p. 15.
29. *Chicago Tribune,* August 29, 1929, p. 21.
30. *Sheboygan Press* (Sheboygan, WI), August 30, 1932, p. 13.
31. *Spalding Official Base Ball Guide* (New York, NY), 1930 p. 69.
32. *Pittsburgh Post-Gazette,* January 26, 1930, p. 30.

33. *Pittsburgh Post-Gazette,* February 8, 1930, p. 13.

34. *Coshocton Tribune* (Coshocton, OH), April 4, 1930, p. 2.

35. *The Register* (Sandusky, OH), April 18, 1930, p. 15.

Chapter 7

1. *St. Louis Post-Dispatch,* June 16, 1930, p. 2B.

2. William B. Mead, *Two Spectacular Seasons* (New York: Macmillan, 1990), p. 89.

3. *St. Louis Post-Dispatch,* December 9, 1985, p. 7C.

4. Frederick G. Lieb. *The St. Louis Cardinals: The Story of a Great Baseball Club* (New York: G.P. Putnam's Sons, 1944, 2001), p. 143.

5. Clippings File, Clear Lake Historical Museum, Clear Lake, WI.

6. *New York Times,* September 25, 1930, p. 32.

7. *Ibid.*

8. *St. Louis Post-Dispatch,* December 9, 1985, p. 7C.

9. *New York Times,* September 30, 1930, p. 36.

10. *Manitowoc Herald-News* (Manitowoc, WI), October 1, 1930, p. 7.

11. *Ibid.*

12. Charles Bevis, *Mickey Cochrane: The Life of a Baseball Hall of Fame Catcher* (Jefferson, N.C.: McFarland, 1998), p. 74.

13. *Coshocton Tribune* (Coshocton, OH), October 2, 1930, p. 13.

14. *Ibid.*

15. Bevis, *Mickey Cochrane,* p. 75.

16. *Baseball Magazine,* November 1931, p. 543.

17. *Ibid.*

18. Broeg. *Bob Broeg,* p. 50.

19. Clippings File, National Baseball Hall of Fame and Museum, Cooperstown, NY.

20. *Capital Times* (Madison, WI), November 24, 1930, p. 8.

21. *New York Times,* March 13, 1931, p. 31.

22. *Chicago Tribune,* May 19, 1931, p. 27.

23. Sam Levy, "They Called Him Old Stubbleboard (Burleigh Grimes)," *Baseball Digest* (Evanston, IL), January–February 1955, p. 51.

24. *Sporting News* (St. Louis, MO), September 25, 1976, p. 6.

25. John Carmichael, *My Greatest Day in Baseball* (New York: A.S. Barnes, 1945), p. 154.

26. Rawlings Sporting Goods Company Staff, "Evolution of the Ball," *Baseball Digest* (Evanston, IL), July 1963, pp. 69–70.

27. *New York Times,* September 8, 1931, p. 30.

28. *Ibid.*

29. *Ladysmith News* (Ladysmith, WI), May 22, 1980, p. 1B.

30. *Wisconsin Rapids Daily-Times* (Wisconsin Rapids, WI), October 17, 1931, p. 7.

31. *Ibid.*

32. *New York Times,* October 5, 1931, p. 24.

33. *Chicago Tribune,* October 6, 1931, p. 25.

34. *Corsicana Daily Sun* (Corsicana, TX), October 6, 1931, p. 8.

35. *Chicago Tribune,* October 6, 1931, p. 28.

36. *Chicago Tribune,* October 6, 1931, p. 28.

37. *Ibid.*

38. *Ibid.*

39. *New York Times,* October 6, 1931, p. 35.

40. *New York Times,* October 6, 1931, p. 36.

41. *Pittsburgh Post-Gazette,* October 7, 1931, p. 16.

42. *Ibid.*

43. *New York Times,* October 10, 1931, p. 20.

44. *New York Times,* October 11, 1931, p. S9.

45. *St. Louis Globe-Democrat* St. Louis, MO), December 10, 1931, sec. 2, p. 1.

Chapter 8

1. Stout, *The Cubs* (New York: Houghton Mifflin, 2007), p. 143.

2. *Chicago Tribune,* July 27, 1932, p. 19.

3. Charles C. Alexander. *Rogers Hornsby: A Biography* (New York, NY: H. Holt and Co, 1995), p. 177.

4. *Chicago Tribune,* August 3, 1932, p. 19.

5. *Chicago Tribune,* August 4, 1932, p. 15.

6. *Chicago Tribune,* August 3, 1932, p. 17.

7. *Reading Eagle* (Reading, PA), August 6, 1932, p. 6.

8. *Chicago Tribune,* September 28, 1932, p. 19.

9. *Chicago Tribune,* September 30, 1932, p. 21.

10. *Chicago Tribune,* October 2, 1932, p. A1.

11. *Chicago Tribune,* October 2, 1932, p. 1.

12. Peter Golenbock, *Wrigleyville: A Magical History Tour of the Chicago Cubs* (New York: St. Martin's Press, 1986), p. 235.

13. Honig, *The Man in the Dugout,* p. 45.

14. *Chicago Tribune,* October 3, 1932, p. 23.

15. *Ibid.*

16. *Los Angeles Times* (Los Angeles, CA), January 6, 1933, p. A10.

17. *Ibid.*

18. *Chicago Tribune,* August 1, 1933, p. 21.

19. *Chicago Tribune,* August 6, 1933, p. A6.

20. *Joplin Globe* (Joplin, MO), August 25, 1933, p. 10.

21. Clippings File, Clear Lake Historical Museum, Clear Lake, WI.

22. Susan Cayleff, *Babe: The Life and Legend of Babe Didrikson Zaharias* (Urbana: University of Illinois Press, 1995), p. 109.

23. *Montana Butte Standard* (Butte, MT), August 7, 1934, p. 6.

24. *Ibid.*

Chapter 9

1. *Manitowoc Herald-Times* (Manitowoc, WI), April 22, 1946, p. 9.

2. *Hammond Times* (Hammond, IN), August 1, 1935, p. 11.

3. *Freeport Journal Standard* (Freeport, IL), August 8, 1935, p. 13.

4. *Hutchinson News* (Hutchinson, KS), July 3, 1935, p. 3.

5. Bill Steinbacher-Kemp, "Minor League Baseball During the Great Depression: The 1935 Illinois-Indiana-Iowa League Season," 24th Annual Illinois History Symposium, Springfield, IL, December 2003, p. 14.

6. *Portsmouth Times* (Portsmouth, OH), April 7, 1936, p. 10.

7. Clippings File, Clear Lake Historical Museum, Clear Lake, WI.

8. *Baseball Digest* (Evanston, IL), January–February 1955, p. 51.

9. *New York Times,* November 6, 1936, p. 31.

10. Honig, *The Man in the Dugout,* p. 51.

11. Kelly Rusinack and Chris Lamb, "A 'Sickening Red Tinge': The Daily Worker's Fight Against White Baseball," *Cultural Logic,* Volume 3, Number 1 (Fall 1999), p. 3.

12. *Ibid.*

13. *Miami Daily News-Record* (Miami, OH), February 16, 1937, p. 9.

14. Graham, *The Brooklyn Dodgers,* p. 142.

15. *Chicago Tribune,* June 5, 1937, p. 17.

16. *The Lima News* (Lima, OH), March 31, 1937, p. 14.

17. Bob McGee, *The Greatest Ballpark Ever: Ebbets Field and the Story of the Brooklyn Dodgers* (Piscataway, NJ: Rutgers University Press, 2005), p. 125.

18. *Chicago Tribune,* April 30, 1937, p. 24.

19. *New York Times,* August 29, 1937, B1.

20. *New York Times,* August 29, 1937, p. 84.

21. Meany, *Baseball's Greatest Pitchers,* p. 76.

22. *New York Times,* September 8, 1937, p. 19.

23. Graham, *The Brooklyn Dodgers,* p. 157.

24. *Ibid.*

25. *Ibid.,* p. 162.

26. *Windsor Daily Star* (Windsor, Ontario), April 30, 1938, p. 1C.

27. *St. Petersburg Times* (St. Petersburg, FL), May, 6, 1938, p. 14.

28. *Ibid.*

29. Ettie Ward, *Courting the Yankees: Legal Essays on the Bronx Bombers* (Durham, N.C.: Carolina Academic Press), p. 193.

30. McGee, *The Greatest Ballpark Ever,* p. 138.

31. Graham, *The Brooklyn Dodgers,* p. 165.

32. Tom Stanton, *Ty and The Babe: Baseball's Fiercest Rivals: A Surprising Friendship and the 1941 Has-Beens Golf Championship* (New York: Thomas Dunne, 2007), p. 155.

33. Golenbock, *Wrigleyville,* p. 239.

34. *Chicago Tribune,* August 3, 1938, p. 19.

35. *Berkeley Daily Gazette* (Berkeley, CA), September 1, 1938, p. 10.

36. *Pittsburgh Press* (Pittsburgh, PA), September 23, 1938, p. 40.

37. William Brown, *Baseball's Fabulous Montreal Royals* (Montreal: Robert Davies, 1996), p. 60.

38. Clippings File, Clear Lake Historical Museum, Clear Lake, WI.

39. *The Daily Courier* (Connellsville, PA), September 9, 1939, p. 7.

40. *Racine Journal-Times* (Racine, WI), July 22, 1940, p. 10.

41. *Ludington Daily News* (Ludington, MI), July 30, 1940, p. 6.

42. *Ibid.*

43. *Turtle Lake Times* (Turtle Lake, WI), August 7, 2008, p. 5A.

44. *Owen Enterprise* (Owen, WI), September 18, 1941, p. 1.

45. *Lowell Sun* (Lowell, MA), February 7, 1942, p. 12.

46. *Pittsburgh Post-Gazette,* September 9, 1943, p. 14.

47. *Syracuse Herald-Journal* (Syracuse, NY), April 16, 1942, p. 36.

48. *Pittsburgh Post-Gazette,* September 9, 1943, p. 14.

59. *The Record-Argus* (Greenville, PA), May 19, 1942, p. 7.

50. *Syracuse Herald-Journal* (Syracuse, NY), April 27, 1943, p. 15.

51. *The Calgary Herald* (Calgary, Alberta), September 22, 1944, p. 12.

52. Jim Mandelaro and Scott Pitoniak, *Silver Seasons: The Story of the Rochester Red Wings* (Syracuse: Syracuse University Press, 1996), p. 76.

53. *Ibid.*

54. Phil Schlarb, Interview with Rex Gray, Grundy County Museum and Historical Society, June 6, 2008.

55. *Wisconsin State Journal* (Madison, WI), August 10, 1947, p. 30.

56. *Wisconsin State Journal* (Madison, WI), July 16, 1952, p. 18.

57. *Janesville Daily Gazette* (Janesville, WI), March 15, 1955, p. 11.

58. Clippings File, Clear Lake Historical Museum, Clear Lake, WI.

59. *The Bee* (Danville, VA), March 31, 1955, p. 25.

60. *Lebanon Daily News* (Lebanon, PA), April 2, 1956, p. 11.

Chapter 10

1. Don Rhodes, *Ty Cobb: Safe at Home* (Guilford, CT: Lyons Press, 2008), p. 154.

2. Clippings File, Clear Lake Historical Museum, Clear Lake, WI.

3. *Clear Lake Star* (Clear Lake, WI), May 21, 1964, p. 1.

4. Jerry Poling, "Collector Keeps Grimes's Legend Alive in Hometown," *Sports Collector Digest* (Palm Coast, FL), August 20, 1999, p. 110.

5. *Clear Lake Star* (Clear Lake, WI), August 6, 1964, p. 1.

6. *Ibid.*

7. Several members of the Grimes family, including Burleigh's parents, are buried at Riverside Cemetery in Withee, Wisconsin.

Chapter 11

1. In 1972, Nixon named Grimes as a pitcher on his 1925–1945 National League All-Time team.

2. Interview with Charles Clark, Clear Lake, WI, June 3, 2012.

3. Interview with Charles Clark, Clear Lake, WI, September 18, 2010.

4. *Clear Lake Star* (Clear Lake, WI), August 30, 1979, p. 1.

5. *Sporting News* (St. Louis, MO), February, 24, 1938, p. 4.

6. *Ibid.*

7. Clippings File, National Baseball Hall of Fame and Museum, Cooperstown, NY.

8. *Cedar Rapids Gazette* (Cedar Rapids, IA), August 21, 1983, p. 3B.

9. Interview with Charles Clark, Clear Lake, WI, September 18, 2010.

10. *Life* (New York, NY), August 1984, p. 94.

11. *St. Louis Post-Dispatch,* December 9, 1985, p. 1C.

12. Ken LaZebnik and Steve Lehman. *Base Paths: The Best of the Minneapolis Review of Baseball* (Dubuque: William C. Brown, 1991), p. 156.

13. *Ibid.*

14. Interview with Charles Clark, Clear Lake, WI, June 3, 2012.

15. Clippings File, Clear Lake Historical Museum, Clear Lake, WI.

Bibliography

Books

Adair, Robert Kemp. *The Physics of Baseball.* New York: Harper & Row, 1990.

Alexander, Charles C. *Rogers Hornsby: A Biography.* New York: H. Holt, 1995.

_____. *Ty Cobb.* New York: Oxford University Press, 1984.

Bevis, Charles. *Mickey Cochrane: The Life of a Baseball Hall of Fame Catcher.* Jefferson, N.C.: McFarland, 1998.

Broeg, Bob. *Bob Broeg: Memories of a Hall of Fame Sportswriter.* Champaign, IL: Sagamore, 1995.

Brown, William. *Baseball's Fabulous Montreal Royals.* Montreal: Robert Davies, 1996.

Carmichael, John. *My Greatest Day in Baseball.* New York: A.S. Barnes, 1945.

Cayleff, Susan. *Babe: The Life and Legend of Babe Didrikson Zaharias.* Urbana: University of Illinois Press, 1995.

Clear Lake Centennial 1875–1975. Clear Lake, WI: Publication Committee, 1975.

Daniel, W. Harrison, and Scott P. Mayer. *Baseball and Richmond.* Jefferson, NC: McFarland, 2003.

Einstein, Charles, ed. *The Third Fireside Book of Baseball.* New York: Simon & Schuster, 1968.

Forr, James, and David Proctor. *Pie Traynor: A Baseball Biography.* Jefferson, N.C.: McFarland, 2010.

Forrester, George. *Historical and Biographical Album of the Chippewa Valley Wisconsin.* Chicago: A. Warner, Publisher, 1891–1892.

Gelman, Steve. *The Greatest Dodgers of Them All.* New York: Putnam, 1968.

Golenbock, Peter. *Wrigleyville: A Magical History Tour of the Chicago Cubs.* New York: St. Martin's, 1986.

Graham, Frank. *The Brooklyn Dodgers: An Informal History.* New York: G.P. Putnam's Sons, 1947.

Hittner, Arthur D. *Honus Wagner: The Life of Baseball's Flying Dutchman.* Jefferson, N.C.: McFarland, 2003.

Honig, Donald. *The Man in the Dugout: Fifteen Big League Managers Speak Their Minds.* Chicago: Follett, 1977.

_____. *The October Heroes.* New York: Simon & Schuster, 1979.

Jones, David. *Deadball Stars of the American League.* Dulles, VA: Potomac Books, 2004.

Keene, Jennifer D. *World War I: The American Soldier Experience.* Lincoln: University of Nebraska Press, 2011.

LaZebnik, Ken, and Steve Lehman. *Base Paths: The Best of the Minneapolis Review of Baseball.* Dubuque: William C. Brown, 1991.

Lieb, Frederick G. *Baseball as I Have Known It.* Lincoln: University of Nebraska Press, 1996.

_____. *The Pittsburgh Pirates.* Carbondale: Southern Illinois University Press, 2003.

_____. *The St. Louis Cardinals: The Story of a Great Baseball Club.* New York: G.P. Putnam's Sons, 1944, 2001.

Mandelaro, Jim, and Scott Pitoniak. *Silver Seasons: The Story of the Rochester Red Wings.* Syracuse: Syracuse University Press, 1996.

McGee, Bob. *The Greatest Ballpark Ever: Ebbets Field and the Story of the Brooklyn Dodgers.* Piscataway, NJ: Rutgers University Press, 2005.

McGowan, Frank, and Zipp Newman. *The*

House of Barons: Record of the Barons Since 1900. Birmingham: Cather Brothers, 1948.

Mead, William B. *Two Spectacular Seasons*. New York: Macmillan, 1990.

Meany, Tom. *Baseball's Greatest Pitchers*. New York: A.S. Barnes, 1951.

New Richmond Centennial, 1857–1957. New Richmond, WI: Dairyland Press, 1957.

Okrent, Daniel, and Steve Wulf. *Baseball Anecdotes*. New York: Oxford University Press, 1989.

Poling, Jerry. *A Summer Up North: Henry Aaron and the Legend of Eau Claire Baseball*. Madison: University of Wisconsin Press, 2002.

Rhodes, Don. *Ty Cobb: Safe at Home*. Guilford, CT: Lyons Press, 2008.

Seymour, Harold, and Dorothy Seymour Mills. *Baseball: The Golden Age*. New York: Oxford University Press, 1971.

Simon, Tom. *Deadball Stars of the National League*. Dulles, VA: Potomac Books, 2004.

Skipper, John C. *Dazzy Vance: A Biography of the Brooklyn Dodger Hall of Famer*. Jefferson, N.C.: McFarland, 2003.

Stanton, Tom. *Ty and The Babe: Baseball's Fiercest Rivals: A Surprising Friendship and the 1941 Has-Beens Golf Championship*. New York: Thomas Dunne, 2007.

Stout, Glenn. *The Cubs*. New York: Houghton Mifflin, 2007.

_____. *The Dodgers: 120 Years of Dodgers Baseball*. New York: Houghton Mifflin, 2004.

Ward, Ettie. *Courting the Yankees: Legal Essays on the Bronx Bombers*. Durham, N.C.: Carolina Academic Press, 2003.

Wiggins, Robert Peyton. *The Federal League of Baseball Clubs: The History of an Outlaw Major League, 1914–1915*. Jefferson, N.C.: McFarland, 2009.

Newspapers

Atlanta Constitution

Austin Daily Herald

The Bee (Danville, PA)

Berkeley Daily Gazette (Berkeley, CA)

Billings Gazette (Billings, MT)

Birmingham News

Brooklyn Daily Eagle

Burnette County Enterprise (Webster, WI)

The Calgary Herald (Calgary, Alberta)

Capital Times (Madison, WI)

Cedar Rapids Gazette

Chicago Tribune

Clear Lake Star

Cleveland Plain-Dealer

Corsicana Daily Sun (Corsicana, TX)

Coshocton Tribune (Coshocton, OH)

The Daily Courier (Connellsville, PA)

Detroit Free Press

Eau Claire Leader

Freeport Journal Standard (Freeport, IL)

Hammond Times (Hammond, IN)

Hutchinson News (Hutchinson, KS)

Janesville Daily Gazette

Janesville Gazette

Joplin Globe

Ladysmith News

Lawrence Journal-World (Lawrence, KS)

Lebanon Daily (Lebanon, PA)

Lima News (Lima, OH)

Los Angeles Times

Lowell Sun (Lowell, MA)

Ludington Daily News (Ludington, MI)

Manitowoc Herald-News

Miami Daily News-Record (Miami, OK)

Milwaukee Journal

Montana Butte Standard (Butte, MT)

Montreal Gazette

New York Times

New York Journal-American

New York Journal Constitution

Ottumwa Daily Courier

Owen Enterprise

Philadelphia Inquirer

Pittsburgh Press

Pittsburgh Post-Gazette

Portsmouth Times (Portsmouth, OH)

Racine Journal-Times

Reading Eagle (Reading, PA)

The Record-Argus (Greenville, PA)

The Register (Sandusky, OH)

St. Louis Globe-Democrat

St. Louis Post-Dispatch

St. Paul Daily Globe

St. Paul Pioneer Press

St. Petersburg Times (St. Petersburg, FL)

Sheboygan Press

Syracuse Herald-Journal

Times-Dispatch (Richmond, VA)

Turtle Lake Times

Washington Post

Windsor Star (Windsor, Ontario)

Wisconsin Rapids Daily-Tribune

Magazines/Journals
Baseball Digest
Baseball Magazine
Cultural Logic
Life
Spalding's Official Base Ball Guide
Sporting Life
Sporting News
Sports Collectors Digest
Sports Illustrated
The Sports Magazine

Websites

www.baseball-almanac.com
www.baseballhall.org
www.baseball-reference.com

www.encyclopediaofalabama.org
www.retrosheet.com
www.sabr.org

Interviews

Charles Clark
Rex Gray

Other

Clippings File, Clear Lake Area Historical Museum, Clear Lake, WI.
Clippings File, National Baseball Hall of Fame and Museum, Cooperstown, NY.
24th Annual Illinois History Symposium, Springfield, IL, December 2003.

Index